C000268702

AN INTELLIGENT PERSON'S GUIDE TO PSYCHOTHERAPY

By the same author

Archetype: A Natural History of the Self

Withymead

The Roots of War

On Jung

The Two Million-Year-Old Self

Jung

Private Myths: Dreams and Dreaming

Ariadne's Clue: A Guide to the Symbols of Humankind

And with John Price

Evolutionary Psychiatry: A New Beginning

AN INTELLIGENT PERSON'S GUIDE TO PSYCHOTHERAPY

Anthony Stevens

Duckworth

First published in 1998 by
Gerald Duckworth & Co. Ltd.
61 Frith Street, London W1V 5TA

A catalogue record for this book is available from the British Library

ISBN 0 7156 2820 8

Printed and bound in Great Britain by
Redwood Books Ltd, Trowbridge

Contents

Acknowledgements

This book is the result of a professional lifetime spent in the practice of psychotherapy, and, inevitably, I have sometimes drawn on material previously written and published by me. I should, consequently, like to express my thanks to the Oxford University Press for permission to use material from my *Jung*, published in their Past Masters Series in 1993, and to Routledge for material from *Archetype: A Natural History of the Self* published in 1982 and from *Evolutionary Psychiatry: A New Beginning*, written in collaboration with John Price, and published in 1996. In addition, I must thank Routledge and the Princeton University Press for permission to quote from *The Collected Works of C.G. Jung*, Pantheon and Harper Collins for permission to quote from *Memories, Dreams, Reflections by C.G. Jung*, recorded and edited by Aniela Jaffé, and the Hogarth Press for permission to quote from *Attachment and Loss: Volume 1, Attachment*, by John Bowlby.

I should also like to thank all those friends, colleagues, and patients, who have over the last three-and-a-half decades contributed to the thoughts and opinions presented in this book. My special thanks go to Dr Verena Kast, Dr Wolfram Keller, Dr Tom Kirsch, Dr Guido Mattanza, Dr Frank Margison, Professor David Orlinsky, Professor Paul Roazen, Dr Seth Isaiah Rubin, Dr Mario Schlegel, Dr Anthony Storr, and Dr Margot Waddell for their valuable guidance and advice, and to Professors Paul Gilbert, Spencer Milham, and Andrew Samuels, who kindly read and commented on portions of earlier drafts. I hasten to add that none of these kind people should be taken to task for any of the views expressed in the Chapters that follow: except where otherwise stated, these are my own and I accept full responsibility for them.

Finally, I must thank my indispensable secretary, Norma Luscombe, for word processing numerous drafts, and for her unfailing good humour and good sense.

1

What is Psychotherapy?

It is a truth universally acknowledged that an unhappy person in possession of a good fortune must be in want of a psychoanalyst. That, at any rate, is the *New Yorker*'s view of the matter: the cartoon patient invariably ends up in a sparsely furnished study, framed diploma on the wall, 'free associating' on a couch, at the head of which sits a bearded man with a bewildered expression on his face and a note pad on his knee – the classic psychoanalytic situation.

To most people terms like psychologist, psychiatrist, psychoanalyst, Freudian, and psychotherapist are virtually synonymous, but to the specialist they mean very different things, and it will be helpful to be aware of these distinctions. A *psychologist* is a pure scientist who studies all behaviour, whether normal or abnormal, human or animal; a *psychiatrist* is a medically qualified practitioner who specializes in the treatment of all mental disorders, using drugs as well as psychological and social means; a *psychoanalyst* is a professional (who may or may not be medically qualified) who specializes in treating carefully selected patients using the theories and techniques devised by Sigmund Freud and his followers; while a *psychotherapist* may belong to any one of more than 400 different 'schools' of therapy, each with its own theoretical and methodological approach to the psychological treatment of people.

That all these different disciplines should be parcelled together in the common imagination and labelled 'psychoanalysis' bears eloquent testimony to the fame attained by Freud in his lifetime and maintained since his death. This is precisely as he would have wished it, for, as we shall see, he was a man driven by a single-minded determination to achieve professional distinction at all costs. It is not an exaggeration to say that psychoanalysis, and the many psychotherapeutic branches that have grown off the original Freudian shoot, is a major manifestation of twentieth century cultural life – 'the central imagination of our age' Harold Bloom, the literary critic, called it. What started as an esoteric movement among a small central European clique has become a growth industry which, in recent decades, has threatened to run out of control, as more and more people present themselves for treatment and more and more prospective therapists seek to be trained, or set themselves up in practice without any training at all.

The flowering of new therapeutic methods, based as they usually are on the theoretical assumptions of the charismatic figures who founded them (rather than on sound empirical evidence of their efficacy), have grown into mutually exclusive 'sects', prone to entertain uncharitable and somewhat paranoid feelings about one another. In response to pressure from the European Union, recent years have seen an attempt in Great Britain to define the various therapies available and to establish their professional and legal status. These efforts have been co-ordinated by the United Kingdom Council for Psychotherapy and the British Confederation of Psychotherapists which, as may be imagined, have had to referee battles which at times assumed such bitterness as to make Waterloo and Gettysburg resemble scuffles on a village green.

So psychotherapy cannot be regarded as a single entity: it is a term that covers a wide range of therapeutic philosophies or 'cultures', some of which retain the psychoanalytic model of unconscious motivation and the analysis of significant experiences from the patient's childhood or infancy, while others focus on the patient's conscious experience and behaviour in the here and now. However, all psychotherapists of whatever school broadly agree with the view that psychotherapy is an interpersonal process involving some form of contract between a trained professional and a patient, which is designed to bring about change in the ideas ('cognitions'), feelings, attitudes, and behaviour which have proved troublesome to the person seeking help.

What, then, are the main forms of therapy on offer? For the sake of clarity they may be broadly classified and briefly described under six headings (Parry, 1996; Roth and Fonagy, 1996):

Psychoanalytic and psychodynamic therapies
Behaviour and cognitive therapies
Humanistic and existential therapies
Family therapy
Group therapy
Counselling

Psychoanalytic and psychodynamic therapies

Both these forms of therapy are designed to enable patients to gain insight into their conscious and unconscious motives so as to resolve the conflicts considered responsible for their personal difficulties. The distinctions between the two forms of therapy are becoming blurred, but they mainly reflect differences in the intensity and time scale of the treatment programme: psychoanalysis requires patients to attend 3-5 times a week and is open-ended; psychodynamic therapy requires 1 or 2 sessions a week and treatment is often limited to an agreed and pre-set period of time. The majority of practitioners of both kinds of therapy adhere to Freudian, neo-Freudian or Kleinian models of psychopathology and treatment. The minority adhere to a Jungian model.

The 'cathartic' approach, originally developed by Freud in collaboration with the Viennese physician Joseph Breuer, advocated a fairly brief form of therapy intended to do no more than remove 'hysterical' symptoms. Classical psychoanalysis, as Freud later developed it, became a longer, more intensive treatment designed not only to eliminate symptoms but to bring about fundamental changes in the personality of the patient. Whether this objective was ever satisfactorily achieved is now open to debate; it nevertheless remains an acknowledged goal of psychoanalytic treatment.

In Britain, until the outbreak of the Second World War, psychoanalysis, whether Freudian, Kleinian, or Jungian, was virtually the only form of psychological treatment available and, of necessity, was confined to a small patient population. The [Freudian] Institute of Psycho-Analysis was founded in 1919, the [at first Freudian but later Kleinian] Tavistock Clinic in 1920, the [Jungian] Society of Analytical Psychology in 1936 and the Anna Freud Centre in 1952. Analysis did not become available for patients under the National Health Service until 1948 and was effectively restricted to those living in the London area. Since then the cost-effectiveness of analytic treatment has increasingly become an issue, and the emergence of briefer, more focused types of psychodynamic therapy has been in part due to the uncertain results of classical psychoanalysis but most of all to the excessive time and expenditure involved.

Behaviour and cognitive therapies

Behaviour therapy was developed in Britain during the 1950s and 60s at the Maudsley Hospital and the Institute of Psychiatry in London. It was derived from classical learning theory and from conditioning experiments conducted on animals. Patients were treated for a variety of conditions, such as phobias, obsessive-compulsive disorders, alcoholism, and homosexuality, by such techniques as negative reinforcement, desensitization, 'flooding', and response-inhibition. True to the tenets of academic behaviourism, symptomatic 'responses' were the focus of therapeutic attention, and cognitive processes were ignored as irrelevant. By the 1970s, behavioural treatments were widely available under the NHS, mostly administered by clinical psychologists, many of whom had abandoned their ancillary role (as technicians applying diagnostic tests) in order to participate actively in the treatment of patients.

However, by the late 1960s, academic psychologists began to liberate themselves from the yoke of behaviourism and to acknowledge that people actually had minds to think with. This was the so-called 'cognitive revolution'. As a result, behaviour therapists started to take account of the cognitive processes occurring in their patients. Reluctantly at first, they came to share certain assumptions with psychodynamic therapists, namely, that the cognitive processes involved in symptom-formation may be unconscious as well as conscious, and that people can be self-destructive because of negative convictions about themselves, the world, and the future. Such negative cognitions are understood to have developed through learning and to be maintained by reinforcement; and cognitive therapy aims to change them through a range of therapeutic techniques, such as identifying and challenging negative assumptions and encouraging patients to monitor their responses in the light of what they have learned in the therapeutic situation. Here again the influence of psychodynamic therapy is apparent.

Humanistic and existential therapies

Until the 1970s patients had a choice, if they had a choice at all, between submitting to psychoanalytic therapy on the one hand or behavioural therapy on the other. The gap between these two approaches was filled by the rapid emergence of new therapies based on the humanistic, existential, and phenomenological ideas of Nietzsche, Sartre, and Husserl. These ideas were taken up by clinicians such as Abraham Maslow, Fritz Perls, Carl Rogers, and Eric Berne, who were part of what came to be known as the 'human potential movement'. Treatment was mainly available privately, though Carl Rogers's 'client centred counselling' now features in some NHS services.

All these approaches eschew the 'deterministic-explanatory' model of psychodynamic therapies, maintaining that emotional problems arise when individuals are inhibited by social circumstances from actualizing their full potential. Instead of 'insight' or the removal of symptoms, 'clients' are helped to develop self-awareness while working towards the goal of self-determination. Therapists attempt to facilitate change through 'unconditional regard' for their clients, being open and receptive to their communications, and empathizing with their feelings. Initially, humanistic therapists maintained that it was their role to provide clients with a series of growth experiences rather than with treatment *per se*, stressing the importance of the therapist's attitudes rather than the use of therapeutic techniques. Gradually, however, specific techniques began to merge in such forms as psychodrama, role playing, and various kinds of abreaction (discharge of emotions).

Though apparently very different from psychoanalytic therapies, there is an evident overlap between the humanistic approach and certain fundamental concepts of Jungian analysis, namely the idea that patients are in part suffering the consequences of unactualized psychic potential, that psychic development does not reach its peak in early adulthood but continues through the course of the entire life-cycle, and that the goal of life is *individuation* – to become as whole and as complete a human being as one's circumstances allow.

Family therapy

As with humanistic therapies, this approach concerns itself less with symptom-removal or with insight into personal psychodynamics but more with the social system responsible for the patient's difficulties. This 'systemic' approach is derived from the science of cybernetics, with its concepts of homeostatic equilibrium and positive and negative feedback. While it can be used in analysing a number of social situations, it has found its most fruitful application in treating members of families. Each member is considered as a unit within the family system, and the task of therapy is to examine the strategic role that the patient's problem has been playing within the context of that system. Having identified this role, family therapists place emphasis on the positive and negative contributions that the patient's symptoms are making to the family system as a whole, and use advice, suggestion, and the re-definition of boundaries between family members in order to render the system less dysfunctional. Although psychodynamic formulations are not encouraged, they nevertheless have a tendency to intrude into family therapy sessions, providing further evidence of the pervasive influence of psychoanalytic ideas.

Group therapy

This approach came into prominence during the Second World War when understaffed military hospitals were forced to use group treatment to deal with large numbers of psychiatric casualties. Though initially rooted in psychoanalytic concepts, group therapy rapidly became an eclectic procedure, transcending different theoretical orientations. It was enthusiastically adopted in the 1960s by the community mental health movement in the United States, with the subsequent development of short-term therapies designed to deal with here-and-now interpersonal problems, to promote self-awareness, reduce emotional dependency, and enhance social competence. In both Britain and the United States, this coincided with the emergence of such 'movements' as the therapeutic community movement, the encounter group movement, group applications of transactional analysis, Esalen, and EST.

Counselling

Counsellors, like psychotherapists, are people possessing varying degrees of competence, experience, and training, and it is difficult to make hard and fast distinctions between them. On the whole, counsellors tend to work with people on their problems in dealing with the practical issues of life rather than attempting to treat their mental or emotional disturbances. While this constraint looks workable in theory, it is often difficult to sustain in practice, and counsellors not infrequently find themselves struggling to cope with psychiatric disorders which they are not adequately qualified to treat. Moreover, a complication arises when psychotherapists are euphemistically referred to as 'counsellors', especially within the NHS, where it is believed that general practice patients will find the idea of consulting a counsellor less of a social stigma.

***

While these six groups represent the main psychotherapeutic orientations discernible at the present time, there is, inevitably, some degree of overlap between them. In some instances this congruence has been exploited to develop new 'integrative therapies', such as the 'cognitive analytic therapy' of Anthony Ryle, which provides a structure in which to make a precise formulation of patients' problems in terms of their characteristic modes of relationship. Ryle's combination of cognitive and psychodynamic elements is not only attracting new candidates for training but stimulating the interest of practitioners of both approaches. Since all psychotherapeutic orientations are attempts to conceptualize the same phenomena, it is understandable that they should influence one another; and research in the form of outcome studies designed to determine 'what works for whom' may serve to promote greater integration between all schools of therapy in the future. Should this be so, it will help to compensate in some measure for the serious decline in respect for psychoanalysis – and all forms of psychodynamic theory derived from it – which has resulted from the recent intellectual shipwreck of their founding father, Sigmund Freud.

The present status of psychoanalysis

Everyone has heard of Freud: his books and papers are the most cited by any author in contemporary literature. His influence, as we have already noted, has not only pervaded the practice of psychological therapies but has entered the very fabric of our culture. In W.H. Auden's words, 'To us he is no more a person/Now but a whole climate of opinion.' The idea that personality is the product of early childhood events, that human actions are unconsciously motivated, that a fulfilled sex life is crucial for human happiness, and that we tend to repress or deny frightening or disagreeable facts, are notions that have come to be generally accepted as self-evident truths, yet they are largely products of Freud's inventive and persuasive genius.

As will become clear in the Chapters which follow, analytic theories are speculative and deeply subjective phenomena, imbued with the psychology and professional ambitions of their originators. Consequently, the history of psychodynamic therapy has been stormy and dramatic – of great personal achievements, intense political rivalries, inflammatory rhetoric between warring factions, and the emergence of independent 'schools', Jungians, Kleinians, Adlerians, Lacanians, Ego Psychologists, Object Relations Theorists, Self Psychologists, and so on, each tending to have its own constitution, bureaucratic organization, official doctrine, specialist journals, initiation rituals, and exclusive membership lists. Since there is little scientific evidence to justify such diversity these different groups have been compared to religious sects or Athenian schools of philosophy. Yet despite this proliferation and the elaborate modifications psychoanalytic formulations have undergone, Freud remains a pivotal figure, a central reference point for all discussions and developments in psychodynamic discourse. This is unfortunate, for, as we shall see, Freud's scientific notions were already out of date when his psychoanalytic thinking began, and the evidence he produced to underpin his theoretical propositions was not infrequently of his own invention. Recognition of these facts has brought about a radical reassessment of Freud's reputation.

Whereas for the greater part of this century informed and intelligent opinion has been sympathetic to Freud, this is no longer the case. Increasingly, attitudes are hardening against him, and many are beginning to share Sir Peter Medawar's bleak view of psychoanalysis as 'the most stupendous intellectual confidence trick of the twentieth century.' Telling indictments come off the presses with increasing frequency: Frederick Crews's devastating articles in the *New York Review of Books* in 1993 and 94, Allen Esterson's *Seductive Mirage: An Exploration of the Work of Sigmund Freud* (1993), Robin Tolmach Lakoff and James C. Coyne's *Father Knows Best: The Use and Abuse of Power in Freud's Case of "Dora"* (1993), Jeffrey Masson's *Against Therapy: Emotional Tyranny and the Myth of Psychological Healing* (1993), Richard Webster's *Why Freud Was Wrong* (1995), Malcolm Macmillan's *Freud Evaluated* (1997) and Robert Wilcocks's *Maelzel's Chess Player: Sigmund Freud and the Rhetoric of Deceit* (1997) – these and others have contributed to the landslide decline in Freud's scientific status and have effectively diminished respect for all schools of dynamic psychotherapy. This has struck a note of alarm throughout the profession: for if Freudian theory is without foundation, what is to stop the whole psychotherapeutic edifice from collapsing into quicksands on which it is built?

Nor has that other charismatic figure, C.G. Jung, proved immune to attack. Although attempts to convict him of Nazi anti-semitic sympathies have been largely discredited, Richard Noll's *The Jung Cult: Origins of a Charismatic Movement* (1994) and *The Aryan Christ: The Secret Life of Carl Jung* (1997) have been widely noticed and praised. Noll accuses Jung's followers of establishing 'an institutionalized capitalist enterprise' with training institutes and local psychology clubs distributed throughout the world. Jungian psychology, Noll argues, is a 'secret church', a religious cult, centred on the 'pseudo-charismatic' figure of Jung, and run by an elitist group of acolytes, who sell initiation into the 'fantasy of individuation' at an exorbitant price. Moreover, Noll seeks to prove that Jungian psychology shares precisely the same Germanic, Aryan, 'völkisch', Nietzschean, sun-worshipping roots as National Socialism – though Noll acknowledges that Jung put this tradition to the service of 'religious' rather than political ends. While this is a biased and largely refutable examination of the shadow side of Jungian practice as I have shown in the second edition of my *On Jung* (in press), it fits well with a growing prejudice against psychotherapy which sees it as a dubious activity – as snake-oil pedalled by hucksters.

As the Freudian clinician and theoretician J.A. Arlow wrote in 1982: 'We are approaching a postapostolic era in psychoanalytic history. In a few years, we will no longer have with us colleagues who had direct or indirect contact with the founding fathers. Our confidence in our work will have to rely not on the memories of bygone heroes but on solid observational data, meticulously gathered in the analytic situation and objectively evaluated, for it is upon this set of procedures that the claim of psychoanalysis to a place among empirical sciences is based.'

The most serious charge to be made against psychoanalysis is not just that it is protracted and very expensive but that it is ineffective, in that it does not bring about the radical improvements that its practitioners claim. This is an issue that can only be decided by painstaking research. But research has been slow in coming, and the results have not been encouraging, as we shall see in Chapter 8. Consequently, psychoanalysis now finds itself in a perilous position.

From being the authoritative father of the psychotherapeutic movement, it has become its problem child. Since there is little or no research evidence to support the view that psychoanalysis brings about more radical or lasting improvements than other less expensive forms of psychotherapy (though the absence of evidence does not necessarily mean that it does not produce such improvements), and since its theoretical foundations have been exposed as less than sound, many critics have argued that the entire psychoanalytic edifice should be pulled down and the site cleared for redevelopment. Others maintain that such drastic action is impractical because psychoanalytic thinking has become deeply enmeshed in our culture and extensively implicated in all psychotherapeutic practices. We have no alternative, they argue, except to assess what, if anything, is of lasting value in the psychoanalytic tradition and build on it, while calling in the bulldozers to get rid of those parts of the structure which are evidently jerry-built or have already collapsed.

Nevertheless, it is important to stress that the profession of psychotherapy will survive because there exist in our society so many people in distress, having major difficulties in their lives, who need the help of someone sympathetic to listen to their troubles and enable them to sort them out. The anxiety, self-doubt and despair that large numbers of people carry is very real, and the help that psychotherapy can provide is no less real, as much careful research has demonstrated. There is nothing wrong with the one-to-one therapeutic relationship as a procedure; what is defective is the theoretical context within which much psychotherapy is practised. And since theoretical considerations are of central significance in psychodynamic therapy – my own particular area of concern – they will feature largely throughout the course of this book.

The problem is that if we abandon psychoanalytic theory altogether, psychodynamic therapists are left with no unitary, integrative paradigm in terms of which to make interpretations, propose hypotheses, or proceed with any confidence in their work. Research then becomes entirely focused on 'outcomes' while saying nothing about the theoretical basis of the procedures whose outcomes are being measured. The solution to this predicament must surely be to replace psychoanalytic theories with a new paradigm.

Does this new paradigm exist? I believe it does, as I hope to demonstrate in Chapter 9. Before it is possible to appreciate the explanatory value of the new paradigm, however, we must first examine the history of the old one. Since readers of this book may well be contemplating psychotherapy for themselves, the historical overview which follows should help them to appreciate what they may be letting themselves in for. *Caveat emptor*!

2

Psychoanalysis and Sigmund Freud (1856-1939)

Though Freud is rightly credited with the creation of psychoanalysis, the therapeutic relationship as a one-to-one interaction between a healer and a patient is a great deal older: we cannot know precisely when it began because its origins are shrouded in the mists of prehistoric time. As a species, we evolved in circumstances of great vulnerability, threatened by predators, natural disasters, hostile neighbours, malevolent spirits, diseases and death. It is not surprising that in such conditions a figure should emerge, whom anthropologists have detected in human settlements throughout the world, whose function it is to heal the infirm and bring comfort to those who are frightened, depressed, ill or sick at heart. The ubiquitous presence of the healer, priest, shaman, guru, or witch doctor, and the practices and rituals of healing, are among the most striking of all cultural universals; and it is from these primordial roots that modern medicine, psychiatry, and psychotherapy have grown.

What have patients always wanted of their healers? The ethnographic evidence points to four main requirements: the healer should (1) possess *authority* or charisma, (2) provide personal *attention* so that patients are given time for the nature of their complaints to be understood, (3) possess *knowledge* – a corpus of theory and practice from which a diagnosis, an explanation, and appropriate treatment can be derived, and (4) possess the ability to *restore patients to health* and to full participation in the community. This still provides a good summary of what is expected of psychotherapists at the present time.

A broad consensus also exists across a large number of different cultures concerning ideas about the cause of diseases and the best means of treating them. Two basic theories of pathology are apparent: (1) the idea that something has got out of the patient which *ought* to be there, and (2) that something has got into the patient which ought *not* to be there. Each of these theories is linked with an appropriate principle of treatment: if something has got out, replace it; if something has got in, remove it.

Patients who are ill because 'something has got out' are usually considered to have lost that ghostly entity which in our culture we call the soul; the function of the healer is to track down the errant soul and restore it to its rightful owner. Clinical descriptions of people considered to be suffering from loss of soul reveal a condition closely akin to what we diagnose as 'depression' or bereavement following the loss of someone beloved. The sufferer feels that something indispensable is missing; recovery is experienced when the vital spark of life returns. In *Modern Man in Search of a Soul* (1933) Jung diagnosed our whole culture as suffering from loss of soul. As we shall see, he believed he cured the condition in himself through what he called his 'confrontation with the unconscious', a form of shamanic initiation from which he was to derive the theory and practice of what has come to be known as *analytical psychology* (to distinguish it from Freud's *psychoanalysis*).

More commonly, illness is regarded as an evil intruder, an alien force or demon that has taken possession of the patient. Healing consists of excising or exorcising it. Among the Nepalese, for example, the healer will suck the illness from a patient and spit out something which on subsequent examination proves to be a piece of animal or vegetable tissue. In the Philippines, so-called psychic surgeons carry out 'operations' without the use of instruments. With their bare hands they knead the abdomen of patients and appear to remove tissues which have the appearance of internal organs. However, when the 'extracted' tissues are analysed, they again prove to be of animal origin. These observations are instructive. Clearly, traditional healers are not above the use of bare-faced trickery; but not only do they get away with it, it also works. Charlatanism heals! How can this be?

Evidently the object extracted by the healer serves as a symbol of the disease. What matters is that the healer should possess the necessary power to make patients believe that their disease has been accurately diagnosed and cured. This is apparently what exorcists and hypnotists do, and it explains why so many traditional healers make use of trance. The patients' conviction that they are being cured is also at the bottom of the 'placebo effect', which modern doctors do their best to eradicate rather than put it to therapeutic use.

Healing by exteriorization – the discharge of something inside that needs to be got out, as in the release of pus, the removal of foreign bodies, or the exorcism of demons – is a healing procedure as old as time, as is the use of *suggestion*, the chief therapeutic instrument of healers right up to the present. The greatest modern exponent of these arcane practices, which he expertly disguised beneath an intricate web of scientific-sounding terminology, was Sigmund Freud.

***

The numerous accounts of Freud's life agree on his most salient qualities: his intellectual brilliance, his obsessive dedication to hard work, his outstanding gifts as a writer and extempore lecturer, his virtuoso ability to play with ideas and juggle them into new syntheses, his intolerance of criticism or dissent, his over-riding ambition and his single-minded determination to succeed.

Freud was not unaware of these characteristics in himself, though, naturally, he sometimes sought to play them down. He attributed his powerful ambition to several influences. First, there was the special love lavished on him by his young and beautiful mother, his elderly father Jacob's third wife. At the height of his fame, Freud wrote: 'A man who has been the indisputable favourite of his mother keeps for life the feeling of being a conqueror, that confidence of success which often induces real success' (*SE* 17, p.156). Then there was a childhood event which occurred when he was 7 or 8. For some reason he had urinated in his parents' bedroom. In an uncharacteristic flash of anger, his usually doting father cried, 'That boy will never amount to anything!' Recalling the incident, Freud commented, 'This must have been a terrible affront to my ambition, for allusions to this scene occur again and again in my dreams, and are constantly coupled with enumerations of my accomplishments and successes, as if I wanted to say: "You see, I have amounted to something after all."' (Jones, Vol. 1, p.93, Penguin edition).

Another memory that stayed with him, spurring him to succeed was an event recounted by his father: 'When I was a young fellow, one Saturday,' Jacob Freud told him, 'I went for a walk in the streets of your birthplace, beautifully decked out, with a new fur cap on my head. Along comes a Christian, knocks off my cap into the muck with one blow, and shouts, "Jew, off the sidewalk!".' Shocked, Freud asked him how he responded to this insult. His father meekly replied, 'I stepped into the road and picked up my cap.' The spectacle of his father grovelling in the gutter released fantasies of revenge in the young Sigmund and fuelled his determination to achieve celebrity in his chosen profession.

At school he proved a brilliant pupil, being first in his class seven years running, and his parents and teachers entertained high expectations of his future. In 1873 he enrolled at Vienna University to read medicine. Particularly interested in zoology and neuroscience, from 1876 to 1882 he combined his medical studies with research work at the Physiological Institute directed by Ernst Brücke (1819-1882). Brücke was the first of several exceptional men whom Freud was both to idolize and utilize as mentors to promote his career. Others were Theodor Meynert, Jean-Martin Charcot, Joseph Breuer, and Wilhelm Fliess. A member of the generation that had rejected vitalism, Brücke was an outspoken determinist and materialist, whose declared objective was to reduce psychology to physiology, and physiology to physics and chemistry. Brücke's influence turned Freud into a life-long determinist.

It was at Brücke's Institute that Freud met the eminent physician, Joseph Breuer (1842-1925), who stimulated his interest in hysteria. Freud's initial intention had been to follow a career in neurological research, but since there was no money in it and he lacked private means, he abandoned science, and, having obtained his medical degree in 1881, decided to become a physician. He had fallen in love with his future wife, Martha Bernays, and became engaged to her in June 1882. He embarked on the required three years of hospital residency on a miserably low salary and, although his future prospects were bright, he knew it would be several years before he could expect to be able to support a wife and family – unless he could make an outstanding discovery which would bring him instant fame (Gay, 1988).

From 1883 to 1886 he worked in the Psychiatric Department presided over by the illustrious Theodor Meynert (1833-1892). During this period, Freud experimented on himself and on others, including his fiancé, with cocaine, which at that time was thought of merely as a harmless and potentially useful alcaloid of coca. He found it to be an effective stimulant capable of countering the effects of fatigue, and published a paper proposing its use as a means of overcoming the disagreeable symptoms of withdrawal from morphine addiction. Fleishl, a friend of his, was addicted to morphine as a result of medical treatment for severe neuralgia. Freud took him into treatment. The result was predictable: Fleishl became addicted to cocaine in addition to morphine. Freud nevertheless published the case as a therapeutic success, even though he knew it to have been a miserable failure.

Ironically, Freud overlooked the one property of cocaine whose discovery would have brought him fame – its use as a local anaesthetic. He made a chance remark, however, to a colleague, Carl Koller, that cocaine caused numbness of the tongue. Acting on this hint, Koller tried it as an anaesthetic for operations on the eye with such dramatic success that he shot to the eminence that Freud was craving for himself. Freud, on the other hand, was excoriated by the medical establishment for not recognizing the danger that cocaine could lead to addiction.

Through the intervention of Brücke and Meynert, Freud obtained a travelling bursary which enabled him to spend the winter of 1885/86 in Paris, where he attended the lecture demonstrations on hysteria at the Salpêtrière Hospital given by the famous neurologist Jean-Martin Charcot (1825-1893). Charcot believed that hysteria was a clinical entity with a clear psychopathology, and sought to prove the psychological origin of hysterical paralysis, fits, and anaesthesia by inducing identical symptoms in healthy subjects and removing them through hypnotic suggestion. Freud at once fell under the great neurologist's spell, uncritically accepting his teaching. He seems to have adopted Charcot as a role model of the outstanding medical personality that he wished one day to become. Charcot was an autocrat, given to wild speculation, believing he could solve scientific problems through the force of his personality alone, and he would brook no dissent or criticism from pupils or colleagues.

The crucial idea that Freud brought back to Vienna from Charcot was that pathogenic ideas could lodge in an unconscious part of the mind where they were actually transformed into bodily symptoms. That mental events can have physical consequences was not a startling original insight: it is apparent, for example, in the sexual experience of us all – hence the joke that the penis must be the lightest object in the world since it can be raised by thought alone. What excited Freud was the idea that specifically *unconscious* ideas could give rise to pathology.

Now fascinated by hysteria, he drew closer to Breuer. Together they collected material for a book, *Studies on Hysteria*, which was published in 1895. The first case presented in this book came to assume huge significance in the history of psychoanalysis. It concerned a young woman, aged 21 when she first consulted Breuer in 1880, whom for the sake of confidentiality they called 'Anna O.'

Anna O. had become ill while nursing her father as he was dying of tuberculosis. Her illness began with a severe cough, followed by development of a rigid paralysis and loss of sensation in her right arm and leg, a convergent squint, and impaired vision and hearing. She had brief 'absences' of consciousness, when she would experience hallucinations and exhibit disturbed behaviour, shouting abuse at people and tearing buttons off her clothes. Her speech was disordered and she lost her capacity to speak German, her native tongue, and could converse only in English.

Breuer diagnosed the case as one of hysteria and he treated her until June 1882, when he discharged her from his care as being completely cured. The treatment he gave her became paradigmatic of the psychoanalytic approach. He visited her daily, usually in the evenings, when he encouraged her to recount what she had experienced during the course of the day. This 'unburdening process' had a calming effect and Anna seems to have become emotionally dependent on Breuer and on what she called her 'talking cure'.

One of her more bizarre symptoms was an inability to drink, despite a raging thirst. Under hypnosis, she recalled that this symptom had begun when she discovered her English companion's dog, which she disliked, drinking from a glass. She had said nothing about it at the time, but now she expressed anger, indignation, and disgust at the incident. Following the recollection of this memory and the discharge ('abreaction') of the emotions involved, the symptom disappeared and she was able to drink without further difficulty.

This is said to have been a turning point both for Anna and for Breuer. In his published account of the case, he referred to the process of recall and abreaction as the 'therapeutic technical procedure', which, when systematically applied, should produce successful outcome in all cases of hysteria. He took each of Anna's symptoms in chronological order of appearance, and encouraged her to remember the exact circumstances in which it had first occurred: as a result, he claimed, 'the symptom was permanently removed.'

The apparently successful technique used in the treatment of Anna O. provided Freud with the crucial ideas on which all his future theorizing would be based. It was, he believed, a revolutionary breakthrough in the psychological treatment of a severely debilitating illness. Yet there was little that was new or original about it. The notion that the physical symptoms of hysteria were due to some psychological or emotional trauma suffered in the past was borrowed directly from Charcot, and the idea that 'abreaction' brings 'catharsis' is very old indeed, belonging to the primordial aetiological theory of something bad that has to be got out of the system. Moreover, the 'confessional' aspect of the talking cure had been used by the Catholic Church to relieve guilt for centuries; and for the past twenty years the Viennese physician Moritz Benedikt had been teaching that hysteria was caused by a 'pathogenic secret' rooted in the sex life of the patient (Webster, 1997).

What was new in Breuer and Freud's contribution was the idea that the memory of the trauma responsible for hysterical symptoms was suppressed: for it was the *suppressed* or 'strangulated' affects caused by the trauma which, they believed, were converted into physical symptoms. The 'therapeutic technical procedure' worked, they maintained, because it offered an alternative mode of release for the affect: it could be discharged in words rather than turned into symptoms. This was the seminal idea from which psychoanalysis grew and it was to prove a major influence on psychiatric thinking in the twentieth century, especially in the treatment of war neuroses, such as 'shell shock' and post-traumatic stress disorder.

According to Breuer, Anna's treatment ended when she reported a terrifying hallucination of a snake, 'which constituted the root of her whole illness' and she at once recovered her ability to speak German. She left Vienna and we are told that after a while regained her mental balance entirely. 'Since then', concluded Breuer, 'she had enjoyed complete health.' It was apparently a miraculous cure of a young woman who had suffered a crippling illness; and its publication brought considerable prestige to Freud as well as Breuer. For many years, it was regarded as the classic example of a successful cathartic cure and its achievement did much to support Freud's later claims for the therapeutic effectiveness of psychoanalysis.

However, we now know that the true facts of the case were very different. Anna O.'s real name was Bertha Pappenheim. In later years she was to become a pioneer social worker, taking a leading role in the struggle for women's rights and in providing relief for refugees and orphans. Through brilliant detective work, the psychiatric historian, Henri Ellenberger, has discovered that she was admitted to Kreuzlingen Sanatorium on Lake Constance in July 1882, only a month after Breuer had discharged her as cured. Her medical records, which are still extant, reveal – as Ellenberger caustically observes – that 'the famed "prototype of a cathartic cure" was neither a cure nor a catharsis' (Ellenberger, 1993). On admission to Kreuzlingen the 'completely cured' Bertha Pappenheim was still complaining of hallucinations, convulsions, recurring loss of the ability to speak German, and severe facial neuralgia. As if this were not bad enough, she had also become addicted to morphine, which Breuer had prescribed for her neuralgia.

As Ellenberger's shocking discoveries demonstrate, Breuer's and Freud's claims to have cured Bertha Pappenheim were fraudulent; as fraudulent as Freud's earlier claim to have cured Fleishl's morphine addiction by giving him cocaine. Moreover, many have argued that Bertha Pappenheim was not suffering from hysteria at all, and have offered alternative diagnoses, such as a left-sided cerebral lesion (which might account for her speech disorder and right-sided paralysis and loss of sensation), tubercular meningitis, syphilis, a borderline personality disorder, or even that the entire illness was simulated. It has subsequently emerged that Bertha Pappenheim herself guided and to a large extent controlled her own treatment, and a plausible interpretation of Breuer's actual case notes (as opposed to his published account) is that, once she had been introduced to the cathartic method she used it to hold and manipulate Breuer's attention.

Whether there was an underlying physical illness or not, Breuer certainly did not cure her, and Freud knew it. Not only did she spend $3\frac{1}{2}$ months in Kreuzlingen in 1882, but between 1883 and 1887 she was admitted on three subsequent occasions to the Inzersdorf Sanatorium, altogether for a total of ten months' in-patient treatment. On each admission the diagnosis was 'hysteria'. Freud was intimately aware of these facts, for on two occasions in 1887, Martha Bernays, whom he had married the previous year, wrote to her mother specifically mentioning Anna O. and reporting that although she was normal during the daytime, her hallucinations returned in the evening. Fortunately, by the end of the 1880s, Bertha Pappenheim was free of symptoms and it seems that they never returned, leaving her free to live a socially productive life. But it was little thanks to Breuer or to Freud.

Freud's knowledge of the ineffectiveness of Breuer's treatment of this case did not discourage him from basing his future theoretical formulations on it. The urgency with which he felt himself driven to achieve professional celebrity encouraged him to seize on each new idea as it occurred to him as a 'discovery' of historic significance. Fame was the spur. There was no time to be wasted on the diligent collection of evidence to support (or refute) what he had 'discovered'. The 1890s were for Freud a period of theoretical exuberance.

With a disregard for correct scientific procedure which was to prove characteristic of him, and giving free wing to an imagination fuelled with regular doses of cocaine, Freud proceeded to outline the basic concepts of what, in 1896, he first referred to as 'psychoanalysis'. These concepts – *repression*, *resistance*, *conflict*, *transference*, and the use of *free association*, and *dream analysis* as a means of advancing the 'talking cure' – were all elaborations of the fundamental principle of catharsis, which was erroneously alleged to have been so successful in the treatment of Bertha Pappenheim.

Like Breuer, Freud at first used hypnosis, not to implant positive suggestions for health, but to assist patients to recall the origins of their symptoms, for 'hysterics', maintained Breuer and Freud, 'suffer mainly from reminiscences.' The reminiscences concerned were often shameful or disagreeable and consequently people were understandably reluctant to recall or reproduce them. This reluctance Freud called 'resistance'. The mechanism responsible for making the reminiscence unconscious (active forgetting), he called 'repression', and the concept of repression became the cornerstone of psychoanalytic theory. Repression was responsible for 'intrapsychic conflict' – the struggle between the emotion which sought its own discharge in consciousness and the forces of repression that kept it unconscious. The repressed affect, denied all other forms of expression, discharged itself in the production of neurotic symptoms. Treatment required the use of techniques to release what was repressed. The symptoms should then disappear. This again was the primordial story of something pathological inside a patient that had to be let out, like pus inside an abscess requiring surgical release.

Finding the induction of hypnosis an unreliable method, Freud sought other techniques for rendering the emotionally charged reminiscences conscious. In the course of treating 'Elizabeth von R.', the first full-length analysis of hysteria that he undertook, he hit on the use of 'free association' which was to provide the 'basic rule' of psychoanalysis. Lying relaxed on a couch, patients were instructed to report whatever came into their minds, rather like a passenger in a railway train reporting on the scene as it passes before the window. *Everything* had to be reported, however trivial, embarrassing, or offensive it might be.

In the case of Elizabeth von R., the crux was reached when, according to Freud, he offered her the interpretation (which she strenuously resisted) that she was in love with her brother-in-law and that she had repressed wicked desires for her sister's death. Freud reported that when he was able to overcome her resistance and she eventually accepted his interpretation, her symptoms disappeared. This again seems to have been untrue. Elizabeth von R.'s real name was Ilona Weiss and, many years later, she told her daughter that contrary to Freud's claims she had not been helped by seeing him. '[He tried] to persuade me that I was in love with my brother-in-law', she said, 'but that wasn't really so' (Webster, 1997).

Charcot had given Freud the idea that hysterical symptoms were caused by sexual traumata in the past: 'C'est toujours la chose sexuelle. Toujours! Toujours!' he declared in his excited, emphatic manner. Freud was evidently determined to capitalize on this idea and use it as the basis for his own theory of neurosis. The trouble was that many patients would not oblige him by producing sexual memories to order. To solve this problem he took one of the theoretical leaps so characteristic of him. The failure of patients to confirm his theory would not be allowed to persuade him that the theory was wrong. Rather the patient must be held responsible for covering up and concealing the truth. Failing to produce the required sexual memory was entirely due to resistance. Building on this idea Freud went on to assert that resistance to reproducing the memory was the same force that had driven the memory out of consciousness in the first place. Thus, resistance and repression were two aspects of the same dynamic principle responsible for keeping unpleasant sexual memories unconscious and for keeping the patient ill; and successful treatment must depend on overcoming the resistance, undoing the repression, and making the traumatic memory conscious.

Developing these hunches into the basic theoretical framework for the practice of psychoanalysis, Freud displayed the sleight of hand of an accomplished magician, who, having covertly slipped a rabbit into his hat, proceeds to produce it to the gratifying applause of his audience. Generations of psychoanalysts have been applauding this imposture ever since, believing that Freud's 'discovery' of the sexual aetiology (cause) of the neuroses was derived from his acute clinical observation of a large number of cases. In fact, it was a conjecture formed while treating a small number of cases, whose clinical details were constantly recycled in the psychoanalytic literature.

There can be little doubt that while patients were undergoing treatment at the hands of Breuer or Freud some of their symptoms would have disappeared. This could certainly have been due to the rapport that they established with their patients, but it could equally have been because neurotic symptoms tend spontaneously to come and go over a period of time. Freud was reluctantly forced to acknowledge, as he treated more and more patients by his method, that symptoms had an unfortunate habit of returning. This put him in something of a quandary: how was he to explain it? It must be, he decided, because there were earlier and certainly nastier sexual experiences that the patient was refusing to remember. Inevitably, these must be sexual, and probably, Freud assumed, due to a premature and precocious introduction of the patient as a child to a form of sexual involvement that she was incapable of accepting and therefore experienced as traumatic. With this hunch Freud's theory of *sexual seduction* was born. It was a piece of theoretical guesswork, which, resurrected by Jeffrey Masson, was to bring misery to thousands of families through the 'recovered memory syndrome' and its attendant industry run by therapists who claimed to be able to diagnose and treat the trauma which they insisted had been inflicted on their patients, even though the patients had no recollection of the alleged abuse.

Jeffrey Masson's *The Assault on Truth* (1993) was well named, for his book is as much a travesty of clinical reality as anything perpetuated by Freud. Masson puts into emotive language the hitherto widely accepted belief that Freud's theory of sexual seduction was based upon factual memories recalled by his patients in analysis: 'Freud's female patients had the courage to face what had happened to them in childhood – often this included violent scenes of rape by a father – and to communicate their traumas to Freud, no doubt hesitating to believe their own memories and reluctant to remember the deep shame and hurt they had felt. Freud listened and understood and gave them permission to remember these terrible events.'

It is now clear, however, that far from giving them permission to remember and speak of these terrible events, Freud himself attributed the seduction to his patients, believing that such experiences would provide the 'sexual trauma' which he wished to establish as the indispensable aetiological factor in hysteria. He himself described analytic treatment as a procedure designed to coerce patients to recollect sexually traumatic scenes of which they had no recollection. His whole theory of hysteria rested on the doctrine that sexual seduction in childhood would have pathological consequences *only if the patient had no conscious memory of the event*. The patient then had to be forced into acknowledging that she had indeed experienced such a trauma. Her resistance to having such disagreeable incidents attributed to her was often so stubborn that to overcome it demanded in Freud's own words 'the strongest compulsion of the treatment'. Masson's argument that Freud *knew* that his patients had been seduced and that he later abandoned the seduction theory out of professional cowardice can thus be rejected.

Freud proceeded to divide the neuroses into two groups: the *actual neuroses*, whose source he considered to reside in the present sex life of the patient, and the *psychoneuroses*, whose source lay in the patient's past sex life. He subdivided the actual neuroses into 'neurasthenia' (whose origin he thought was masturbation) and 'anxiety neurosis' (caused by coitus interruptus), and the psychoneuroses into 'hysteria' and 'obsessional neurosis' (both the result of sexual abuse suffered in childhood). Hysteria occurred mainly in females, who suffered the abuse passively; obsessional neurosis occurred mainly in males, who participated more actively in the abusive experience and felt pleasure (their obsessive ideas being a form of self-reproach for having experience illicit enjoyment). Freud claimed that he had analysed 18 cases of hysteria and 'discovered' that in every case the patient had been seduced in childhood. This, he alleged was a discovery of such enormous importance that he felt justified in comparing it to 'the source of the Nile in neuropathology'. Within a year, however, he was admitting to his friend Wilhelm Fliess that he no longer believed in the truth of this 'discovery'.

The sexual seduction theory provided him with a pat explanation for the aetiology of neurotic conditions, but there were problems with it which made Freud uneasy. To begin with, psychoneurosis is very common. Was he to assume that Viennese children were being routinely abused by their adult caretakers on a pandemic scale? As Freud acknowledged, both he and his brothers and sisters had neurotic symptoms. Did this mean that his kindly old father had sexually interfered with them all in their early years? Moreover, for an impecunious practitioner to embrace such a theory would scarcely encourage the growth of a thriving practice if the fathers who paid him fees to analyse their neurotic daughters received little more for their pains than the accusation of being monsters of sexual depravity. On due reflection, Freud decided that he had better retreat: accordingly, he wrote to Fliess in 1897 to say that he 'no longer believed in [his] *neurotica'* (theory of neurosis).

Forced to abandon the seduction theory, what could he put in its place? Should he renounce the sexual aetiology of the neuroses altogether? Decidedly not, for that would be to defenestrate the baby with the bath water and to reject the teaching of the great Charcot. A solution occurred to him. What if his patients had not been actually seduced in childhood but had produced *fantasies* of being seduced? What if, as young children, they had *wished* to be seduced only to become ashamed of such wishful fantasies and, as a consequence, later repress them? That would provide a satisfactory resolution of the problem. Fathers of his patients would be spared scandalous recrimination, for no one could be held responsible for erotic fantasies concocted by a child. Moreover, if the patients in Freud's care failed to report such fantasies then the remedy was easy: they would be told that it was because they had repressed them. If further free associations on the couch failed to overcome the repression and the memory of such fantasies stubbornly failed to re-emerge then patients would be told it was because they were resisting treatment. As a result, Freud replaced the seduction theory with the more sustainable but no less controversial theory of *infantile sexuality*.

That Freud could be ruthless in overcoming resistance and insistent that patients should produce the repressed sexual traumas he wanted to hear about is apparent from his writings. 'Before they come for analysis', Freud wrote in his paper 'The Aetiology of Hysteria', the patients know nothing about these scenes. They are indignant as a rule if we warn them that such scenes are going to emerge. Only the strongest compulsion of the treatment can induce them to embark on a reproduction of them' (*SE* 3, p.304). When patients on the couch fell silent, this too is to be taken as resistance, and dealt with accordingly. When patients protested that nothing occurred to them to say, that was absolutely not acceptable. 'We must not believe what they say', he wrote in another paper, 'we must always assume, and tell them too, that they have kept something back ... We must insist on this, we must repeat the pressure and represent ourselves as infallible, till at last we are really told something' (*SE* 2, p.279).

The blatant use of such unscrupulous tactics may have enabled him to bully his patients into accepting his interpretations, but clinical arrogance of this degree of magnitude was ill-designed to protect him against the kind of missed physical diagnosis of which all psychotherapists live in dread. Almost inevitably, this fate befell Freud. For example, a little girl was sent to him suffering abdominal pains. He diagnosed her as an 'unmistakable' case of hysteria and 'cured' her with psychoanalysis. Two months after he discharged her she died, the cause being an abdominal lymphoma. Apparently unabashed, Freud denied all culpability, insisting that he had cured the hysteria which, he declared, 'had used the tumour as a provoking cause'.

Freud's famous theory of sexuality which he developed in the years 1897 to 1905 was based on the notion of an instinctual drive which existed *a priori* in the individual as a biological given and passed through three stages in the course of ontogeny (personal development). Here Freud felt he had his feet on solid ground. Not only is sex indispensable to the survival of the species but, under Darwin's influence, Freud understood sexual selection to be a primary factor in evolution. His sexual theory could thus provide psychoanalysis with a sound organic basis in biology and would enable him to create the science of psychobiology which he had set himself to achieve. Sex provided him with the essential link, connecting the body to the mind, and would enable him to fulfil Brücke's prediction that the neuroses would prove to have a physical cause. Inspired with this vision he wrote his 'Project for a Scientific Psychology'. 'In the sexual process', he was to write to Jung in April 1908, 'we have the indispensable organic foundation without which a medical man can only feel ill at ease in the life of the psyche' (*Freud/Jung Letters*, pp.140-41).

In reducing the sum total of human motivations to sex he was adopting an incredibly narrow perspective, but this could not have been so apparent to Freud as it is to us. Ethology, the branch of biological science that studies animal behaviour in natural habitats, had yet to be born, and Freud knew nothing of the rich diversity of instinctual patterns occurring in nature, for the zoology of his time confined its observations to animals in zoos, where opportunities for actualizing the vast repertoire of instinctive potential inherent in all animal species were lacking. When territorial and dominance conflicts are ruled out by lack of space and an absence of competitors, it is little wonder that bored, well-nourished animals pass their days in fornication or 'self-abuse'. That Freud's patients displayed a reluctance to become loquacious when asked about their sexual history and showed signs of embarrassment when the issue was raised is understandable in view of the sexual inhibitions current in the society of his time. That we are less inhibited in this respect is perhaps a measure of the effect that Freud's ideas have had on our culture.

In this manner Freud's association with Charcot and Breuer gave him the inspiration to use sex as the means to graft psychological ideas on to the physiological principles he had acquired from Brücke and, to his own satisfaction, ground the theory and techniques of psychoanalysis in biology. Sex became the bedrock on which his entire edifice was raised. 'My dear Jung', he said on one much quoted occasion, 'promise me never to abandon the sexual theory. That is the most essential thing of all. You see, we must make a dogma of it, an unshakeable bulwark' (Jung, *MDR*, p.173). Neurotic symptoms, the symbolism of dreams, perversions, jokes, slips of the tongue, the psychopathology of every day life, all were made to rest on this single 'indispensable foundation', sex.

Why Freud insisted on this rigid and excessive reductionism was probably out of a misguided belief that he was being scientific and obeying Ockham's razor (namely, that in scientific explanations entities should not be multiplied beyond necessity). Like all nineteenth century physicians Freud was much impressed by the germ theory of disease proposed by Koch and Pasteur, to the effect that all genuine diseases have but a single cause. Charcot had taught him that hysteria was a genuine disease. Freud likewise assumed that other neuroses, such as obsessional neurosis and 'neurasthenia' were also genuine diseases and persuaded himself that he had discovered the single cause responsible for them all. On this discovery he was to rest his hopes of fame. With it he could fulfil his lifelong ambition of 'opening all secrets with a single key.' Henceforth, colleagues or patients who questioned or refused to accept this claim were treated as heretics and cast into outer darkness, as Jung, Adler, Stekel, Rank, Ferenczi, and others were to discover.

Right up to the middle years of his life Freud was prone to hero-worship men whom he perceived as intellectual giants. In addition to Brücke, Meynert, Charcot, and Breuer, he was later to be in thrall to the brilliant and intensely charismatic Swiss psychiatrist, Carl Gustav Jung (1875-1961).

From the standpoint of the development of psychoanalysis, the most influential and certainly the most eccentric of these hero figures was the Berlin ear-nose-and-throat surgeon, Wilhelm Fliess, with whom Freud corresponded through much of the 1890s. This correspondence provides major insights into the course of Freud's thinking, and it also reveals the extent of his credulity. Fliess believed in the essential bisexuality of human beings and maintained that the whole life span of both sexes was determined by different rhythmic cycles, the female cycle being 28 days and male cycle 23 days. These cycles, according to Fliess, controlled the dates of birth, illnesses and death, as well as the regenerative processes on which life depends. He also believed there to be an essential psychophysical correspondence between the genitals and the nasal mucosa and described a syndrome which he called the 'nasal reflex neurosis', which could be relieved by a most unpleasant operation on the nasal septum. All these ideas Freud enthusiastically embraced as the revolutionary discoveries of a scientific genius. As their epistolary relationship progressed, Freud's admiration for Fliess grew, to the extent that he could address him, without embarrassment, as 'the Kepler of Biology' and his 'Messiah'. However, apart from the menstrual cycle, no evidence has ever been forthcoming in support of Fliess's rhythms or his nasal reflex neurosis and they have gone the way of all unsubstantiated conjectures.

***

During the period 1894 to 1899 Freud suffered what Henri Ellenberger (1970) has called a 'creative illness' and his emotional dependence on Fliess intensified. In his letters he complained of feeling isolated in a hostile world, of being unable to shake off worrying psychosomatic symptoms, and of suffering mood swings which alternated alarmingly between elation and despair. His psychosomatic complaints included cardiac arrhythmias, shortness of breath, fear of dying, headaches, and recurrent sinusitis. The mood swings and sinusitis could be accounted for by Freud's psychological dependency on cocaine, while his irregular heartbeat and breathing difficulties are attributable to his addiction to cigars, which he considered a substitute for masturbation. But as Ellenberger points out, it was during this period of 'creative illness' that most of Freud's major insights and theoretical formulations occurred. These were probably inspired, and certainly energized, by cocaine.

The crowning achievement of these years, Freud always maintained, was his 'discovery' of the function of dreams and how to interpret them. Wishing to understand the cause of his symptoms, which he attributed to psychological rather than physical origins, Freud embarked on a protracted course of self-analysis, which included keeping a careful record of his dreams and using free association to elucidate their meaning. In the early morning of July 24th 1895, he dreamt a dream that has gone down in history as 'the dream of Irma's injection.' He was staying with his family at Schloss Belle Vue, a favourite resort on the outskirts of Vienna. As he worked on the dream later that day, the thought suddenly struck him that *it was the fulfilment of a hidden wish*. This flash of illumination brought with it the conviction that he had found the key to unlock the door to the unconscious mind. At that precise moment he knew that the riddle of dreams, which had preoccupied oneirologists for millennia, had been solved, and he entertained the fantasy that one day a marble tablet would be affixed to the façade of the schloss stating that *In this house on July 24th, 1895, the Secret of Dreams was Revealed to Dr Sigmund Freud* – a fantasy which was subsequently implemented in reality.

The Interpretation of Dreams, completed in 1899, was to dominate theoretical approaches to dreaming for much of the twentieth century. Freud offers the dream of Irma's injection as the prototypical example of Freudian dream analysis, and there is a rich irony in this. The dream is about one of Freud's patients who approaches him at a party with the disagreeable information that, despite his treatment, her illness has not improved but got worse. In the dream he deals with this news in a way which we can now see as typical of him: he blames the patient, accusing her of resisting his interpretation of her case. Then he proceeds to pass the blame on to a medical colleague. The crucial wish motivating the dream, as Freud honestly acknowledged, was the desire not to be the one held responsible for Irma's deterioration. Although there is evident sex symbolism in the dream (for example, the colleague responsible for her relapse has given her an injection with a dirty syringe), Freud glosses over this, stressing that the primary wish is to escape blame. This is odd in view of the emphasis on sexual motivation which dominates the rest of his book.

Freud's theory of dreams is an extension of his theory of neurosis. The wish of which the dream is a fulfilment is a repressed wish – repressed because it is unacceptable (usually sexual) and, if permitted to reach dream consciousness, would shock the sleeper into wakefulness. Because of the vigilance of a psychic institution which Freud termed the censor, the repressed wish (the *latent* content of the dream) can only be expressed in disguised form (the *manifest* content). The dream thus circumvents inner tensions that would otherwise wake the dreamer, for dreaming permits the vicarious fulfilment of the forbidden wish. Thus, in Freud's famous formulation, 'dreams are the guardians of sleep.' The purpose of dream analysis is to make the latent content of the dream conscious. Since the use of free association makes this possible, Freud regarded dreams as providing 'the royal road to the unconscious', and, as a result, the analysis of dreams became an essential part of classical psychoanalytic technique.

That dreams might reflect sexual wishes was not a new idea: it had already been noted by such authorities as Charcot, Janet, and Krafft-Ebing. What was ingenious about Freud's approach to dreaming was the use to which he put this idea. Had he maintained that all dreams were overt fulfilments of wishes, his theory could readily have been refuted, but he was careful not to do this. What he claimed was that dreams were *disguised* wish fulfilments and this again put his theory beyond refutation. If, for example, a patient dreamed of something happening that clearly she would not have wished to happen to her, then Freud interpreted the dream as a wish on the part of the dreamer to prove his theory wrong! To engage Freud in an argument was always to be on the losing side. Like the builder of the *Titanic*, Freud designed his brainchild to be unsinkable.

Similar ingenuity is apparent in Freud's whole concept of the unconscious. He could not claim to have discovered the unconscious, for the idea was already current by the time he entered the scene. What was novel about Freud's approach was his idea that the unconscious was the part of the mind whose specific function it was to harbour *repressed* impulses, memories, and thoughts. It was useless for his critics to object that they harboured no such impulses or memories in themselves because Freud would counter that they could not know them precisely because they were unconscious and they preferred to keep them that way. Only psychoanalysis possessed the ability to make them conscious. Thus, his critics were trapped in an ingenious catch-22.

Much of the background to the dream of Irma's injection is revealed in the correspondence between Freud and Fleiss (Masson, 1985). It emerges that Irma was a composite figure, created by Freud's unconscious, based on two young widows who were patients of his. One of these was Emma Eckstein, who suffered from constant pain and bleeding from her nose. Freud's interpretation of these symptoms was that they were psychosomatic manifestations of repressed sexual desire for her analyst – that she was, in fact, 'bleeding for love' of him. Her symptoms persisted, however, and suspecting this was a case of 'nasal reflex neurosis', he called in Fliess, who operated on her, removing her nasal septum. Not only was this traumatic operation entirely unnecessary, but Fliess botched it, carelessly leaving behind a gauze pack in one nasal cavity, which turned septic. When this was found and removed two weeks later by another surgeon, Emma Eckstein had a severe haemorrhage, which in less expert hands may well have proved fatal. This was an evident piece of malpractice which Freud was careful to conceal in his published associations to the dream. But the dream itself is evidence of his continuing unease about the case and his desire to be absolved of guilt and responsibility for his role in it.

In the light of modern dream research, it is now clear that most of Freud's ideas about dreams were wrong. For him, dreams were produced in the same way as neurotic symptoms, and this implied that normal, well-adjusted people would not have them. Dream laboratory studies have established, however, that dreaming sleep is an entirely normal and recurrent state of sleep in all mammals, including ourselves. We spend about a quarter of every night in REM (rapid eye-movement) dreaming sleep. According to Freud, the basic need of mental life was to achieve a state of tranquillity through the complete discharge of all tensions. He later called this the Nirvana principle. For him, the healthy person, untroubled by dreams, was a bonded heterosexual with a regular and satisfying sex life, who could discharge his or her sexual tensions in repeated orgasms and enjoy a recurrent state of tensionless Nirvana. There is little objective evidence to support this view, and much to refute it.

Freud's assumptions about the ways in which the central nervous system functions were deeply flawed, based as they were on the neurobiology of the 1880s. He believed it to be an essentially passive organization, responsive only to outer stimulation, and incapable of generating either its own energy or its own information. The Freudian view of the psyche and nervous system as fuelled by powerful drives (sex and later aggression) like a train driven by coal and steam is hopelessly obsolete and quaint. No one now conceives of human or animal psychology in the engineering terms which still seemed appropriate at the end of the nineteenth century. Although later developments in Freudian 'ego psychology' contributed some advance on Freud's original thinking, its contribution is of dubious significance because it still clung to Freud's mechanistic model. Thanks to the research of the last fifty years, we now know that the nervous system is metabolically capable of generating (and cancelling) its own energy, and genetically capable of producing much of its own information. We also know that episodes of REM sleep and dreaming occur as a result of the spontaneous activity of the central nervous system, acting independently of stimuli arising from the environment.

It seems likely that Freud realized that the neurobiology he had learned from Brücke could become outdated, for he eventually disowned any relationship between neuroscience and psychoanalysis, and suppressed his 'Project for a Scientific Psychology'. He wanted his theories to appear original and to survive any revolutionary or unforeseen developments that might occur in neuroscientific research. Nevertheless, his notion of repressed sexual 'libido' which could discharge itself in the manifest content of dreams, the symptoms of neurotic illness, perverse sexual acts, and inadvertent slips of the tongue, was the product of the now wholly discredited teaching he received in Brücke's laboratory.

But such was the brilliance of Freud's rhetoric, his diligence and powers of political manipulation that his franchise on psychodynamic thinking has persisted to the detriment of psychotherapeutic practice as a whole. Because psychoanalysis has clung onto the outdated *a priori* assumptions of its founder, it has resisted scientific verification (or refutation), and languished in an intellectual time warp of its own making. There are signs, however, that this is beginning to change, with the emergence of a new evolutionary paradigm that could drag psychoanalysis out of its sterile state of self-absorbed isolation. We shall return to this possibility later on.

***

Having abandoned the seduction theory, Freud persisted in his view that neurosis was associated with disturbances of sexual function in the earliest years of childhood, as a result of which the child's sexual development became partially arrested or 'fixated' at an immature stage. To his contemporaries the idea that the 'component instincts' of sexuality became apparent in the 'polymorphously perverse' behaviour and fantasies of infancy, as Freud now maintained, was only marginally less shocking than the idea that neurosis was due to early sexual abuse. But it was a sustainable hypothesis supported by observation, since young children do display such precursors of adult sexual behaviour as penile erections, 'clasping', and pelvic thrust. Where Freud allowed his theoretical enthusiasm to carry him beyond the pale of biological probability was in proposing that development of the sexual instinct proceeds through a series of stages involving the mouth and the anus before reaching the final genital stage, which a child was assumed to reach by the age of about 5.

Observation could certainly confirm that young children derive pleasure from the acts of sucking, feeding, urinating, and defecation; but where Freud put himself on impossibly shaky ground was his uncritical acceptance of Wilhelm Fliess's view that this pleasure was exclusively sexual in nature. This would presume that sex is the only form of pleasure available to us, which is evidently not the case. For good evolutionary reasons, nature has arranged things so that many activities which promote individual survival give rise to pleasure, just as activities or stimuli which threaten survival give rise to fear or pain. Eating, drinking, and playing (by which young animals practice behaviours essential for self-preservation) are all pleasurable in their own right and it is clear that sex is but one of many delights that children and adults can enjoy. It is true that use of the mouth and anus as 'erogenous zones' can be involved in the arousal associated with sexual foreplay in adults, but this in no way proves that the pleasure derived from oral or anal stimulation in childhood is intrinsically sexual.

Yet Freud developed an elaborate theoretical system around this idea, maintaining that a variety of 'perversions' and neuroses, as well as 'oral' and 'anal' character structures, were due to fixations of (sexual) libido in these earlier stages of development and to defences against the unacceptable desires arising from them. In a mischievous lampoon of the sexual theory, Richard Webster has suggested that the feet and hands should be added to Freud's list of 'erogenous zones' to provide 'pedal' and 'manual' stages of libidinal development. A child's delight in having its feet tickled and its evident desire to hold onto its mother's hand would then be diagnosed as manifestations of 'pedal-eroticism' and 'manual-eroticism' respectively; and soccer and handball could be interpreted as polymorphously perverse activities!

As one might expect, Freud's one-track mind determined his understanding of dream symbolism as much as his elucidation of symptom formation. Just as a dream sword being thrust into its scabbard had to be symbolic of intercourse, so an hysterical loss of consciousness symbolized orgasm, appendicitis or vomiting represented pregnancy wishes, dyspnoea (shortness of breath) symbolized coital breathing, a nervous cough represented fellatio, and squeezing blackheads the act of masturbation. 'It is fair to say', declared Freud, 'that there is no group of ideas that is incapable of representing sexual facts and wishes.' He felt justified in reducing a vast array of objects to their supposed male or female sexual symbolism:

> All elongated objects, such as sticks, tree-trunks and umbrellas (the opening of these last being comparable to an erection) may stand for the male organ – as well as all long, sharp weapons, such as knives, daggers and pikes. Another frequent though not entirely intelligible symbol of the same thing is a nail file – possibly on account of the rubbing up and down.

> Boxes, cases, chests, cupboards and ovens represent the uterus, and also hollow objects, ships, and vessels of all kinds. Rooms in dreams are usually women; if the various ways in and out of them are represented, this interpretation is scarcely open to doubt ... A dream of going through a suite of rooms is a brothel or harem dream ... Steps, ladders or staircases, or, as the case may be, walking up or down them, are representations of the sexual act.
>
> In men's dreams a necktie often appears as a symbol for the penis ... nor is there any doubt that all weapons and tools are used as symbols for the male organ: e.g. ploughs, hammers, rifles, revolvers, daggers, sabres, etc. (Freud, 1976, pp.470-73).

The banal reductiveness of such interpretations robs these symbols of all their other implications. While all these objects may indeed represent the human genitals and sexual activities, they may also represent a lot of other things as well. As Jung once quipped, the penis is itself a phallic symbol. Nature clearly intended it to represent power and virility as well as male sexuality (this could explain why the human penis is proportionately three times larger than in any other primate, Diamond, 1991).

The fundamentally reductive approach which characterized the Freudian attitude to the phenomena of life – what Jung was to caricature as the 'nothing but' approach, which boiled all things down to their lowest common denominator – helped to spread what many have seen as the disenchantment and spiritual impoverishment endemic in our culture. The more perceptive of Freud's disciples recognized their complicity in this misfortune: 'We must grudgingly admit', wrote Erik Erikson (1962), 'that even as we were trying to devise, with scientific determinism, a therapy for the few, we were led to promote an ethical disease among the many.'

A highly significant 'unacceptable desire' was thought to occur at the phallic stage when, Freud maintained, a boy becomes sexually interested in his mother, wishes to possess her, and to displace his father in her affections. However, this 'Oedipal situation' gives rise to fears that his father will retaliate and punish him by castration. The resulting 'castration complex' is reinforced by the boy's discovery that girls lack a penis and by the thought that this deficiency could be the result of castration.

On what evidence did Freud base this apparently far-fetched scenario? The Fliess correspondence once more gives us the lead. On October 15th 1897 Freud wrote: 'A single idea of general value dawned on me. I have found, in my own case too, [the phenomenon of] being in love with my mother and jealous of my father, and I now consider it a universal event in early childhood ...'

As with his other major 'discoveries', Freud managed to present this 'universal event in early childhood' in such a way as to make it seem a phenomenon which he had detected in the course of studying large numbers of cases. In fact, it was based on two speculations: (1) that he *may* have been sexually aroused when he saw his mother undressing (*if* he had seen her undressing, he was not sure) when he travelled with her from Leipzig to Vienna in a railway sleeping compartment as a young child of $3\frac{1}{2}$ years-old, and (2) that the erections which Fliess reported observing in his one-year-old son, Robert, *may* have been caused by seeing his mother in the nude. From these intuitive guesses, Freud generalized a family drama to the whole of humanity and formally dedicated the Oedipus complex as the keystone of the arch of psychoanalytic theory.

Despite its insubstantial origins, the Oedipus complex and its resolution by the castration complex became psychoanalytic dogmas accepted without question by generations of Freud's followers. One of the very few to express dissent was the 'independent' British psychoanalyst, John Bowlby, who argued that while it was undeniable that children become strongly attached to their mothers, this has little if anything to do with sex and everything to do with the ubiquitous, naturally occurring mother-child bond apparent in a great number of animal species. Sons may indeed perceive fathers as rivals for their mother's love, but on the whole fathers do not subject their offspring to threats of castration in order to eliminate the competition for their wives' affections.

In an important reassessment of Freud's case histories, Frank Sulloway (1991) reveals the extent to which they are all characterized by arbitrary interpretations and ineffective outcome. Indeed, Frederick Crews has questioned whether Freud himself ever practised psychoanalysis in the manner which he recommended to others. Rather than allowing patients' free associations to lead naturally to repressed material, 'he sought to "nail" the client with hastily conceived interpretations which he then drove home unabatingly.'

Perhaps the most upsetting of Freud's case histories, particularly to feminists, is that of 'Dora' (Ida Bauer), published by Freud in 1905 as a 'Fragment of an Analysis of a Case of Hysteria'. This was regarded by generations of psychoanalysts as 'the classical analysis of the structure and genesis of hysteria' (Erik Erikson, 1962).

Ida Bauer was an attractive young woman of 18 when she was brought reluctantly to see Freud. She suffered from numerous tics, suicidal thoughts, and had become extremely impertinent to her parents. The dramatis personae involved in the story she unfolds are her parents and their friends Herr and Frau K. Herr Bauer, Ida's father, was having an affair with Frau K., while Herr K. had shown sexual interest in Ida since she was 14, when he had forced a kiss on her, which she found disgusting. Herr K. followed this up by offering Ida a direct sexual invitation two years later, for which she slapped his face. She told her mother about these incidents, insisting that her father should break off relations with the K.s. When Herr Bauer tackled him, however, Herr K. denied the incident had ever occurred and attributed Ida's story to a fevered imagination stimulated by romantic literature. To Ida's fury, Herr Bauer accepted Herr K.'s assurances and refused to give way to her pressure to stop seeing the K.s. Ida retaliated by accusing her father of colluding with Herr K. in his designs so that he could continue his affair with Frau K. Deeply embarrassed by this 'insubordinate' line of reasoning, Herr Bauer brought his troublesome daughter to Dr Freud.

What is shocking about Freud's approach to this case is that he did not take his patient's part in this steamy drama, but rather that of her father and Herr K. Freud told Ida that she was really in love with Herr K. and that her disgust when he kissed her was an hysterical reaction to feeling his erect penis pressing against her (this was entirely Freud's supposition of which Ida denied all knowledge). Freud went on to suggest that when Ida slapped Herr K.'s face, it 'was by no means a final No.'

Not for a moment does Freud entertain the possibility that a 14-year-old girl might appropriately be disgusted by the advances of a much older man. Rather he attributes her behaviour to psychosexual pathology based on the usual Freudian credo of repressed homosexuality, fantasies of pregnancy and oral sex, memories of childhood masturbation, and an early witnessing of the 'primal scene' of her parents having sexual intercourse. But Ida would have none of this, and, totally rejecting Freud's interpretations, she broke off the treatment. In his published account, Freud has the gall to regret her premature departure because it deprived him of the possibility of overcoming her sexual inhibitions sufficiently to enable her to succumb to Herr K.'s advances (and thus render him less prone to object to Herr Bauer's attention's to Frau K., Lakoff and Coyne, 1993).

A famous case that Freud claimed to have cured, knowing perfectly well that he had not, was that of the 'Wolf Man' (Sergei Pankeev) which Freud published in 1918. Because Pankeev lost his family fortune in Russia, Freud treated him for nothing and provided him with financial assistance during the five years of his analysis. Although Freud claimed to have cured his depression and obsessional neurosis, Pankeev was to remain in and out of analytic treatment for many years. He seems to have become something of a psychoanalytic rentier, subsidized financially and supported emotionally by one analyst after another perhaps in the hope that he would not tell his true story to outsiders. However, in the 1970s, he eventually spilled the beans to an Austrian journalist,

Karin Obholzer, reporting that his disagreeable symptoms had persisted and that analysis had not particularly helped him.

As a critical reading of the published account of the case makes clear, Freud did not hesitate throughout the course of the analysis to impose his theoretical assumptions on the clinical data. His theory of neurosis demanded a 'primal scene', to provide the sexual trauma necessary to account for Pankeev's symptoms, and Freud found it in a dream which Pankeev remembered from the age of 4. Freud's interpretation of this dream provides a telling illustration of the ease with which he would invent aetiological fantasies which were based on his own experiences of childhood and not on those of his patient.

In Pankeev's childhood dream, six white wolves with large tails (actually they were dogs) sat perfectly still in a tree outside his bedroom window. The wolves, Freud told him, were his parents. That they were white was an evident association with bed linen, and their stillness meant the opposite, vigorous copulation. Their large tails, by the same mysterious logic, meant castration. It was clear, declared Freud, that about the age of 1, Pankeev from his cot had observed his parents copulating, doggy fashion, on three successive occasions, and he had soiled himself in horrified disgust. Pankeev himself never accepted Freud's explanation: it was, he said, 'terribly far-fetched.' He had no recollection of ever seeing his parents having sex or of soiling himself on such an occasion. In any case, he argued convincingly, it would not have been possible, since no child of his class and background ever slept in a cot in his parents' bedroom. But, of the two people engaged in this analysis, one of them did sleep in his parents' bedroom, did believe he had witnessed the 'primal scene', and did have a traumatic memory of urinating there, and that was not Sergei Pankeev but Sigmund Freud ('That boy will never amount to anything!').

***

Of all the concepts introduced by Freud during his 'creative illness' (which he referred to as his period of 'splendid isolation'), the one that has had a most profound and lasting influence on the development of psychodynamic therapy is that of 'transference'. 'What do you think of the transference?' Freud demanded during an early exchange with Jung. 'That it is the alpha and omega of psychoanalysis', replied Jung. 'Then you have understood the main thing', said Freud.

Freud introduced the term transference to describe the process by which a patient unconsciously *transfers* on to the person of the analyst feelings and attitudes that were, in fact, possessed by significant people, particularly parents, in the past. This gives rise to the so-called *transference relationship* between patient and analyst. This has to be distinguished from the *analytic relationship* or the *therapeutic alliance*, which refers to the total relationship between analyst and patient as actual people.

Freud came to see transference as an artificially induced neurosis in which patients repeated all the attitudes, assumptions, feelings, and modes of relating which they had developed in relation to their parents. This was an insight of the greatest significance. To this day, 'analysis of the transference' is the defining characteristic of all psychodynamic treatment which distinguishes it from other forms of psychotherapy.

Being a somewhat schizoid personality, Freud did not welcome the strong feelings patients often experienced, and expressed, in relation to himself. 'As for the transference', he wrote in 1910, 'it is altogether a curse.' On the face of it, the clinical approach he advocated might seem designed to circumvent such feelings, but, as we shall see, it only served to generate them. 'I cannot advise my colleagues too urgently', wrote Freud, in his 'Recommendations to Physicians Practising Psychoanalysis', 'to model themselves during psychoanalytic treatment on the surgeon, who puts aside all his feelings, even his human sympathy, and concentrates all his mental forces on the single aim of performing the operation as skilfully as possible' (*SE* 12, p.115). He advocated 'emotional coldness' on the part of the analyst, who should be opaque to his patients, and like a mirror show them nothing but what is shown to him.

Adopting his historical perspective to telling effect, Henri Ellenberger has pointed out that Freud's attitudes to his patients must be understood in the light of what neuropathologists wrote at the end of the nineteenth century about the 'diabolical cleverness' employed by hysterics to deceive their doctor and draw him into their own devious strategies: 'It is as if each rule of Freudian technique was devised to defeat the cunning of these patients' wrote Ellenberger.

One might add that each rule was also devised to strengthen the doctor's position in coercing his patients. The rule that all appointments must be paid for in advance, whether kept or not, prevents the patient from punishing the analyst or *resisting* the analytic process through absenteeism and non-payment. This also renders the analyst's livelihood more secure and further strengthens his ability to control the patient. By sitting behind patients, out of view, the analyst deprives them of an audience and of the satisfaction of being able to see his reactions. By insisting on analysing the transference, the analyst defeats the hysteric's concealed but always present purpose of seducing him. For this reason, any kind of 'acting out' or physical contact is prohibited, as is social contact outside the therapeutic situation. And because of the hysteric's determination to defeat the analyst by all means at her disposal, even at the cost of remaining ill and socially incapacitated, a cure must never be promised and the patient told that improvement will depend entirely on her own efforts. In this way, the analyst neatly absolves himself of all responsibility for failure. As we shall see, similar rules apply in Kleinian analysis, where failure to benefit from analysis is attributed to the patient's 'destructive envy' of the 'good breast' proffered by the analyst.

Application of these rules by an emotionally cold analyst, going about his business with the objective precision of a surgeon, treating his patients' emotional responses to him as being nothing but repetitions from the past, had a number of consequences not always helpful for the patients. To begin with, it meant that any genuine feelings they might be experiencing as adults in the here and now were uniformly discounted. Secondly, Freud's charismatic authority, combined with his insistence that he 'knew' what was going on in their minds had the effect of infantilizing them and resurrecting in them feelings that they had indeed experienced long ago in relation to their parents. Ashamed of such feelings, patients were understandably reluctant to talk about them – a reluctance which Freud invariably interpreted as 'resistance' and took as confirmation of his theory of sexual repression.

Most importantly, the whole Freudian technique put patients in a position of extreme emotional vulnerability. Having encouraged them to reveal the most intimate, guilty and embarrassing secrets of their lives, the analyst offered no reassurance, no emotional support, and, above all, no reciprocation, which in any normal human relationship they would have had every right to expect. This again deepens patients' sense of helpless dependency on the analyst and increases the strength of their longings for his reassurance and his love.

These criticisms of classic Freudian technique are not new. They were made very cogently in a 'secret diary' kept in 1932 by one of Freud's hitherto most trusted lieutenants, Sandor Ferenzci. Significantly, the diary was suppressed for over fifty years and was published for the first time in a French translation in 1985. In it, Ferenzci frankly acknowledges the feelings of power the analyst can enjoy over 'numbers of helplessly worshipful patients, who admire the analyst unreservedly'; he can prolong their treatment as long as he likes and turn them into lifelong taxpayers. For, however extreme their sufferings and however unsuccessful the treatment, the infantilized patient cannot walk out of the analysis – 'just as it is impossible for a child to run away from home, because, left on its own, it would feel helpless.' He records Freud as saying, 'patients are only riffraff', and that all they were good for was to help the analyst to make a living and to provide material for concocting theories. 'He looms like a god above his poor patient, who has been degraded to the status of a child. We claim that the transference comes from the patient, unaware of the fact that the greater part of what one calls the transference is artificially provoked by this very behaviour.'

In the course of his life, Freud subjected the transference concept to a number of revisions. Perhaps the most important of these was in *Beyond The Pleasure Principle* (1920) where he shifted the emphasis of analytic work away from exploration of unconscious motives to the analysis of the ego's mechanisms of defence. Since unconscious drives were experienced as threats, the ego defended itself against the consequent anxiety by protecting itself behind a battery of defences such as denial, repression, reaction-formation, projection, rationalization, etc. The task of the analyst must be to dismantle these defences and to assist the patient in 'working through' the underlying anxiety, while relating the process to the existence and subsequent removal of neurotic symptoms. The patient was then expected to develop more appropriate defences and to achieve a better adjustment to the issues of life. However, the dismantling of patients' defences could be an extremely painful process and it had the inevitable consequence of further increasing their emotional vulnerability and their dependence on the analyst.

It was not until publication of *Analysis Terminable and Interminable* in 1937 that Freud finally acknowledged that it was not always possible to terminate an analysis after a definite period with a lasting cure. Some patients had to re-enter analysis from time to time while others had to continue indefinitely through life. He did not, of course, consider the possibility that this might be because psychoanalysis was ineffective in these cases. On the contrary, it was due to deficiencies in the patient, such as weakness of the ego or to the constitutional power of the unconscious drives, especially of the death instinct. In his posthumous *Outline of Psychoanalysis*, Freud added 'psychic inertia' to the list of defects shared by unresponsive patients, together with a weak capacity for the sublimation of sexual and destructive impulses.

Since Freud's death, the transference concept has undergone many further revisions, and it is true to say that contemporary psychodynamic therapists attribute neurosis less to repressed drives than to a failure on the part of the patient to make satisfactory and lasting human relationships. Analysis of the transference now involves the interpretation of the patient's modes of relating to the analyst in the present. The early origins of these patterns are examined but the main emphasis is on revealing how the patient's difficulties in relating to others are reflected in the analytic relationship. The success of this delicate procedure depends in great measure on the sensitivity of the analyst in shifting the focus of attention between the transference relationship and the real relationship of the 'therapeutic alliance'. We shall be returning to this crucial theme at a later stage.

Inevitably, analysts as well as patients bring unconscious baggage with them when embarking on the analytic encounter. At first Freud assumed that the analyst would, through his own self-analysis or his training analysis, be so aware of the unconscious material he brought with him from the past that he would be incapable of transferring it to his patients. With time and experience, however, Freud and his colleagues acknowledged that this was by no means always the case and it was necessary to monitor the unconscious reactions their patients released in them if they were not to distort the therapeutic alliance in unintended ways. These unconscious projections by the analyst on to the patient make up what Freud called the *countertransference*. Introducing the term in a paper published in 1910, Freud insisted that it was essential for the analyst to recognize his countertransference and overcome it: 'Anyone who fails to produce results in a self-analysis of this kind may at once give up any idea of being able to treat patients by analysis' (1910, pp.144-45).

Unfortunately, the emphasis placed in recent decades on the importance of analysis of the transference as a means of solving problems of relationship has led to such an extension of the meanings attributed to these useful terms as to render them virtually redundant. Thus, transference has come to refer to the patient's total emotional *attitude* to the analyst, while countertransference has come to cover the total emotional *reaction* of the analyst to the patient. The unfortunate consequence of this totalistic application of the terms has been to crowd out the no less important concept – research would indicate that it is the more important concept – of the therapeutic alliance. We shall return to this issue when we consider the implications of 'object relations theory' for psychodynamic therapy.

***

We must conclude that Freud's most extraordinary achievements were neither clinical nor scientific but personal and promotional. With impressive tactical skill he was able to present himself as a fearless searcher after truth, a lonely genius surrounded by lesser men and beset with the hostility of a dismissive, anti-Semitic medical establishment, a selfless scientist of impregnable integrity, totally incapable of fraud or malpractice. Now that this self-serving myth has been torn away, he stands exposed as an ambitious quack, an unscrupulous clinician, capable of bullying his patients into providing the data he needed to 'prove' his aetiological fantasies, and of generating an extensive literature which used and re-used a tiny number of 'classic' cases with such consumate cunning as to create the illusion of an enormous clinical database.

Yet, for all that, he remains an outstanding historical figure, more famous by far than any of his critics or detractors. How did he do it? Knowing what we now know, how could it be that Freud was destined to become the most celebrated psychological architect of the twentieth century? How could he get away with using a few half-baked bricks and much crumbling mortar to build a fantastic Manhatten of the mind, where thousands queued up to secure leases?

The cultural success of psychoanalysis can be understood, as we have already seen, as due to its apparent ability to meet the desire for an all-inclusive explanatory system to replace the religious belief systems which Western society had lost. Freud and Jung were both personally seeking a psychological substitute for their lost religious faith, and far from being alone in this, they articulated the cultural plight of millions, and seemed to provide a solution. Accordingly, Freud did not confine himself to the treatment of neurosis, but strove throughout his life to create a coherent system of ideas capable of explaining the psychosocial functions of art, literature, religion, and the traditional institutions of society.

Largely because of the myth Freud created round himself, psychoanalysis was seen as a brilliant scientific achievement that had arisen *de novo* from his own empirical observations. Until the publication of Ellenberger's *Discovery of the Unconscious* in 1970, it was not realized how many of Freud's original discoveries were in fact ideas he had adapted from such luminaries as Darwin, Haeckel, Schopenhauer, Fechner, and Nietzsche, as well as Brücke, Meynert, Charcot, Breuer, and Fliess. Darwin's vision of psychology as a science based on the biology of instinct was adopted by Freud as his basic premise, while Haeckel's now discredited 'biogenic law' that 'ontogeny recapitulates phylogeny' (that individual development goes through the same phases as the evolutionary development of the species) was accepted by Freud without question. He used it in *Totem and Taboo* (1913) in order to explain the Oedipus complex as an individual recapitulation of a primordial crime which Freud believed had actually occurred in the ancestral past when a tyrannical Father, ruler of the primal horde, was murdered by his sons.

Schopenhauer's *The World as Will and Idea* had an enormous success in the second half of the nineteenth century and deeply influenced the work of such figures as Wagner, Nietzsche, and Thomas Mann, as well as Freud and Jung. What Schopenhauer called the 'Will' was the blind force that prevailed throughout the universe and guided the life of humanity; the 'idea' constituted the conscious realm of phenomena. This was an extension of the distinction made by Kant between the thing-in-itself (*das Ding-an-sich*) and the phenomena to which the thing-in-itself gives rise. Schopenhauer's 'Will', the irrational force which drives us but of which we are largely unaware, consists of two instincts: preservation and sex. Of the two, sex is much stronger: 'Man is incarnate sexual instinct', wrote Schopenhauer, 'since he owes his origin to copulation and the wish of his wishes is to copulate'. Freud's attribution of sex as the central motivating force of the unconscious psyche and his later distinction between the id (the 'Will') and the ego (the 'idea') are evident transpositions of Schopenhauerian metaphysics into Freudian metapsychology.

But of all the cultural influences helping to shape Freud's thinking, none were greater than the ideas of Friedrich Nietzsche (1844-1900), which permeated the intellectual climate of the 1880s and 90s. Characteristically, Freud attempted to disown Nietzsche's influence, insisting that he developed his theories independently and empirically. He even had the audacity to write condescendingly of Nietzsche as a philosopher 'whose guesses and intuitions often agree in the most astonishing way with the laborious findings of psychoanalysis'! And he makes the ingenuous claim that he had avoided reading Nietzsche for many years so as to keep his mind free of all Nietzschean influences! Even if this were true, it would not have been possible for any educated man of the period to remain in ignorance of Nietzsche's ideas, since they were constantly being quoted and discussed in café's, newspapers, periodicals, and journals throughout the German-speaking world.

One of Nietzsche's aphorisms could have provided the justification of Freud's life: 'Against positivism, which halts at phenomena – "There are facts" – I would say: No, facts are precisely what there are not, only interpretations.' Nietzsche's lifelong emphasis on the unconscious, orgiastic, self-destructive (Dionysian) side of human nature, apparently to the detriment of the calm, conscious, orderly, and rational (Apollonian) side, finds echoes in Freud's distinction between primary and secondary process thinking, between the pleasure principle and the reality principle, between the id and the ego.

Like Nietzsche, Freud was to prove an accomplished exponent of the 'uncovering' or 'unmasking' psychology that strips all human phenomena to the lowest common denominator. This trend began with the French moralists of the seventeenth century, achieving its most dazzling expression in the Maxims of La Rochefoucauld, with their witty exposure of virtuous pretension as disguised self-advancement. It is unfortunate for the well-being of our culture that one of the most contagious of psychoanalytic prejudices has been that which views human ideals and aspirations as defensive sublimations designed to conceal what is most base in us. Freud's *Civilisation and Its Discontents* (1930) has many parallels with Nietzsche's *Genealogy of Morals* (1887), both being inspired by Diderot's idea that civilisation makes men sick by inhibiting fulfilment of their primordial instincts. Nietzsche's passionate atheism and violent attacks on Christianity may well have encouraged Freud to publish his own iconoclastic views in *Moses and Monotheism* (1939) and *The Future of An Illusion* (1927), in which he dismisses monotheistic religion as the fulfilment of regressive infantile longings for an all-powerful, all-protecting parent.

Though he sought to deny all these influences, Freud nevertheless acknowledged a debt to Gustav Theodor Fechner (1801-1887), from whom he developed his topographical concept of mind, and the concept of mental energy, as well as the principles of pleasure-unpleasure and of repetition. But, on the whole, Freud preferred to annexe ideas without acknowledgement, dress them up in his own impressive terminology, and recycle them as empirical discoveries made on his own couch. Thanks to Ellenberger, Macmillan, Webster, and others, we know that they came less from Freud's consulting room than from his library. Freud's achievement was to weave these ideas into a new synthesis, devising new rituals for the treatment of neurotic disorders via the analytic situation, the analytic relationship, and the analysis of ego-defences and the transference.

That so many of the root ideas of psychoanalysis were current in the culture of Freud's time goes a long way to explain the readiness with which psychoanalytic doctrines were eventually accepted. One area in which psychoanalysts continue to claim primacy for Freud's achievement is in his fearless introduction of novel sexual theories at a time when discussion of anything sexual was considered 'taboo'. But this again is not the case. It is true that there existed a dread of venereal infection, especially syphilis, which inhibited open discussion of sexual topics in polite society, but this does not mean that sex was a taboo subject in intellectual, particularly medical, circles, as is evidenced by the wide circulation and discussion of books by a new breed of sexologists such as Krafft-Ebing, Magnus Hirschfeld, and Havelock Ellis.

Freud's success in making psychoanalytic ideas accessible to a huge international constituency was due to his undoubted brilliance as a writer. Over the years he developed a wonderfully patrician literary style which lent his utterances great authority, and as an extempore lecturer, speaking for hours without notes, he was unsurpassed. When he presented a case history, he described the unconscious processes responsible for its symptomatology so convincingly that few members of his audience even suspected that what they were being fed was a highly inventive series of speculations. And those who did suspect, had often abandoned their disbelief by the time Freud brought his discourse to a close.

His technique, both as writer and lecturer, was to begin with a beguiling show of tentativeness, designed to lull the reader into a sense of being led through dense thickets of complex material by an open-minded guide. Anticipating every possible objection he was careful to disarm each in turn. Then, very gently, he proceeded to persuade his audience to accept as firmly established what had been only tentatively suggested. And, like his hero Sherlock Holmes, formulate the case and present his conclusions in a manner so convincing as to make them seem the only possible deductions from the facts.

Above all psychoanalytic writers he had *Sprachgefühl* (feeling for language) and few were surprised when he received the Goethe prize for literature in 1930. He admired Shakespeare, Goethe, Schiller, Heine, and the Greek tragedians, whom he called 'his masters', and it is possible that had he devoted his life to literature instead of psychoanalysis he could have been an important creative writer. It is perhaps because of his literary gifts that psychoanalysis is closer to fiction than to science. In an interview with the Italian author Giovanni Papini in 1934, Freud said: 'Though I have the appearance of a scientist, I was and am a poet and novelist.' Bilingual commentators say that something of the high literary merit of the German originals is irretrievably lost in translation, but Freud is, nevertheless, always a pleasure to read in English. So lucid and persuasive is his prose that it possesses *instant* credibility. Even though Freud invariably preferred arcane explanations to obvious ones, he somehow manages to make one accept his preferences as yet further examples of the percipience and profundity of his thinking.

Why was Freud so casual with the truth and so willing to doctor his facts? Was it entirely due to overweaning ambition and an obsessive determination to succeed? Not entirely. One of Freud's severest critics, Richard Webster, offers the most charitable explanation: he maintains that Freud was totally convinced of the validity of his theories and genuinely believed that psychoanalysis would make so great a contribution to the relief of suffering in the world that the matter of providing evidence to substantiate his beliefs seemed trivial by comparison and wasteful of his energies. If this is so, then Freud is similar to many other charismatic leaders of esoteric movements, whose appeal to their followers lies in the total conviction with which they express their views.

In his book *Feet of Clay* (1996), Anthony Storr has no hesitation in classifying Freud as a guru (a Sanskrit term meaning both 'weighty' and 'one who brings light out of darkness'; in India it is used to designate a Hindu or Sikh religious teacher). In this fascinating study, Storr characterizes gurus as people who believe they have been granted some special, life-transforming insight. This usually comes to them at some time in their 30s or 40s and typically follows a period of mental or physical illness (which has variously been described as a 'mid-life crisis', a 'creative illness', or 'dark night of the soul'). The Eureka experience may come on gradually or like a thunderbolt, in the manner of a religious conversion, a scientific discovery, or the intact delusional system of a psychotic illness. As a result, the guru becomes convinced that he has discovered 'the truth', and this conviction, as well as the passion with which he proclaims it, gives him the charisma which makes him attractive to potential followers. Good looks and the ability to speak fluently in public are invaluable additional assets.

In a study published by John Price and myself in the same year as Storr's book appeared, we described charismatic leaders, based on our reading of the available literature, as possessing personal characteristics which would readily satisfy the internationally recognized psychiatric diagnostic criteria of 'borderline', 'schizoid', 'schizotypal' or 'paranoid' personality disorders. Of these, Freud would most readily fit in to the schizoid category, as for that matter would Jung. Freud, as we have seen, had no great opinion of humanity, and throughout his life he preferred correspondence to actual meetings with people. In his *Autobiographical Study*, he confines himself to the development of his ideas; he hardly mentions his relations with other people. This is in line with his theoretical focus on drives, their sublimation and repression *within* the individual, and with his lack of interest in 'object relations', which were to preoccupy the 'neo-Freudians' who came after him.

As Storr points out, gurus are more interested in what goes on in their minds than they are in their relationships with others, and being of an authoritarian, anti-democratic disposition, they tend to attract followers rather than friends, their relations with followers being based not on fellowship but on dominance. Accordingly, Freud maintained his ascendancy over other psychoanalysts by keeping his distance from them, while at the same time demanding their loyalty and their love. Gurus require disciples as much as disciples need a guru, for the guru's conviction in the truth of his message is not always as absolute as it appears, and his confidence requires the constant boost that followers can bring. For this reason, gurus are extremely intolerant of criticism, feeling that anything less than total agreement with their views is equivalent to overt hostility. It was Freud's dogmatic certainty, combined with his refusal to tolerate dissent, that drove unsycophantic colleagues away from him and bound the rest to him with hoops of steel. His insistence that sexuality was the causal factor in every case of hysteria, for example, destroyed his collaboration with Breuer, and guaranteed the eventual estrangement between himself and Jung.

Psychoanalysis thus demonstrates many of the features of that complex relationship between love, power, and submission which is characteristic of all messianic movements. Freud's somewhat masochistic submission earlier in life to men such as Brücke, Breuer, and Fliess was the reverse of the dominance he later exerted over disciples like Jones, Ferenczi, and Rank. Paul Roazen, that perceptive historian of psychoanalytic vicissitudes, has described how many of Freud's disciples and patients, hungry for his love, so identified with him as to mimic his verbal and physical mannerisms. Hans Sachs, for example, became obsessional about catching railway trains in the same way as Freud, while Theodor Reik adopted Freud's manner of smoking cigars, his style of writing and talking, and grew an identical beard. For them Freud came to represent what Jung was to call an archetype – the archetype of the sage, prophet, healer, and, ultimately, the wise old man. But what kept all his followers in line was the fear of being perceived as deviant or doctrinally unsound, for the consequences of Freud's pronouncement of anathema and excommunication for heresy could, as we shall see, be terrible indeed.

With Freud there was always a tendency for enmity to follow friendship. This happened not only in his relations with Meynert, Breuer, and Fliess, but with Jung, Adler, Stekel, and other colleagues who were at one time close to him. Alfred Adler (1870-1937), a Viennese physician, was one of the first disciples to be attracted to Freud, and he remained active in Freud's psychoanalytic circle until differences between them brought about his departure in 1911. Like Jung, Adler came to disagree with the exclusive emphasis Freud placed on sexual development in the aetiology of neurosis, and became increasingly convinced that social instincts, and compensatory power strivings, were more fundamental motivations than sexuality.

As will become clear in the next and later Chapters, the intellectual differences which arose between the pioneers of psychoanalysis were invariably related to their personal biographies. Disagreements over the importance of the Oedipus complex is a case in point. Whereas Freud's mother had been a beautiful young woman who lavished love and attention on him, Jung's mother, as we shall see, was a homely soul who was prone to attacks of depression, which caused her to spend at least one long period in hospital during her son's early childhood. Freud's concept of the Oedipus complex and its central role in human development grew directly out of his fantasies about his own childhood experience. That neither Jung nor Adler accepted the universality of the Oedipus complex was due to their quite different childhood circumstances. Events in Adler's early history caused him to place great emphasis on the developmental influence of birth order in siblings, and on the individual's need to compensate for early feelings of inferiority, while Jung's sense of maternal deprivation, and a religious crisis experienced during adolescence in relation to his father, caused him to turn inwards and seek spiritual security within himself.

But to Freud, these dissidents were intolerable, and it was in order to protect him from them that Ernest Jones proposed in 1913 that a secret committee should be formed of Freud's most loyal adherents to act as a kind of Praetorian Guard. The objective of this group of intellectual heavies, which we might call the 'Freud Squad', was to engineer the ejection of Jung from the International Psychoanalytic Association, to protect Freud from heretics, and to police the theoretical purity of psychoanalysis.

Freud took to the idea at once, for it offered him some hope that his work might survive after his death: 'I was so uneasy about what the human rabble would make out of it when I was no longer alive', he later recalled. The secret committee was inaugurated on May 25th that year in Freud's consulting room at Berggasse 19 and consisted of Ernest Jones, Sandor Ferenzci, Max Eitingen, Hans Sachs, Otto Rank, and Karl Abraham, as well as Freud himself. Freud presented each of them with an ancient intaglio from his collection of antiquities, which they had mounted on gold rings and wore as pledges of eternal brotherhood. Freud's was incised with the head of Jupiter! All this was done behind Jung's back and while he was still President of the International Association.

It was that summer of 1913 that Freud wrote *Totem and Taboo*, perhaps his most fantastic and controversial book, which demonstrated the extent to which he conceived family dynamics to be based on conflict. Before civilization began, so Freud's fantasy ran, an all-powerful father had possessed all the women of the tribe. His sons eventually banded together, killed him, and ceremonially ate his body. The brothers then quarrel among themselves, and out of remorse for their parricide, decide to accept their father's prohibition against incest. In his secret committee, Freud was, apparently without realizing it, setting up a similar situation: it was as if he were unconsciously inviting its members to kill him and quarrel among themselves. Though Freud survived until 1939, serious tensions certainly developed between members of the committee. Ferenzci and Rank eventually rebelled, and suffered the inevitable excommunication.

***

What then may we conclude about the consequences of Freud's contribution to psychotherapy and to our culture? The debate about this will continue for a long time to come, some maintaining that he liberated us from sexual inhibition and prudery, others that he seriously eroded the ethical codes of self-discipline and social responsibility on which Western society has hitherto depended. The idea that Freud was the first to stress the importance of sex in neurotic aetiology at a time when all mention of sex was prohibited is, as we have seen, part of the Freudian legend. As already noted, at the turn of the century Vienna was awash with sexual theorizing. The works of Moritz Benedikt, Richard von

Krafft-Ebing, Otto Weininger, Havelock Ellis, and Magnus Hirschfeldt were well known and a source of much discussion in intellectual circles at the time. But in the wider, less sophisticated culture there was still much sexual guilt and shame, against which the rising influence of psychoanalysis had to struggle. The eventual triumph of Freudian theory, however, contributed to the twentieth century obsession with sex – to the exaggerated emphasis on the importance of a satisfied sexual appetite for human happiness, to the salacious public interest, inflamed by media titillation, in the private sexual life of all celebrities, and to the uncritical acceptance of the idea that most human actions, however altruistic, are sexually motivated.

By setting himself up as the unmasker of hypocrisy and pretension, advocating a systematic exposure of the mechanisms people use to defend themselves against their real desires, Freud generated the belief that peoples' true motives are always less creditable than they seem, and that their actions are less inspired by public spirited ideals than driven by selfish, greedy, aggressive, destructive, and lustful passions.

This jaded and cynical view of human nature, which has been promoted so enthusiastically by the media, has had unfortunate consequences for both the private and the public domains of contemporary existence. It has led to that seamy atmosphere of suspicion and distrust that would assert that anyone who delights in the company of children must be a paedophile. It has brought us to the sad point where fathers are fearful of expressing love for their daughters lest it be seized on as 'evidence' of incest or abuse; doctors are fearful of offering physical comfort to distressed patients by putting an arm round their shoulder or holding their hand lest this be construed as an attempt at seduction; and employers are fearful of complimenting their young employees on their appearance lest it exposes them to an accusation of sexual harassment. It is of course true that children are sometimes abused, patients seduced, or young people are sexually harassed, but when interest in these matters becomes exaggerated or obsessive, it can have most unhappy consequences for ordinary social life.

Perhaps Freud's major bequest to his followers was that form of convincing yet spurious authority which Robyn Dawes (1994) has called the 'myth of expertise' – the self-assumed justification to claim special knowledge about patients which is not only unavailable to less qualified practitioners but also inaccessible to the patients themselves. Taking Freud as their model, generations of psychoanalysts, therapists, and social workers have felt justified in making assumptions on theoretical grounds as to the nature of the unconscious and repressed material responsible for making them ill, and, in the name of therapy, 'helping' their clients to 'remember'. The philosopher, Isaiah Berlin, foresaw this danger many years ago. To assume that one knows someone better than they know themselves, and that one is justified in over-riding their protests in the interests of their own good, can readily become a justification to 'bully, oppress, torture them in the name, and on behalf, of their "real" selves.'

Freud repeatedly reassured his readers and audiences that he had abandoned hypnosis and the use of suggestion in the early 1890s, preferring to allow his patients, through their free associations, to lead him, like an explorer without a map, through the jungle of their unconscious memories to the sexual traumata at the root of their disorder. As a result, psychoanalysts, and indeed all psychodynamic therapists, have tended grossly to underestimate the power of suggestion in therapy, and have too uncritically accepted the belief that true memories can be unearthed, uncontaminated by the prejudices and preoccupations of the practitioner. The many terrible instances of injustice which have resulted from faith in the 'recovered memory syndrome' have demonstrated the extent to which the human psyche is vulnerable to suggestion. As research has overwhelmingly demonstrated it is evident that psychotherapy is still too primitive a discipline to be able to claim that it can use signs, symptoms, and symbols to detect the existence of unconscious events and repressed memories of which patients declare they know nothing. At the present state of knowledge, any therapist who does this automatically stands convicted of professional malpractice.

It would hardly be fair, however, to blame Freud for all the ills which have overtaken Western society in the twentieth century. The sociologists and political ideologues must take their share of the blame. Moreover, much social advocacy and legislation has been based on misinterpretations of Freud's views. The 'liberation philosophy' of the 1960s, for example, was promoted by media pundits who, having absorbed a distorted version of Freudian theory, genuinely believed we had such certain knowledge of human nature as to justify changing laws and institutions so radically as to liberate people from social constraint and set them free to seek their individual self-fulfilment, uninhibited by the repressive machinery of the State. Unfortunately, the intellectual steam driving the 60s revolution was generated by the wholly erroneous idea that Freud had proved sexual repression to be the cause of all social ills.

What Freud actually maintained, on the contrary, was that the suppression and sublimation of instinctual forces into socially responsible modes of behaviour actually made civilization possible. Now that the truth of this realization is beginning to dawn, the time has passed when it is possible to do much to rectify the damage. Nostalgic for the old certainties, we have lost the vocabulary for articulating them and the political will to re-establish or redefine them. Not only have we dismantled the laws which underpinned these certainties but we have rejected the religious authority and the historical traditions out of which these laws were derived and authenticated.

The central flaw in Freud's theorizing and his promotion of 'an ethical disease among the many' is the fact that he set himself the goal of creating a science of human nature before the time for such an achievement had arrived, and that he then used all his skill as a communicator to persuade the world that he had created it. Too many influential people took him at his word. We shall continue to suffer the consequences of this misfortune far into the twenty-first century.

But has no good come out of what Richard Webster calls this 'complex pseudo-science which should be recognized as one of the great follies of Western civilization'? Although he did not always practice what he preached, Freud's advocacy of an objective, non-judgemental attitude to patients and their problems contributed to the development of a more tolerant and humane approach to neurosis and to sexual deviation. His influence helped to persuade the medical profession, as well as the public at large, that these were essentially developmental disorders and not the result of hereditary 'taints', constitutional 'degeneration', or inherent wickedness. By introducing the formal ritual of the psychoanalytic '50-minute hour', he established the fundamental psychotherapeutic principle of providing what no other human relationship provides – a safe environment in which a qualified professional gives individual patients undivided and sympathetic attention, getting to know them intimately without judging or rejecting them, but respecting their essential humanity.

The majority of people who seek psychotherapeutic help feel they have seldom if ever been accepted or valued for what they are. To be able to reveal their social anxieties, personal doubts, and feelings of low self-esteem to another human being not only enables them to objectify their troubles and find solutions to them but to embark on a process of self-discovery and self-affirmation which is itself experienced as healing. In all forms of mental distress the crucial remedy is to find oneself accepted, understood, reaffirmed, and valued as a member of the human race. Insofar as Freud was responsible for rediscovering this therapeutic principle and making it available to vulnerable people in our society we must be forever in his debt.

3

Analytical Psychology and Carl Gustav Jung (1875-1961)

A widely accepted view of Jung is that of a woolly-minded defector who betrayed the strict scientific principles of psychoanalysis in order to found a mystical cult of his own. This distortion, which started with Freud and his inner circle, has proved remarkably resilient, and has recently resurfaced in the writings of Richard Noll. The truth is very different. As will become clear, the basic hypotheses postulated by Jung during and after his break with Freud have stood the test of time better than those of his erstwhile mentor. For example, Jung's theory of 'archetypes' making up the 'collective unconscious' of a phylogenetically (evolutionary) endowed psyche, his ideas about psychopathology and the adaptive nature of psychiatric symptoms find close parallels in the ideas current in contemporary evolutionary psychiatry.

Jung went to Vienna to meet Freud for the first time in March 1907. They were so captivated by one another that they talked without stopping for thirteen hours. Freud was 50 and still struggling to establish his reputation as the founder of psychoanalysis; Jung was 31, a promising psychiatrist on the great Eugen Bleuler's staff at the Burghölzli Hospital in Zurich, who had already achieved recognition through his demonstration of the existence of unconscious complexes through his use of the word association test, originally devised by the English physicist, Sir Francis Galton. Following this first encounter, an intense friendship developed between them which lasted – mostly through letters – for 6 years.

On the face of it this was an odd relationship between two men of different age, character and background. Jung, a rural Protestant, son of a Swiss pastor, conventionally educated, was steeped in theology and Romantic idealism; while Freud, an urban Jew, was educated in a progressive tradition that led him naturally into science and atheism. Jung's published work on the association test and his book *The Psychology of Dementia Praecox* (1906), as well as his position as Bleuler's second-in-command at the Burghölzli, meant that he was both well known and highly regarded in international psychiatric circles. Freud, on the other hand, was a much more controversial figure because of his ideas on the polymorphous perversity of infants and the sexual aetiology of neurosis. Of the two, Jung was at that time considered the better scientist. For Jung to throw in his lot with Freud was personally and professionally risky and, as we shall see, he was destined to emerge from the relationship psychologically scarred, his reputation in tatters.

What drew them to one another? From the start, it was clear that each felt the other could help further his professional ambitions; but gradually both began to find fulfilment of deeper personal needs in their burgeoning friendship. Freud's closest associates in Vienna quickly became envious of the affectionate attention he lavished on Jung and resented the special relationship that was growing up between them. Freud was irritated by this reaction, which he regarded as the sort of petty-mindedness typical of the second rate individuals who made up his small Viennese clique. Jung, by contrast, so supremely able and well placed in the psychiatric world, had the added advantages, in Freud's view, of being neither Jewish nor Viennese. Freud hoped that his new ally might rescue psychoanalysis from the ever present threat of anti-Semitic hostility, draw it out of its parochial obscurity, and gain for it a place on the international stage.

From their very first meeting, Jung was fascinated by Freud: 'Freud was the first man of real importance I had encountered', he wrote in his memoir *Memories, Dreams, Reflections*:

> in my experience up to that time, no one else could compare with him. There was nothing the least trivial in his attitude. I found him extremely intelligent, shrewd, and altogether remarkable. And yet my first impressions of him remained somewhat tangled; I could not make him out.
>
> What he said about his sexual theory impressed me. Nevertheless, his words could not remove my hesitations and doubts. I tried to advance these reservations of mine on several occasions, but each time he would attribute them to my lack of experience. Freud was right; in those days I had not enough experience to support my objections. I could see that his sexual theory was enormously important to him, both personally and philosophically ... When he spoke of it, his tone became urgent, almost anxious, and all signs of his normally critical and sceptical manner vanished. A strange, deeply moved expression came over his face, the cause of which I was at a loss to understand (*MDR*, pp.146-147).

As Jung saw it, Freud, who made no secret of his atheism, had turned his sexual theory into a pseudo-religious dogma: in place of Jaweh, whom he had lost, he substituted another daemonic force: 'sexual libido', a *deus absconditus*, a numinous principle which Freud claimed as scientific and removed from all religious taint.

Two days after their first encounter, Jung returned for a second meeting with Freud, this time bringing with him another young Swiss psychiatrist, Ludwig Binswanger. Freud asked them both about the dreams they had had the night before, and proceeded to interpret Jung's dream as involving a wish to dethrone him and take his place. The mood of the meeting was, however, extremely congenial: 'Freud's dislike of all formality and ceremony,' recorded Binswanger afterwards, 'his personal charm, simplicity, natural openness, and kindness, and not least his humour, left no room for constraint. And yet one could not for a moment deny the impression of greatness and dignity that emanated from him. To me it was a pleasure, albeit somewhat sceptical, to see the enthusiasm and confidence with which Freud responded to Jung, in whom he immediately saw his scientific "son and heir".'

Jung, evidently pleased by the esteem in which Freud held him, was drawn to his older colleague as to a mentor whom fate had provided at a critical moment in his career. To Jung, Freud represented the intellectually courageous father that his own timid, reticent, and self-doubting father could never have been. In contrast to the rather tragic, spiritually inadequate country pastor, who had suffered the catastrophe of losing his faith, Freud was a towering figure who spoke with total conviction out of his hard-won experience. Jung was happy to accept the subordinate position in their relationship, for, as he acknowledged, he still had much to learn. Soon after their first meeting, he wrote to Freud: 'Let me enjoy your friendship not as one between equals but as that of father and son.' While in a letter to Jung, Freud wrote of his 'long years of honourable but painful solitude' and of the 'serene certainty which finally took possession of me and bade me wait until a voice from the unknown multitude should answer mine. That voice was yours.'

If Jung needed a father, Freud needed a son whom he considered worthy to inherit his kingdom and continue his rule. Unfortunately, this was not the sort of relationship that could last. On his side, Freud was not particularly keen to see his 'son' grow up: he would have preferred a devoted disciple willing to accept his doctrines and respect his authority without reservation. For several years, he continued to make fulsome allusions to Jung's brilliance as a psychoanalyst and to his crucial importance for the future of the movement. This embarrassed Jung, because as he increasingly realized, he would never be able to uphold Freud's ideas in their entirety. Nevertheless, in accordance with Freud's wishes, he allowed himself to become the first President of the International Psychoanalytic Association, and chief editor of the first psychoanalytic journal, the *Jahrbuch*.

What Jung really needed was a father-figure whom he could admire sufficiently to overcome the spiritual doubts that had tormented him since childhood, discover his own masculine authority, and establish himself as a major figure in the world of psychiatry. Freud, it is true, was as much caught up in a father-son complex as Jung, but with the added fact that in Freud's personal myth the son was equated with thrusting ascendancy and the father with inexorable decline. As a consequence, as is evidenced by Freud's interpretation of Jung's first dream, he readily detected the parricide in Jung, and it deeply upset him – to the extent that he fainted on two separate occasions when Jung happened to mention to him the subject of death.

***

During the years of their association, Jung was able to make significant contributions to psychoanalytic theory and practice. Not only did his word association experiments provide hard empirical evidence for the existence and power of unconscious complexes, but his work with schizophrenics at the Burghölzli carried psychoanalytic concepts into areas beyond Freud's reach. In addition, Jung infected Freud with an enthusiasm for the study of mythology and comparative religion, though not, as it turned out, with happy consequences, for the conclusions that both men drew from these studies were explosively at variance with one another.

As time passed, Jung's differences with Freud became harder to conceal. Two of Freud's basic assumptions were unacceptable to him: that human motivation is exclusively sexual, and that the unconscious mind is entirely personal and peculiar to the individual. Jung found these and other aspects of Freud's thinking reductionist and narrow.

Instead of conceiving psychic energy (or *libido* as Freud called it) as wholly sexual, Jung preferred to think of it as a more generalized 'life force', of which sexuality was but one mode of expression. Moreover, beneath the personal unconscious of repressed wishes and traumatic memories posited by Freud, Jung believed there lay a deeper and more important phylogenetic layer that he was to call the *collective* unconscious, which contained *in potentia* the entire psychic heritage of mankind. The existence of this ancient basis of mind had first been hinted to him as a child when he realized that there were things in his dreams that came from somewhere beyond himself. He believed that the reality of the collective unconscious was confirmed when he and his colleagues studied the delusions and hallucinations of schizophrenic patients and found them to contain symbols and images which also occurred in myths and fairy-tales all over the world. He concluded that there must exist a dynamic psychic layer, common to all humanity, on the basis of which each individual builds his or her private experience of life.

Whenever Jung attempted to express these ideas to Freud, however, they were firmly discounted and attributed either to youthful inexperience or to 'resistance'. 'Don't deviate too far from me when you are really so close to me, for if you do, we may one day be played off against one another', Freud admonished him, adding a sinister little threat: 'my inclination is to treat those colleagues who offer resistance exactly as we would treat patients in the same situation'! Jung was irked by such a condescending attempt at intimidation and a row became unavoidable. It was heralded in 1911 by the publication of the first part of Jung's *Transformations and Symbols of the Libido*. As if warning Freud of the heresies to come, Jung wrote to him saying 'It is a risky business for an egg to be cleverer than the hen. Still what is in the hen must find the courage to creep out.'

The row finally erupted in 1912 with the publication of part 2 of *Transformations*. This time Jung wrote to Freud quoting Zarathustra: 'One repays a teacher badly if one remains only a pupil.' In this work and in a series of lectures given in New York in September 1912, Jung spelled out the heretical view that libido was a much wider concept than Freud allowed and that it could appear in 'crystallized' form in the universal symbols or 'primordial images' apparent in the myths of humanity. Jung drew special attention to the myth of the hero, interpreting the recurrent theme of his fight with a dragon-monster as the struggle of the adolescent ego for deliverance from the mother. This led Jung to interpretations of the Oedipus complex and the incest taboo which were very different from those proposed by Freud. In Jung's view, a child became attached to his mother not because she was the object of incestuous passion, as Freud maintained, but because she was the provider of love and care – a view which anticipated the theoretical revolution wrought some forty years later by the British psychoanalyst and psychiatrist John Bowlby.

Publication of these views provoked a major rift with Freud which resulted in the formal termination of their relationship early in 1913. Jung resigned his Presidency of the Association, his editorship of the *Jahrbuch*, his lectureship at the University of Zurich, and withdrew altogether from the psychoanalytic movement. He was now entirely on his own.

Given the characteristics of both men it was inevitable that their intellectual union would end in divorce. To Jung, the ultimate goal in life was to realize one's potential, follow one's own vision of the truth, and become as complete a human being as one's personal circumstances would allow (*i.e.*, to achieve what he was later to call the goal of *individuation*). He had to go his own way. It was Freud's misfortune that his intolerance of dissent meant that he often ended up by provoking it: he was a strange mixture of autocrat and masochist. The loss of Jung was a tragic blow to him and it took him a long time to get over it, but once it had happened, there could be no going back and, henceforth, he regarded Jung as both a traitor and an implacable enemy. Early on, he had confessed to Jung that his emotional life demanded the existence of an intimate friend and a hated enemy and that, not infrequently, both coincided in the same person. This pattern was apparent in his childhood relationship with his nephew John (who happened to be his own age), and in his relationship with Wilhelm Fliess. A similar fate overtook his friendships with Breuer, Meynert, Adler, Stekel, Silberer, Tausk, and Wilhelm Reich. Such was the power of Freud's personal charisma that his anathema could have appalling consequences for the excommunicant: Reich, for example, developed a psychotic illness, from which he recovered only temporarily, while Silberer and Tausk eventually committed suicide.

For Jung the disaster was almost as dire: he fell into a protracted 'state of disorientation', at times verging on psychosis, which lasted 4 or 5 years. Although profoundly disturbing – to his family no less than to himself – this proved to be a period of intense creativity which Jung referred to as his 'confrontation with the unconscious' and Ellenberger has diagnosed as a further, well documented example of a 'creative illness'.

It is interesting that Jung suffered his 'creative illness' at an identical period of his life to Freud, between the ages of 38 and 43, though in Jung's case the symptoms were more incapacitating and their origins more profound. Ellenberger describes the illness as being prone to strike after a time of intense intellectual activity and it resembles a neurosis or, in severe cases, a psychosis. Still struggling with the issues that were a prelude to the condition, the sufferer is convinced that he is beyond outside help, becomes socially isolated, and turns deeper into himself. As with Jung, the disturbance can last 4 or 5 years. When recovery sets in it occurs spontaneously and is associated with euphoria and a transformation of the personality. The subject feels that he has gained insight into important truths and believes that he has a duty to share these with the world.

At times the disturbance was so severe in Jung's case as to bring him to the edge of madness. He played in his garden like a child, heard voices in his head, walked about holding conversations with imaginary figures, and, during one episode, believed his house to be crowded with the spirits of the dead. However, he did not lose touch with reality altogether and it is a measure of his unusual quality that he regarded this disaster as if it were an experiment being performed on himself. To be a psychiatrist in the grip of a breakdown gave him an opportunity for research! He could study the whole experience at first hand and then use it to help his patients:

> This idea – that I was committing myself to a dangerous enterprise not for myself alone, but also for the sake of my patients – helped me over

several critical phases ... It is, of course, ironical that I, a psychiatrist, should at almost every step in my experiment have run into the same psychic material which is the stuff of psychosis and is found in the insane. This is the fund of unconscious images which fatally confuse the mental patient. But it is also the matrix of a mythopoeic imagination which has vanished from our rational age (*MDR*, pp.172, 181).

There are close parallels between Jung's experience and anthropological descriptions of the initiatory illness passed through by Siberian, African, and North American shamans. The Tungus noun saman means 'one who is excited, moved, raised.' As a verb, it means 'to know in an ecstatic manner.' Ethnological studies reveal the majority of shamans to be borderline personalities if not, on occasion, frankly schizophrenic. As with all charismatic leaders and gurus, their influence arises from the uncanny, hypnotic power of their personalities, and their apparent ability to put themselves in close touch with the unconscious and articulate its contents in a way that convinces their followers that they are inspired.

Jung was to look back on the years of his 'confrontation with the unconscious' as the most important of his life: 'in them everything essential was decided' (*MDR*, p.191). They provided him with the basis of the psychotherapeutic discipline that bears his name. 'It all began then; the later details are only supplements and clarifications of the material that burst from the unconscious, and at first swamped me. It was the *prima materia* for a lifetime's work' (*MDR*, p.191).

If Jung was not a guru before his break with Freud, he was to become one now, and following publication of his first major work in which he announced his new insights, *Psychological Types* (1921), people flocked to Zurich from other continental countries, from Britain, and from North America to be analysed by him. Some returned whence they came, but many, especially women, stayed to join the ranks of the entourage surrounding Jung, known to local wits as the *Jungfrauen*.

***

Jung shared many of the characteristics common to gurus. In addition to the 'shamanic initiation' induced by his creative illness, he experienced himself as solitary, even when surrounded by his family and admiring followers, and placed greater emphasis on his inner life of dreams, fantasies, and ideas than on his relationships and social encounters. This pattern became established early in childhood. An only child for the first 9 years of his life (his sister Gertrud was born in 1884), he withdrew into himself because of the 'unbreatheable' home atmosphere of 'death, melancholy and unease', caused by the unhappy state of his parents' marriage.

Jung's mother was an uncanny, at times witch-like figure, whom he loved, admired, and feared. Emotionally unstable, she spent several months in hospital, apparently for treatment of a depressive illness, when Carl was 3, and this enforced separation at a critical stage in his development seems to have affected Jung for the rest of his life. As John Bowlby was later to demonstrate, the despair displayed by young children on the loss of their mother is a normal response to frustration of their absolute need for her presence. Although children usually manage to survive this trauma it is often at the cost of developing a defensive attitude of emotional detachment, and by becoming self-absorbed and self-reliant to an unusual degree. Typically, they are left with lasting doubts about their capacity to elicit care and affection. They also tend to become rather odd and aloof in manner, which does not endear them to others.

Although Carl was cared for by an aunt and a young maid while his mother was away, he recalled being 'deeply troubled' by her absence: he suffered from nervous eczema and had terrifying dreams. 'From then on,' he says, 'I always felt mistrustful when the word "love" was spoken. The feeling I associated with "woman" was for a long time that of innate unreliability' (*MDR*, p.23). Jung's later reputation as a womanizer was probably in part due to his need to find 'safety in numbers.'

His father, a pastor in the Swiss Reformed Church, was a gentle, tolerant man, but Carl experienced him as powerless, and emotionally immature. Quite early in his ministry, Paul Jung seems to have lost his faith, but, lacking any alternative source of income, felt compelled to persevere with his parish duties. Carl found this enforced hypocrisy extremely embarrassing, especially when he had to bear the discomfort of hearing his father preach on Sundays. Inevitably, when Paul Jung prepared his son for confirmation it was a disaster: it had the effect of alienating Carl from the church forever, and starting him on a life-long quest to find a spiritually satisfying substitute. Whenever Carl attempted to discuss his religious doubts, his father behaved much as Freud was to behave when his younger colleague attempted to express reservations about the sexual theory: both told him to stop questioning and *believe*. This was never acceptable to Jung, who had to *know* – i.e., discover the truth for himself.

At school he was unhappy because his somewhat schizoid (withdrawn, aloof, self-absorbed) manner made him unpopular, and his sense of personal singularity was aggravated when a master accused him of plagiarizing an essay he had written with meticulous care. For a long period he dropped out of school altogether by dint of producing fainting spells after a blow to the head. He spent as much time as he could on his own: 'I remained alone with my thoughts. On the whole I liked that best. I played alone, day-dreamed or strolled in the woods alone, and had a secret world of my own' (*MDR*, p.58).

This secret world compensated for his isolation. The fantasies and rituals common to childhood assumed a heightened intensity for him, and they influenced the rest of his life. For example, his adult delight in studying alone in a tower which he built as a retreat for himself at Bollingen on the upper lake of Zurich was anticipated by a childhood ritual in which he tended a manikin in a pencil box hidden in the attic. Each time he visited the manikin he presented him with a scroll written in a secret language to provide him with a library for his private study. This gave Carl a deep feeling of security: 'No one could discover my secret and destroy it. I felt safe, and the tormenting sense of being at odds with myself was gone' (*MDR*, p.34).

But not all his secret experiences were agreeable. When he was 3 or 4 he had a terrifying dream of an enormous phallic god erect on a throne in an underground cave, from which he deduced that there were more sinister aspects to God then the meek, sexless image of Christ purveyed by the church. This understanding was confirmed by a later vision of God defecating on His cathedral at Basel and smashing in the roof with an enormous turd. This indicated that God had no greater opinion of His church than Carl had. Such experiences convinced him that he had an inner relationship to God which was denied to his spiritually bereft father.

A favourite fantasy with which he entertained himself during the long walk to school was of a fortified citadel with a tall keep, which contained a wonderful secret that he alone knew. Inside the tower was a copper column which extracted a 'spiritual essence' from the atmosphere and drew it down into the cellar, where there was a laboratory in which Carl transformed the airy substance into gold. This seems to have been an early prefiguration of his adult preoccupation with alchemy.

The need to create a citadel in which to hide from the world is characteristic of people with a schizoid disposition. Within his own defensive fortifications, Carl experienced himself as made up of two separate personalities, which he referred to as 'No.1' and 'No.2' respectively. No.1 was the son of his parents who went to school and coped with life as well as he could, while No.2 was much older, remote from the world of human society, but close to nature and animals, to dreams, and to God. As a psychiatrist he formed the opinion that these two personalities were not unique to himself but present in everyone and he called them the ego and the Self. He believed that the play and counterplay between them constituted the central dynamic of personality development. Throughout his adolescence, Carl experienced the Self as God-like and his commitment to this internal 'other' took precedence over all outer relationships. He did not feel himself to be among people, but alone with God.

It is against this background that Jung's 'confrontation with the unconscious' between 1913 and 1918 has to be understood. Having no faith in orthodox Christianity, and having lost faith in Freudian psychoanalysis, he turned to the 'God within' and to the guru and 'anima' figures who emerged in his trance-like fantasies. This use of fantasy, which he later called 'active imagination', resembled the trance state induced by spiritualist mediums. For his doctoral dissertation at Basel University, Jung had attended and recorded the seances held by a young medium, his cousin Hélène Preiswerk. His mother's family, the Preiswerks, produced numerous ministers of religion, many with a keen interest in spiritualism and paranormal phenomena – an interest which Jung shared.

Two aspects of his cousin's performances during her seances particularly impressed Jung. One was how real her 'spirits' seemed to her: 'I see them before me', she told him, 'I can touch them, I speak to them about everything I wish as naturally as I'm talking to you. They must be real' (*CW* 1, para.48). The other was the way in which a quite different, more dignified personality emerged when Hélène was in a trance. Her 'control' spirit, who said her name was 'Ivenes', spoke in perfect High German instead of Hélène's customary Basel dialect. Jung concluded that Ivenes was the mature, adult personality that was developing in Hélène's unconscious. The seances provided a means through which this development could proceed.

In these observations we can detect the origins of two ideas which were to become central to the practice of analytical psychology: (1) that part-personalities or 'complexes' existing in the unconscious psyche can 'personate' in trances, dreams, and hallucinations, and (2) that the real work of personality development proceeds at the unconscious level. These ideas, in turn, gave rise (1) to a therapeutic technique (*active imagination*) and (2) a teleological concept (*individuation*) – the notion that the goal of personal development is *wholeness*, to become as complete a human being as personal circumstances allow.

Jung's 'confrontation' with his own unconscious was conducted in the manner he had learned from Hélène Preiswerk. 'In order to seize hold of the fantasies', wrote Jung, 'I frequently imagined a deep descent. I even made several attempts to get to the very bottom. The first time I reached, as it were, a depth of about a thousand feet; the next time I found myself at the edge of a cosmic abyss. It was like a voyage to the moon, or a descent into an empty space. First came the image of a crater, and I had the feeling that I was in the land of the dead. The atmosphere was that of the other world' (*MDR*, p.174).

Going down the steep descent was akin to entering a state of trance during which unconscious personalities emerged with sufficient clarity for him to hold conversations with them. Essentially, what he had discovered was a knack – the knack of descending into the underworld, like Odysseus, Heracles, or Orpheus, while remaining fully conscious.

On one occasion he encountered an old man with a white beard together with a beautiful young girl. They told him their names were Elijah and Salome and that they belonged together for all eternity. Jung came to understand these figures as the embodiment of two archetypes – the wise old man and the eternal feminine and he identified them with the Logos and Eros principles. Soon, another personage arose out of the Elijah figure, and Jung called him Philemon.

Philemon appeared to him on numerous occasions and Jung declares that he learned many things from him, the most important being that there were events in his psyche that produced *themselves* as if they had a life of their own. 'In my fantasies I held conversations with him, and he said things which I had not consciously thought. For I observed clearly that it was he who spoke, not I. He said I treated thoughts as if I generated them myself, but in his view thoughts were like animals in the forest, or people in a room, or birds in the air, and added, "if you should see people in a room you would not think that you have made those people, or that you were responsible for them" '(*MDR*, p.176).

Like 'Ivenes' for Hélène, Philemon represented 'superior insight' for Jung. 'At times he seemed to me quite real, as if he were a living personality. I went walking up and down the garden with him, and he told me he was what the Indians call a guru' (*MDR*, p.176). Like 'Ivenes' he was an 'attempt of the future personality to break through'.

It was also in the course of these fantasies that Jung first discovered the reality of what he was to call the 'anima' as an autonomous complex within himself. One day he asked himself, 'What am I really doing? Certainly it has nothing to do with science. But then what is it?' Whereupon he clearly heard a female voice within him say, 'It is art.' He was irritated by this interjection and replied emphatically, 'No, it is not art! On the contrary, it is nature' (*MDR*, p.178). He resented the imputation that what he was doing was 'art' because if his unconscious emanations were contrived, then they were not the spontaneous productions of the 'natural mind' that he took them to be. He came to the conclusion that she must be the personification of his soul. In many traditions the soul is conceived of as feminine, and for this reason he gave her the Latin name 'anima'. 'I came to see that this inner feminine figure plays a typical, or archetypal, role in the unconscious of a man', and 'anima' seemed the most appropriate name for her (*MDR*, p.174).

In one episode of active imagination Jung reported that a most disagreeable thing happened: 'Salome became very interested in me, and she assumed I could cure her blindness. She began to worship me.

I said "Why do you worship me?" She replied, "You are Christ." In spite of my objections she maintained this. I said, "This is madness", and became filled with sceptical resistance.' (Seminars, Vol.3). In the course of this imaginary episode, Jung reported that a snake approached him, encircling and gripping his body. He assumed the attitude of the Crucifixion and felt that his face had taken on the aspect of a lion or a tiger. Years later, in a seminar with a select group of students, Jung amplified this experience in terms of Mithraic symbolism, identifying the lion-headed god gripped in the coils of a snake as Aion, *Deus Leontocephalus*, a statue of which exists in the Vatican Museum.

In his book *The Aryan Christ* (1997) Richard Noll has attempted to argue that Jung was so crazy that he believed he had actually been 'deified' by this experience and become a god, the 'Aryan Christ', capable of saving the world. This interpretation is completely at variance with Jung's understanding of symbolic experience and contrary to Jung's specific warnings to his patients and colleagues not to become identified with the powerful figures that can emerge during the course of active imagination.

At times when unconscious events threatened to overwhelm him he understood how essential it was to keep a hold on reality. He would repeat to himself, 'I have a medical diploma from a Swiss university; I must help my patients; I have a wife and 5 children; I live at 228 Seestrasse in Küsnacht,' in order to remind himself that he really existed and that he was not 'a blank page whirling about in the winds of the spirit, like Nietzsche', who went mad when he had similar experiences (*MDR*, pp.181-182). What prevented these inner events from driving Jung mad was the creative attitude he adopted to them: 'I took great care to try to understand every single image, every item of my psychic inventory, and to classify them scientifically – so far as this was possible – and, above all, to realize them in actual life. That is what we usually neglect to do. We allow the images to rise up, and may be we wonder about them, but that is all. we do not take the trouble to understand them, let alone draw ethical conclusions from them' (*MDR*, p.184).

A culmination was reached soon after the Armistice in 1918 when Jung acted as commandant of a camp for British internees. A gifted amateur artist, his military duties being undemanding, he worked every morning on drawings in a notebook. These usually took the form of a 'mandala' (a Sanskrit term for a circular configuration incorporating the idea of quaternity and emphasizing the centre). He felt that these drawings enabled him to objectify and observe the transformations which his psyche was undergoing from day to day.

Jung began to understand that the goal of all psychic development was realization of what he called the Self. He conceived this as the central nucleus of the entire personality. It contains the phylogenetic potential with which each of us is born and the purpose of life is to actualize this potential in reality. To open oneself up to the dynamic resourcefulness of the Self is to transcend the petty concerns of the conscious ego and to enable intrapsychic healing to occur. This came to him with the force of a gnostic revelation: he *knew* it to be true. As a result, the stability that had eluded him for years came within his grasp: 'Gradually my inner peace returned' (*MDR*, p.188).

Finally he had a dream in which he found himself in Liverpool (which literally means 'pool of life'). The various quarters of the city were arranged radially about a square (*i.e.*, in the form of a mandala). 'In the centre was a round pool, and in the middle of it a small island. While everything round about was obscured by rain, fog, smoke and dimly lit darkness, the little island blazed with sunlight. On it stood a single tree, a magnolia, in a shower of reddish blossoms. It was as though the tree stood in the sunlight and was at the same time the source of light' (*MDR*,p.189).

This dream brought him a sense of finality. He felt that the unpleasant black of the fog represented what he had gone through up to that point. But now he had an image of great beauty with which he could go on living in the 'pool of life'. He experienced the whole episode as a profound process of personal transformation resulting in a radical shift in consciousness. Now he saw his way ahead. 'When I parted from Freud,' he wrote, 'I knew that I was plunging into the unknown. Beyond Freud, after all, I knew nothing; but I had taken the step into darkness. When that happens, and then such a dream comes, one feels it as an act of grace' (*MDR*, p.190).

***

Freud remained bitter about Jung's 'defection' to the end of his life, accusing Jung of 'cowardice' in the face of the facts of sexuality. (Yet of the two, Freud was the sexually frustrated one. As Paul Roazen has said, 'Jung may have rejected Freud's concepts of sexuality, but then he had less personal need to make sex seem all-important.') For years members of the 'Freud Squad' continued to level accusations of 'cowardice', 'resistance', and 'flight from the unconscious' at all those whom they convicted of betraying orthodox Freudian ideology. It was the sort of charge that Melanie Klein was later to repeat against John Bowlby. Such attacks were made with a humourless, carping insistence, which revealed a remarkable lack of psychological insight and an incredible capacity for unconscious projection. Freud never considered that he may have done harm to others, but was intensely aware of the wrongs other people had done to him. As he wrote in 1915, 'I have never done anything shameful or malicious, nor do I find in myself any temptation to do so ... others are brutal and unreliable ...' (Roazen, 1992, p.262). When, on one occasion, Jung mildly commented how ambitious Freud was, Freud said, 'Me? I'm the most humble of men and the only man who isn't ambitious.' With wry wit, Jung replied, 'That's a big thing – to be the only one!'

On recovery from their creative illnesses, both Freud and Jung published major works: Freud's *The Interpretation of Dreams* in 1899 and Jung's *Psychological Types* in 1921. In *Psychological Types* Jung began to organize his ideas about the structure and function of the psyche and to examine the basis of his differences with Freud. From a wide-ranging review of cultural history he concluded that two fundamental psychological orientations are apparent, which he called *introverted* and *extraverted attitudes*. Introversion is characterized by an inward movement of interest away from the outer world to the inner world of the subject, extraversion by an outward movement of interest away from the subject to the outer realm of objective reality. This distinction between introverted and extraverted attitude types has found wide acceptance, even among academic psychologists hostile to analysis, like Hans Eysenck.

Jung recognized that every psychological system, whether that devised by Freud, by Adler, or by himself, grew out of the psychology of its originator: it was in the nature of a subjective confession. 'Even when I am dealing with empirical data', he wrote, 'I am necessarily speaking about myself' (*CW* 4, para.774). In advanced old age, he added: 'My life is what I have done, my scientific work; the one is inseparable from the other. The work is an expression of my inner development' (*MDR*, p.211). What had drawn him into psychiatry in the first place was the idea, expressed in Krafft-Ebing's *Textbook of Psychiatry*, that mental illnesses were 'diseases of the personality' and that to treat them meant that the psychiatrist must engage them with his whole personality. Inevitably, his enthusiasm for this idea engendered a personal approach to the analytic relationship which was much warmer, more intimate, and emotionally committed than that advocated by Freud.

Because of his introverted concern with subjective experiences such as he had encountered in his 'confrontation with the unconscious', Jung's approach to psychology has been generally discounted as 'less scientific' than Freud's. This is doubly unfair: not only have Freud's scientific credentials been seriously impugned but Jung is seldom given adequate acknowledgement for his attempt to ground his own concepts in biology. By adopting a transpersonal perspective, Jung sought to examine the life of the individual, not only in the context of his or her culture, but in the context of human existence as a whole. 'Ultimately', he wrote, 'every individual life is at the same time the eternal life of the species' (*CW* 11, para.146). As a consequence, Jung's model of the psyche is imbued with biological assumptions. Not only did he consider the archetypal structure of the collective unconscious to have an evolutionary origin but he maintained that the psyche functioned in accordance with the biological principles of adaptation, homeostasis, and epigenesis. Thus, in Jung's view, the human infant, far from being a *tabula rasa*, is a highly complex creature, endowed with a huge repertoire of built-in expectations, demands and patterns of response, whose fulfilment depends on appropriate stimuli arising in the environment. The sum total of this endowment, as we have already seen, Jung called the Self, which he often referred to as the archetype of archetypes. The other psychic structures that he described – the ego, persona, shadow, animus or anima – all develop out of this matrix and remain under the guiding influence of the Self. The goal of the Self is wholeness and it is this life-long quest that Jung called *individuation* – the attainment of the fullest possible Self-realization in the psyche and in the world. In religious terms this is symbolized by the incarnation of God in the human form of Christ.

Though Jung felt the anima (the contrasexual complex in the male) to be identified with the soul, it, like the animus in the female, is at the same time part of an evolved system responsible for initiating and maintaining the heterosexual bond. Seen in this light, both animus and anima are indispensable to the survival of the species. Together they represent a supreme pair of opposites, the *syzygy*, 'giving the promise of union and actually making it possible'.

That the psyche is an efficient organ of adaptation is because it evolved in the context of the world. The laws which prevail in the cosmos also prevail in the psyche because the psyche is, in his words, 'pure nature'. For this reason, Jung referred to the collective unconscious as the *objective* psyche, because it is as real and as existent as anything in nature. This explains why fundamental natural laws, like the principles of adaptation, homeostasis and growth, apply to the psyche just as surely as to any other biological phenomenon.

Homeostasis is the principle of self-regulation. It is the means by which biological systems keep themselves in a state of balance in the interests of survival. Natural environments on our planet are constantly changing, and no living organisms could have evolved had they not possessed within themselves the capacity to maintain a steady state. Accordingly, Jung viewed the psyche, like the body, as a self-regulating system, which strives perpetually to maintain a balance between opposing propensities, while, at the same time, actively seeking its own individuation. Just as the body possesses control mechanisms to keep its vital functions in balance, so the psyche has a control mechanism in the compensatory activity of dreams.

Here again, it is true to say that Jung's approach to the psychology of dreaming was more compatible with biological thinking than Freud's. He viewed the function of dreams as being to promote better adaptation to life by compensating the one-sided limitations of the dreamer's conscious attitudes, and he rejected Freud's idea that the dream is a façade concealing its true meaning: 'the so-called façade of most houses is by no means a fake or a deceptive distortion; on the contrary, it follows the plan of the building and often betrays the interior arrangement' (*CW* 7, para.319). In other words, 'dreams are the direct expression of unconscious psychic activity'(*CW* 7, para.295). They provide a view of the dreamer's situation and mobilize the potential of the personality to meet it. The compensatory function of dreams is derived from the rich capacity of the unconscious to create symbols, to think laterally, and to derive information from a pool of data far more extensive than that directly available to consciousness.

One of the most eminent of modern dream researchers, J. Allan Hobson of Harvard University has come round to a position very close to Jung's: 'I differ from Freud in that I think that most dreams are neither obscure nor bowdlerized, but rather that they are transparent and unedited', Hobson declares, 'They reveal clearly meaningful, undisguised and often highly conflictual themes worthy of note by the dreamer (and any interpretive assistant). My position echoes Jung's notion of dreams as transparently meaningful and does away with any distinction between manifest and latent content' (1988, p.12).

As an efficient adaptive, homeostatic system, the psyche, in Jung's view, possessed the capacity to heal itself, and it was in the compensatory function of the unconscious that this power for self-healing resided. For him, a vital expression of this propensity was the way in which the unconscious gave rise to symbols capable of reuniting conflicting tendencies which seemed irreconcilable at the conscious level. Jung called this phenomenon the transcendent function. He argued that we are never able to solve the most crucial problems in life, but we can, if we are patient, transcend them. Describing this, Jung wrote: 'here and there it happened in my practice that a patient grew beyond the dark possibilities within himself, and the observation of the fact was an experience of foremost importance to me. In the meantime, I had learned to see that the greatest and most important problems of life were all fundamentally insoluble. They must be so, because they express the necessary polarity inherent in every self-regulating system. They can never be solved, but only outgrown' (*Jung*, 1962, p.91).

Growth, development, individuation, Self-realization, these are the themes to which Jung returned again and again. He saw the whole life cycle as a continuing process of metamorphosis which was regulated by the Self. Conducting us through the life cycle, the Self causes us to

in 388.68

out 371-56

17-12

5-97

11-15

1-15

CARROTS

BROCCOLI

FRIDAY
MORNING

recreate images, ideas, symbols and emotions similar to those that human beings have always experienced since our species began and wherever on this planet we have taken up our abode. As the life cycle unfolds, so we accept and incorporate into our personalities our personal experience of living. But we are aware only of our personal history; we are unconscious of the evolutionary blueprint on whose basis our personal experience proceeds. This helps to explain how it is that some of the best minds of the twentieth century have rejected an evolutionary approach to human nature in favour of behaviourist theories which looked no further than the conditioning to which each individual is subjected in his or her own lifetime. By ignoring the archetypal dimension, they neglected the biological bedrock on which each human personality is built. But there are signs that at last this is beginning to change.

***

Of all Jung's ideas, none has proved more controversial than his theory of a collective unconscious. Yet it is a hypothesis which has been rediscovered and reproposed by specialists in a number of different disciplines. Jung used it to explain the existence in human beings of certain psychic and behavioural characteristics which, while achieving unique expression in each individual are, at the same time, universally present in all members of our species. 'I have chosen the term "collective" because this part of the unconscious is not individual but universal; in contrast to the personal psyche, it has contents and modes of behaviour that are more or less the same everywhere and in all individuals' (*CW* 9i, para.3).

Jung related this 'common psychic substrate of a suprapersonal nature' to the structure of the brain: 'Every man is born with a brain that is profoundly differentiated, and this makes him capable of very various mental functions, which are neither ontogenetically developed or acquired … This particular circumstance explains, for example, the remarkable analogies presented by the unconscious in the most remotely separated races and peoples.' It is apparent, he says, in the extraordinary correspondence which exists between the myths, folk tales, religious beliefs and rituals that occur throughout the world. 'The universal similarity of human brains leads us then to admit the existence of a certain psychic function, identical with itself in all individuals; we call it the collective psyche' (*CW* 9i, paras.453-54). This is such a reasonable position to adopt that it is a puzzle to understand why Jung's proposal encountered as much opposition as it did.

A major difficulty was that it subverted the prevailing academic consensus (what has been called the Standard Social Science Model or

SSSM), which eschewed biological thinking altogether and was deeply hostile to the idea that innate structures could have any part to play in human psychology or human social behaviour. In many quarters the SSSM still prevails, though there are signs that its global influence is beginning to wane, together with its principle article of faith that in human affairs 'cultural evolution has replaced biological evolution'.

Another difficulty arose from Jung's terminology. For many, the term 'collective unconscious' had an unmistakably mystical ring to it, as if Jung believed in the existence of a 'group mind' or 'world soul'. Initially, he also used the term 'primordial image' for what he was later to call an 'archetype', and this suggested a Lamarckian belief in the inheritance of intact and pre-formed innate images – a notion quite unacceptable to biologists. Jung later corrected this error by making a clear distinction between the archetype-as-such and the ideas, images, and behaviour patterns that the archetype-as-such gave rise to.

Though he remained all his life primarily interested in the psychic aspects of archetypes, he nevertheless understood that a strictly scientific approach would make more headway if it concentrated on their behavioural manifestations. As he himself insisted, the archetype 'is not meant to denote an inherited idea, but rather an inherited mode of functioning, corresponding to the inborn way in which the chick emerges from the egg, the bird builds its nest, a certain kind of wasp stings the motor ganglion of the caterpillar, and eels find their way to the Bermudas. In other words, it is a "pattern of behaviour". *This aspect of the archetype, the purely biological one, is the proper concern of scientific psychology*' (*CW* 18, para.1228; italics added).

In my *Archetype: A Natural History of the Self* (1982), I drew attention to the many striking parallels which exist between the concepts of analytical psychology and those of ethology (the branch of behavioural science that studies animals in their natural habitats) and suggested a fruitful interaction between the two disciplines would become more feasible if Jung's terminology were modified: I proposed the term *phylogenetic psyche* to replace 'collective unconscious' and *innate neuropsychic units* or *potentials* to replace 'archetypes'. I went on to argue that if Jungians wish to place analytical psychology on a sound scientific basis they would do well to draw closer to the ethologists and become aware of the discoveries which were being made not only in the observation of animal behaviour but in the cross-cultural studies of human communities throughout the world. Since then, a number of evolutionary psychologists and psychiatrists on both sides of the Atlantic have detected and announced the presence of neuropsychic propensities which are virtually indistinguishable from archetypes. These have been variously termed 'response patterns', 'master programmes', 'propensity states', 'response strategies', 'evolved psychological mechanisms', and 'modules': all are held responsible for the crucial, species-specific patterns of behaviour and psychological functions that evolved because they maximised the fitness of the organism to survive, and for its genes to survive, in the environment in which it evolved. These strategies are inherently shared by all members of the species, whether they be healthy or ill.

The significance of these developments for all psychotherapeutic disciplines cannot be overemphasized, and we shall return to them in Chapter 9. They provide the theoretical basis for a science of human development and for a systematic approach to human psychology. Psychopathology can then be understood to occur when 'archetypal' strategies malfunction as a result of environmental insults or deficiencies at critical stages of development. A sound theoretical basis in terms of which hypotheses can be formulated will enable these insults and deficiencies to be empirically investigated and defined. Though Jung is seldom mentioned by evolutionary psychologists, his primacy in introducing the archetypal hypothesis into psychology must be acknowledged: it is one of the truly seminal ideas of the twentieth century.

Another area in which Jung has not been given his due is his contribution to the actual practice of psychotherapy. The innovations he introduced have had an influence which extends far beyond his own school, and it is fair to say that this influence has been benevolent and humane. Though his initial formulations arose mainly out of his own creative illness, they were also a conscious reaction against the stereotype of the classical Freudian analyst, sitting silent and aloof behind the couch, occasionally emitting *ex cathedra* pronouncements and interpretations, while remaining totally uninvolved in the patient's guilt, anguish, and need for reassurance and support. Instead, Jung offered the radical proposal that analysis is a *dialectical* procedure, a two-way exchange between two people, who are equally involved. Although this was a revolutionary idea when he first suggested it, it is a model which has influenced psychotherapists of most schools, though many seem not to realize that it originated with Jung.

Jung's attitude to patients, his approach to mental illness, the principles and techniques he advocated in treatment, and his views on the role of the therapist were all radically different from those of Freud. In place of Freud's surgical detachment, Jung advocated a warmer, more welcoming atmosphere in the consulting room. Many people who consulted him have testified to the cordiality with which they were received. His sense of humour was always in evidence and he made no secret of his own vulnerabilities and shortcomings. For example, one deeply worried woman was immediately reassured when he greeted her with a grin and said, 'So you're in the soup, too!' He believed patients should be treated with the same courtesy that one would extend to any respected visitor and that every appointment should be regarded as a social occasion as well as a clinical interview. Accordingly, he never used a couch or any obvious techniques or tricks of the trade, treating people as essentially normal and healthy, while giving serious attention to any problems they might bring. 'If the person has a neurosis', he told his London colleague E.A. Bennet, 'that is something extra, but people should be regarded as normal and met socially.'

My own analyst, Irene Champernowne, who was herself analysed by Jung, told me that what struck her most was the extent to which he committed his whole attention to the material that emerged in the analytic hour: he was completely there, she said, not aloof and out of sight, not a screen for projections, not a transference manipulator, but there as a *real* person. What was more, he gave you the feeling that he was working with you not just because he was your analyst but because, through you, he was pursuing his own research, and was learning from the process. This gave a sense of heightened importance to the proceedings. Jung confirmed this in his memoir: 'My patients brought me so close to the reality of human life that I could not help learning essential things from them. Encounters with people of so many different kinds and on so many different psychological levels have been for me incomparably more important than fragmentary conversations with celebrities' (*MDR*, p.143).

Unlike Freud, Jung did his best to eschew dogma. When E.A. Bennet told him in 1951 that he was writing an article about him for *The British Medical Journal*, Jung said at once: 'Whatever you say, make it clear that I have no dogma, I'm still open and haven't got things fixed.' His advice to Irene Champernowne and to all his students was, 'Learn your theories, and then, when the patient walks in through the door, forget them.'

In evolving his approach to mental illness, Jung was reacting not only against the concepts of Freudian psychoanalysis but also against the ideas that prevailed, and to a large extent still prevail, in conventional psychiatry. The traditional pathological approach describes mental illnesses as distinct entities, each presenting a clearly defined clinical picture. Jung considered this to be rewarding up to a point, but saw that it had the disadvantage of thrusting all the inessential features of the condition to the forefront, while covering up the one aspect that is essential, and that is the patient's intensely personal and individual story: 'To my mind, therapy only really begins after the investigation of that wholly personal story. It is the patient's secret, the rock against which he is shattered. If I know his secret story, I have a key to the treatment … In therapy the problem is always the whole person, never the symptom alone. We must ask questions which challenge the whole personality' (*MDR*, p.118). 'Clinical diagnoses *are* important,' he acknowledged, 'since they give the doctor a certain orientation. But they do not help the patient' (*MDR*, p.124).

Behind all psychiatric symptomatology, even the most bizarrely psychotic, we find age-old human conflicts: 'at bottom we discover nothing new and unknown in the mentally ill, rather we encounter the substratum of our own natures' (*MDR*, p.127). In Jung's view, psychiatric symptoms were persistent exaggerations of natural psychophysiological responses, and this view has been reaffirmed by contemporary psychiatrists who use ethological concepts in their approach to mental illness. For example, Dr Brant Wenegrat of the Stanford University Medical Center in California sees all psychopathological syndromes, whether psychotic, neurotic, or psychopathic, as statistically abnormal manifestations of 'innate response strategies' (his term for archetypes) shared by all individuals whether they are mentally healthy or ill.

Jung carried this insight one very important stage further, arguing that *symptom formation is itself a product of the individuation process*, that illness is, in other words, a creative act, a function of the psyche's imperative to grow and develop even in abnormal circumstances. Neurosis is thus to be conceived as a form of adaptation – albeit an inferior adaptation – of a potentially healthy organism responding to the demands of life. Because certain archetypal needs essential to the programme of development have not been met at the appropriate time in the patient's past he or she experiences difficulty in achieving a mature adjustment and as a consequence individuation follows a course into illness rather than healthy self-completion.

An important distinction has to be made here between Jung's and Freud's approaches to the aetiology of neurosis. Unlike Freud, Jung did not hold that the origins of a neurosis invariably lie in early childhood. On the contrary, Jung maintained that neurosis is caused by a failure to meet the contemporary challenges of life. Neurosis may occur at any stage of the life cycle as a response to outer events, such as going to a new school, losing a parent or spouse, starting a new job, being conscripted into the Army, getting married or divorced, bearing one's first child, and so on. Earlier traumata may predispose an individual to exhibit neurotic symptoms, it is true, but such traumata are not the *cause* of the neurosis. Neurosis is, therefore, in Jung's view, essentially an escape from a challenging life event which the individual feels unequipped to meet. Consequently, Jung taught his students, when confronted with a new patient, to ask themselves, 'What task is this patient trying to avoid?'

A fair proportion of Jung's patients had little that was psychiatrically wrong with them. 'About a third of my cases', he wrote, 'are not suffering from any clearly definable neurosis, but from the senselessness and aimlessness of their lives. I should not object if this were called the general neurosis of our age' (*CW* 16, para.83). To what did he attribute this 'general neurosis'? He put it down to a collective 'loss of soul': to a loss of contact with the great mythic and religious symbols of our culture, and to the emergence of social institutions which alienate us from our archetypal nature.

Jung argued that the more secular, materialistic, and compulsively extraverted our civilization became, the greater the unhappiness, 'senselessness and aimlessness' of our lives. What was the answer? Not a return to the church since his own experience had taught him that organized religion meant spiritual death. Again as a result of his own experience, he felt that we have no other recourse than to abandon the exclusively extraverted quest for meaning in the outer world of material objects and, instead, establish contact with the symbol-forming capacities latent within our own psychic nature.

What was needed was hard psychological work to open our minds to the inner wealth of the unconscious in order to realize in actuality our own capacity for wholeness. In the process, he believed that meaning and purpose would flood back into our lives, as it had into his own. 'I have frequently seen people become neurotic', he wrote, 'when they content themselves with inadequate or wrong answers to life. They seek position, marriage, reputation, outward success or money, and remain unhappy and neurotic even when they have attained what they were seeking. Such people are usually confined within too narrow a spiritual horizon. Their life has not sufficient content, sufficient meaning. If they are enabled to develop into more spacious personalities, the neurosis generally disappears. For that reason the idea of development was always of the highest importance to me.'

One important virtue of conceiving symptom formation as a creative act is that it gives rise to *therapeutic optimism*. Instead of regarding symptoms as futile forms of suffering, they can be understood as the growing pains of a soul struggling to escape fear and find fulfilment. Neurosis, said Jung, in the nearest he came to a definition, is the suffering of a soul that has not found its meaning.

***

If you present yourself for Jungian analysis, what are you letting yourself in for? As a rough guide, Jung divided analysis broadly into four stages, which inevitably overlap and certainly do not always proceed in a regular order. These are *confession*, *elucidation*, *education*, and *transformation*.

Confession is the stage when one shares one's story with the analyst, offering up one's guilty secrets and feelings of self-doubt and personal inadequacy. This is cathartic in that one feels one has shed a burden or discharged a load of poison. One begins to feel less isolated with one's problems and, in Jung's terminology, the integration of the shadow begins (*i.e.*, one starts to acknowledge in consciousness the bad and inferior parts of oneself that have been kept hidden not only from everyone else but from oneself).

Elucidation is roughly akin to Freudian interpretive analysis in that symptoms and transference phenomena are examined, not with a single-minded search for sexual traumata (though these may, of course, emerge), but with a view to detecting areas of failed development or what I have called 'the frustration of archetypal intent' (Stevens, 1982).

In the educative phase, the insights gained in the first two stages are 'amplified' by examining parallels in myth, folk tale, art, and literature, so as to establish the cultural and archetypal contexts of one's personal mythology or, as Adler called it, the 'guiding fiction' which has ruled one's life. One thus begins to experience oneself as a member of the human species, a living part of its history; and this usually goes along with an improved adaptation to the demands of society.

Transformation occurs through one's own 'confrontation with the unconscious': one comes face-to-face with the part-personalities active in one's unconscious psyche. These function in a naturally homeostatic manner in order to compensate for one's previously narrow, neurotic, or one-sided development. By this stage a lot of homework becomes necessary outside the analytic situation, recording one's dreams, working up associations to them, making some representation of their imagery (drawing or painting them or modelling them in clay), amplifying their symbolism by consulting the literature, doing active imagination, and so on. At this stage, the 'transcendent function' of symbols comes into its own, and, provided one can accept full ethical responsibility for what is released from the unconscious, the individuation process is well under way. It is accompanied by a growing sense of 'selfhood', a state reaching beyond mere 'normality' or 'social adaptation' to a full affirmation and acceptance of oneself as a whole entity in one's own right.

To elucidate the analytical process itself, Jung drew analogies from alchemy. Not surprisingly, this was treated with scepticism, often amounting to frank incredulity, especially among academic psychologists and those who liked to see themselves as hard-headed, 'scientific' psychoanalysts. Jung's interest in alchemy arose from his insight that this primordial science could be understood as an imaginative form of 'projective identification' with the transformative processes occurring in matter.

Having little or no objective knowledge of these processes, alchemists projected their fantasies about them into what they were observing, and in so doing were unconsciously revealing those very processes as they occurred in themselves. Alchemy and astrology were of interest to Jung, not because he believed that it was possible to turn base objects into gold or read one's personal destiny in the stars, but because they represented repositories of generations of human psychological investment. They were artefacts produced by the activity of the objective psyche. By studying these projections, he believed he could gain valuable insight into the archetypal structures at the core of psychic experience and functioning.

Though he liked to think that he proceeded in an orderly and scientific manner in collecting material to amplify his concept of a collective unconscious, Jung acknowledged that analysis, like alchemy, is not a science but an art, an *ars spagyrica*. 'Spagyric' is derived from two Greek words, *span* meaning to rend, to separate, to stretch out (*i.e.*, to analyse), and *ageirein*, to collect together (*i.e.*, to synthesize). The alchemical slogan *solve et coagula* (dissolve and coagulate) precisely expresses these two steps: 'The alchemist saw the essence of his art in separation and analysis on the one hand and synthesis and consolidation on the other' (Foreword to *CW* 14). The analytic phase corresponds to the reductive method of Freud and the first two stages of Jungian analysis, and the synthetic phase, to the last two stages.

Whether or not an analysis succeeds in its objectives depends on the raw materials (the alchemical *prima materia*) which patient and analyst bring with them to the analytic situation (the alchemical retort, the *vas*) and the transformation that occurs through their interaction. The first requirement is that both accept full responsibility for themselves and their own contribution to the relationship: 'The doctor must emerge from his anonymity and give an account of himself, just as he expects his patients to do' (*CW* 16, para.23). Initially, many patients find it hard to accept responsibility for themselves and for their problems, preferring to hold others responsible and to adopt a passive or dependent attitude to the analyst. But this has to change if the analysis is ever to progress beyond the second stage: 'The real therapy only begins when the patient sees that it is no longer father and mother who are standing in his way, but himself ...' (*CW* 7, para.88).

The techniques of classical Jungian analysis – the two chairs, the dialectical mutuality between analyst and patient, the practice of instituting relatively frequent breaks in the analysis and a progressive reduction in the number of sessions, the personal work on dreams and 'active imagination' outside the analytic situation – are all designed to heighten a sense of responsibility in the patient for his or her own process of growth. Jung banished the couch from the consulting room because he found it made the patient passive and dependent on the analyst and positively encouraged a Freudian regression to the infantile complexes. This inevitably hindered the onset of the collaborative, prospective adventure that Jung conceived analysis to be. Although he took full account of the patient's experience of the past, he was far more interested in what the patient was in the process of *becoming* in the present and the future. Sitting face-to-face on similar chairs also made it easier for both therapist and patient to experience themselves as colleagues working on a shared task and to test the reality of whatever transference or counter-transference projections they might make on one another.

Interestingly in the light of recent research which would tend to support Jung's view, he was critical of the Freudian practice of seeing patients intensively over long periods of time:

> The psychoanalyst thinks he must see his patients for an hour a day for months on end; I manage in difficult cases with three or four sittings a week. As a rule I content myself with two, and once the patient has got going, he is reduced to one. In the interim he has to work on himself, but under my control. I provide him with the necessary psychological knowledge to free himself from my medical authority as speedily as possible. In addition, I break off the treatment every ten weeks or so, in order to throw him back on his normal milieu ... In such a procedure time can take effect as a healing factor, without the patient's having to pay for the doctor's time. With proper direction most people become capable after a while of making their contribution – however modest at first – to the common work. In my experience the absolute period of cure is not shortened by too many sittings (*CW* 16, para.43).

Contemporary research leads to similar conclusions. Yet many analytic organizations continue to insist that patients must attend at least three or four times a week over long periods of time; otherwise, they insist, the patient is not getting proper analysis and therefore not receiving adequate treatment. Unless these organizations can produce evidence in support of this contention, they should face up to a need to reconsider their position.

One aspect of Jung's practice which most analysts have chosen to ignore (often for financial reasons) is his advice to break off the analysis every ten weeks to throw the patient back into life, to discourage dependence on the analyst, and to encourage reliance on the Self. Then the patient does not live to analyse, but analyses to live. This can be of immense benefit to analysts as well as to patients, for it helps prevent the exhaustion that can so easily afflict hard-working therapists and ensure against their work becoming routine or lifeless. Provided they can afford it, a regular break from clinical responsibilities can enable analysts to follow other pursuits, such as studying, writing, lecturing, painting, pottery, travel, sport, and participating more fully in the lives of their family and friends, so that they can recharge their creative energies and strengthen their immunity to those forms of psychic contagion and 'burn out' that are common among therapists, social workers, and psychiatrists. Jung could afford to do this because he married a rich wife. Others are less fortunately placed, but it remains an ideal goal.

However, a number of patients find it impossible to work in the manner that Jung advocated, especially those who, as a result of defective parenting in childhood, suffer from personality disorders or from what Bowlby called 'anxious attachment'. Such patients need time to establish with their analyst a working relationship through which they can begin to conceive of themselves as capable of sustaining a lasting bond of intimacy and trust. Only when this has been achieved can they benefit from the kind of imaginative work with the unconscious that Jung regarded as the crux of analysis. Apart from these and some other exceptions, the classical Jungian approach seems to be of help to patients with widely differing kinds of personal difficulties and neurotic disorders, although a great deal of research needs to be done to substantiate this.

In Jung's view, the factor of primary importance which determines the success or failure of treatment, is the personality of the analyst. For this reason Jung introduced the training analysis as an indispensable requirement for becoming an analyst, while he was still a member of Freud's psychoanalytic circle. 'You must yourself be the real stuff,' he wrote. 'If you are not, God help you! Then you will lead your patients astray. Therefore you must first accept an analysis of yourself' (*MDR*, p.134). Elsewhere he wrote: 'An ancient adept has said: "if the wrong man uses the right means, the right means work in the wrong way." This Chinese saying, unfortunately, only too true, stands in sharp contrast to our belief in the "right" method irrespective of the man who applies it. In reality, everything depends on the man and little or nothing on the method' (*CW* 13, para.4).

Once again, Jung's opinion is in line with recent research which has established that the personal qualities of the analyst and the quality of the relationship he or she succeeds in forming with the patient contribute more reliably to a positive outcome than the theoretical orientation or the professional qualification of the analyst.

Not only is it necessary, in Jung's opinion, for analysts to be analysed during their training, but they must continue to work on themselves throughout their professional life. The analyst must go on learning endlessly, he wrote, for only what he can put right in himself can he hope to put right in the patient. Continuing self-analysis is necessary because of Jung's conception of what the analytic relationship entails, namely, a commitment on the part of the analyst that is at least as great as that of the patient. At the unconscious level both doctor and patient are participating in what the alchemists termed a *coniunctio*: like two chemical substances, they are drawn together in the analytic situation by affinity, and their interaction produces change: 'When two chemical substances combine, both are altered. This is precisely what happens in the transference' (*CW* 16, para.358).

Jung greatly extended the Freudian view of the transference. He understood that the doctor-patient relationship is an archetypal relationship which has been with us since the beginning of time. In the course of an analysis, archetypal images are stirred up which, when projected onto the person of the analyst, can confer upon him or her great therapeutic (or destructive) power. In Jung's own experience, such numinous figures as the magician, shaman, witch-doctor, guru, priest, and wise old man were commonly projected.

Most importantly from the point of view of therapeutic outcome, the analyst can receive the projection of previously unfulfilled archetypal needs. For example, he may become the powerful father figure which a patient lacked in childhood, and this was clearly a crucial component of Jung's own transference onto the person of Freud. Finally, unconscious activity in the patient causes reciprocal activity in the unconscious of the analyst, with the result that the bond between them is transformed into something much more profound than the conventional doctor-patient relationship. It is this aspect of the transference that makes it essential that the therapist should be thoroughly analysed and made aware of what Jung called his 'personal equation'. It then becomes possible for the analyst to recognize what is unconsciously projected onto the patient (the so-called *countertransference*) and to use this constructively in the therapeutic relationship, instead of allowing it to become disruptive.

Moreover, in contrast to analysts of other schools, Jung laid stress on the vital importance of *feeling* as an indispensable catalyst influencing all transactions between analyst and patient. Jung pointed out that feeling also has to be present in the ego's relationship with the unconscious no less than in the analytic relationship itself. This is particularly true when patient and analyst are both of the same sex, success depending on each being in a feeling relationship with the other's unconscious and the material arising from it. Some over-rational patients try to understand 'with their brains only', observed Jung. 'And when they have understood, they think they have done their full share of realization. That they should also have a feeling relationship to the contents of the unconscious seems strange to them or even ridiculous' (*CW* 16, para.489). Yet unless feeling is present, the prospects for growth and transformation are not good.

Jung's assertion that the personalities of both analyst and patient must be fully committed in a feeling relationship if the analysis is to succeed is contrary to the teaching of both Freudian and Kleinian schools but entirely compatible with recent studies of the essential factors contributing to positive therapeutic outcome. Freudians and Kleinians have always criticized Jung for lacking their scientific objectivity, for abandoning Freud's deterministic and mechanistic outlook, and for rejecting the coherent explanatory system which they believed Freud had developed from a set of strictly scientific propositions. In the light of the recent critical review of the Freudian literature and current studies of psychotherapeutic effectiveness we are now in a position to form a more balanced opinion concerning the appropriateness of Jung's views.

Where Jung continues to leave many people unconvinced and bewildered, however, is when he goes beyond science to eschew the laws of cause and effect, to embrace a universe in which 'synchronistic' events can transcend the barriers of space and time, as in the phenomena of telepathy, clairvoyance, extrasensory perception, reincarnation, spiritualism, and communication with the dead. For one of his background and upbringing it is not surprising that he should always have been interested in such phenomena and more than half-inclined to believe in their actuality. The fact that current scientific laws could not account for them was no reason, in his view, for not giving them due consideration or for declining to propose possible hypotheses to account for them. These ideas, which had preoccupied him as a student when he lectured about them at his University Zofingia Society, returned to haunt him as he approached old age. He sought to penetrate what he perceived to be the unitary reality which underlay all manifest phenomena – the *unus mundus* of mystical tradition the 'eternal ground of all being'. Having conceived the archetypes as possessing a fundamental duality, having both a psychic and a neurological structure (the two poles of 'spirit' and 'matter'), he now began to see archetypes as mediators of the *unus mundus*, responsible for organizing not merely ideas and images in the psyche but the fundamental principles of matter and energy in the physical world as well.

In advancing this proposition, Jung attracted no less a person than the Physics Nobel Laureate, Wolfgang Pauli, who argued that by conceiving archetypes in this way Jung had discovered the 'missing link' between the physical events (which are the legitimate study of science) and the mind of the scientist who studies them. In other words, the archetypes which order our perceptions and ideas are themselves the product of an objective order which transcends both the human mind and the external world. At this supreme point physical science, psychology, and theology all coalesce.

It is hard to escape the conclusion that the alienation between Freud and Jung was a personal misfortune for them both and an historical misfortune for psychoanalysis. Their bitter division drove both men hard in opposite directions, taking their followers with them. It made Freud reaffirm his dedication to the principles of causality and psychic determinism, causing him to concentrate on the psychopathology of childhood and to reject religion as an infantile desire for parental protection. Jung countered by adopting a teleological perspective: he endorsed the freedom of the will, extended the developmental process beyond childhood to the whole span of life, proposed that psychiatric symptoms were themselves an attempt at adaptation, and saw the religious life as the fulfilment of a basic human need. Freud persisted in the view that symbolism was essentially the product of pathological, defensive processes; while Jung conceived it as a natural function of the psyche's quest for meaning, balance, and self-completion, an expression of the self-correcting and self-healing capacities inherent in human nature. To Freud the unconscious was and remained a Zuider Zee of repressed infantile urges to be drained in the service of the ego; to Jung it was an inexhaustible source of life-enriching potential. Where Freud conceived civilization as a consequence of a necessary repression and sublimation of atavistic urges, Jung developed the view that Western society was compounding the mistake of the alchemists, projecting its spiritual aspirations into material things in the delusion that it was pursuing the highest goal.

So it was that in Jung psychoanalysis lost a priceless asset. His continued adherence could have transformed the course of its development, giving it a profounder, broader, more imaginative view of the human psyche. Instead, psychoanalysis was to continue to trudge along the reductive path on which Freud had set it, persisting in an obsessive preoccupation with the real and imagined experiences of infancy, getting locked in conjectural disputes about their supposed significance, while virtually ignoring the formative influences of events occurring throughout the rest of life.

As the century wore on, some psychoanalysts were to move covertly in the Jungian direction (while denying that they were doing so), while some Jungians, like Michael Fordham in England, moved openly in the Freudian direction. As the historian of psychoanalysis, Paul Roazen, has commented, 'Few responsible figures in psychoanalysis would be disturbed today if an analyst were to present views identical to Jung's in 1913.' Such are the ironies of history. However, it is my belief that a true rapprochement will not be achieved between these contrasting traditions until their differences are transcended through the adoption of a new paradigm taking full account of the phylogeny, the evolutionary background, the natural history of the Self.

4

Warring Egos, Bad Breasts, and the Analysis of Children

Anna Freud (1895-1982) and Melanie Klein (1882-1960).

Child analysis was pioneered, first on the continent and subsequently in Britain, by two women: Anna Freud and Melanie Klein. They were rivals from the start. Later, in their country of adoption, this rivalry blossomed into intense mutual hostility and was responsible for splitting the British psychoanalytic movement into two, and eventually three, antagonistic groups. Both women were innovators, but whereas Anna Freud's innovations were largely developments of her father's work and made, on the whole, with his blessing, Melanie Klein's were far more extensive and made without any such blessing at all. Always intensely loyal to her father, Anna Freud saw herself after his death as the custodian of the true cross and accordingly anathematized Klein and her followers as dangerous heretics. Psychoanalysis world-wide, and particularly in America, tended to accept this edict, but in England a substantial number of analysts remained loyal to Melanie Klein.

Though a person of many gifts, Anna Freud, in a sense, never really grew up. Being her father's daughter was not so much a fact of nature for Anna as the vocation of a lifetime. Diminutive in size, there was always something girlish in her manner of speech, movement, and dress; and it is likely that the success she was to enjoy as a child analyst was in some measure due to the ease with which she identified with children and saw things from their point of view. She never married, and does not seem to have had a close relationship with any man, apart from her father. Whether she was gay is a matter of fruitless conjecture. Certainly, all her close relationships were with women, such as Loe Kama, Lou Andreas Salomé, Princess Marie Bonaparte, and her life-long friend and intimate companion, Dorothy Burlingham, whose children by her estranged and mentally unstable husband Anna both analysed and helped to bring up. It is possible, of course, that she went unmarried for the same reason as many other women of her generation:

the carnage on the battlefields of Europe had ensured that there were not enough husbands to go round. But for whatever reason, Anna's was to be a life of service – to her father, to other peoples' children, and to psychoanalysis. Though a fierce defender of the Freudian faith, she nevertheless extended the focus of psychoanalytic treatment beyond the influence of the father on child development (which Freud had emphasized) to that of the mother, and beyond analysis of the id to analysis of the ego and its mechanisms of defence.

Anna's adoration of her father was not balanced by a comparable affection for her mother. This is possibly not unrelated to the fact that, alone among her siblings (3 brothers and 2 sisters), she was not breast-fed, and a few months after her birth her mother went away on holiday, leaving her children at home. When Anna was still very young, her mother's unmarried sister, Minna Bernays (with whom Freud is alleged to have had a protracted affair), moved in to help care for the children. But Anna seems never to have been strongly bonded to her mother or her aunt, both of whom she experienced as rivals for her father's love. She preferred her nurse, Josefine, who joined the family when Anna was born.

Initially, Freud was disappointed by Anna's arrival (he had wanted another son), but she was destined ultimately to become the most cherished of all his children, serving him as companion, secretary, nurse, and gifted exponent of his ideas. So important was she to him that he found himself in a conflict over his feelings about her for the rest of his life: on the one hand he wanted her to leave home, find a husband, and raise a family, but on the other he dreaded the prospect of losing her. As he wrote to Lou Andreas Salomé when Anna was 27, 'Sometimes I urgently wish her a good man, sometimes I shrink from the loss.' Consequently, when possible suitors came along, as did Ernest Jones in 1914 and Hans Lampl in 1920, Freud advised her to reject them, which, without much equivocation, she did.

Probably aware that Freud would have preferred a son to a daughter, Anna seems to have distanced herself from her sisters as well as her mother and aunt (she dismissed their involvement in such feminine pursuits as sewing, knitting, and dressmaking, as a compensatory disguise for their 'genital deficiency'!), trying instead to make herself indispensable to her father by taking a lively interest in his work, listening in to his psychoanalytic discussions with colleagues, and delighting him with what he saw as her masculine appetite and aggression, her intellectual responsiveness, and her dislike of 'purely feminine activity'. Though he encouraged her interest in psychoanalysis, Freud did not send her to the sort of school that would have prepared her for a university education, nor would he countenance her wish to become a doctor.

Initially she trained as a teacher and returned to work at the school where she had been a pupil. In her spare time, she helped her father with work on his psychoanalytic papers, and through the troubled years of the First World War their bond grew ever closer. Though Freud would not permit her to seek a medical qualification, he eventually agreed that she should train as a 'lay' psychoanalyst. The Budapest Psycho-Analytic Congress of 1918 ruled that personal analysis was an essential precondition of training, and, by a piece of extraordinary miscalculation amounting to professional malpractice, Freud decided to undertake Anna's analysis himself. It lasted from 1918 to 1921 and was resumed for a further year in 1924. That both had guilty feelings about this piece of 'psychological incest' is apparent, for neither of them mentioned the analysis except to a trusted inner circle of confidants. The great majority of psychoanalysts were completely unaware of it, and were extremely embarrassed when Paul Roazen made it public in 1969, many privately agreeing that it would have been much better if the truth had never been revealed. Appalled that the secret had been leaked, Anna retaliated by putting an embargo on certain papers in the Freud archive in the Library of Congress which will remain in place until the twenty-second century!

That the psychoanalytic community should share her embarrassment is entirely understandable. Freud, of all people, could not have been unaware of the link between Anna's powerful father complex and her inability to form a sexual relationship with a man. Had he seriously wished her to resolve her 'Electra complex' he would surely have sent her to another analyst. As it was, he committed himself to a daily analytic encounter with his daughter, during which they worked on her masturbatory fantasies of being beaten and analysed her sexual fixation on himself. In so doing, he was not only transgressing a powerful taboo but reinforcing the very incestuous relationship in which Anna was trapped and beyond which she needed to grow. On her side, Anna clearly colluded with him: by accepting her father as her analyst, she effectively gave up all hope of being emotionally free of him and surrendered her sexual independence to his control. As a result, their relationship further intensified. And when, in 1923, Freud was diagnosed as having cancer of the jaw (in all probability related to his heavy cigar consumption), nearly bleeding to death as a result of the first of many operations he underwent for the condition, Anna thereafter seldom left his side.

Murkier still, Anna's qualifying paper, which she presented to the Vienna Psycho-Analytic Society in May 1922, gave an account of her father's interpretations of her own beating fantasies, though she was careful to mislead her audience into believing the case was that of an unnamed patient. At the 1925 Congress, she read another paper, this time by Freud himself, which maintained that a girl's beating fantasies were due to masturbation guilt and narcissistic humiliation induced by not having a penis. Her penis envy, Freud declared, is converted into a wish to have a child, 'and with that purpose in view she takes her father as a love-object' (*SE*19). Very few members of her audience would have been aware of the ironic deception they were being made party to.

When his other two daughters left home in the 1920s to be married, Freud compared his relationship with Anna to that between King Lear and Cordelia. But as his illness progressed, and his dependency on Anna increased, the image that struck him as closer to the truth was of the blind Oedipus at Colonnus with his faithful daughter Antigone, who escorts him and leads him by the hand. The analogy was even more apposite than perhaps he allowed himself to recognize, for, being the product of Oedipus's incestuous union with his mother Jocasta, Antigone was as much his sister as his daughter. And like Anna, Antigone never married.

Anna began using psychoanalytic concepts to understand children when her sister Sophie died in the influenza epidemic of 1920 at the age of 27, and Anna had to help look after her orphaned nephews, Ernst and Heinele. But most of her initial experience of child analysis was gathered while working with Dorothy Burlingham's four children from 1925 onwards. She began lecturing to the Vienna Society about this work, and in 1927 she published her first book, *An Introduction to the Technique Of Child Analysis*.

Anna was spurred to write this by Melanie Klein who gave a paper at the Wurzburg Congress in 1924 in which she presented the case of a 6-year-old child called 'Erna', whom she claimed to have analysed with complete success. In her book, Anna took issue with Melanie Klein over her entire approach to the analysis of children, and thus the first shots were fired in what was to be a Thirty Years' War which only petered out as Melanie Klein neared the end of her life. Though Anna had many valuable insights of her own, much of what she wrote was in reaction to Melanie Klein's theories, and so it will be more convenient to consider Anna Freud's ideas in greater detail when we come to discuss those of her adversary.

Anna's intimacy with Dorothy Burlingham enabled her to continue her observations of the four Burlingham children as they grew into adolescence. She drew on this experience to write another book, the enormously influential *The Ego and the Mechanisms of Defence*, which was published in 1936 as an 80th birthday present for her father. In addition to providing psychoanalytic insights into the developmental problems of adolescence, she took up her father's concepts of the ego, the superego, and the id and filled out his account of how the ego defends itself against anxiety arising from conflicts between the superego and the id. Whereas Freud insisted that the ego's defences were invariably pathological, Anna argued from her child-care experience that these defences could function in an adaptive as well as a maladaptive manner. She proceeded to name and illustrate nine of these 'mechanisms of defence'.

Freud's earliest topographical model pictured a conflict between conscious and unconscious functions whereby sexual impulses battled against the defences that the ego constructed to contain them. The task of treatment was to render the sexual impulses conscious by breaching the defences through use of the 'fundamental rule' of free association. 'ego psychology' as it came to be known, was in no sense a departure from Freudian doctrine but an extension of it following on from Freud's own publication of *The Ego and the Id* in 1923.

In this book Freud introduced a structural model that depicted a more complex struggle occurring between three internal agencies: the id (seeking to gratify infantile wishes), the superego (striving to impose moral constraints on these wishes), and the ego (which has the thankless task of mediating between the demands of the id, the superego, and the outside world). The ego does its work by achieving a compromise between id and superego demands, permitting a degree of instinctual gratification through skilful use of the defence mechanisms at its disposal. In this way, the ego effectively disguises the id impulses in such a way as to outwit the superego and avoid the censure of society. Neurosis arises when a maladaptive compromise is reached between these conflicting tendencies so that the individual develops symptoms. For example, the ego may disguise hostile impulses by the use of reaction-formation, whereby these impulses are transferred into their opposite: the deeply angry person becomes aggressively helpful and suffocatingly kind. But this poses a considerable problem for treatment. How is it possible for the analyst to unmask the ego's defensive cunning, to tell the patient that his niceness is a sham covering up his basic nastiness, and keep him as a patient without destroying his whole adjustment to life?

Anna's point was that the basic mode of personality functioning can be rooted in defensive processes operating at a level outside the patient's awareness and control. To confront these defences head on could be life-threatening to the patient. Successful outcome therefore requires considerable tact and the establishment of a strong therapeutic alliance. The most appropriate attitude for the analyst to adopt, she maintained, was one of neutrality. It was important to allow the demands of the ego, the superego, and the id to be clearly stated, without the analyst taking sides between them. What had to be cultivated was a balanced interest in all three intrapsychic participants so that the patient could become aware of the position adopted by each and achieve a more adaptive resolution of their demands.

One ego psychologist who greatly extended Anna's view of the adaptive function of the ego and its defences was Heinz Hartmann (1894-1970). Hartmann's importance in the history of psychotherapy is that he was the first psychoanalyst to adopt a position which anticipated that of contemporary ethologists. Like them, Hartmann took the standpoint that all animals, humans included, were designed by natural selection to be highly adapted to their surroundings. This was as true of their psychological as of their physical characteristics. He proposed that a child is born with in-built ego potentials which are primed to be activated by 'average expectable' environmental conditions. This was a major step beyond the Freudian position which held that the ego was created out of nothing more than conflict and frustration. What Hartmann was suggesting was that there existed certain *a priori* 'conflict-free ego capacities' whose functions emerged naturally as the young child grew up in an appropriate environment. These capacities included thinking, perception, object comprehension and conservation, language, and so on. Each capacity enabled the child to adapt to its social and physical surroundings.

In Hartmann's proposal we can detect early glimmerings of the 'Swiss Army-knife' conception posited by evolutionary psychologists, the specialized tools and blades corresponding to the 'multiple mental modules' which make up the human mind-brain. Each module is adapted to specific domains of psychological or behavioural functioning. There is also a parallel between Hartmann's idea and Jung's notion, published in 1928, of innate 'subjective aptitudes': 'There is no human experience, nor would experience be possible at all, without the intervention of a subjective aptitude', wrote Jung. 'What is this subjective aptitude? Ultimately it consists of an innate psychic structure which allows men to have experiences of this kind' (*CW* 7, para.300). (Needless to say, Hartmann made no mention of Jung's ideas, nor did he make any radical theoretical excursion into the realm of psychobiology, but his thinking did represent an important step towards a model of the human psyche as an adaptive organ.)

Unfortunately, Hartmann was unable to free himself from the Freudian model of the mind as being structured round drives and defences. Lumbered as he was with Freud's obsolete concepts of mental and nervous energies, Hartmann was stuck with the problem of stating where the energy for his adaptive 'conflict-free' ego capacities came from. Psychoanalytic orthodoxy insisted that all mental activities were fuelled by sex and aggression which manifested themselves in conflict-ridden demands for gratification. From what source could he derive the energy necessary to drive his non-conflictual capacities for language, perception, and learning? For twentieth century neuroscience this is not a problem for it has been established beyond doubt that the central nervous system generates its own energy and has no need to recruit additional energies from glandular or other extraneous sources. Yet Freud's hold on the psychoanalytic imagination was so powerful that ego psychologists were never able to escape from its grip.

In order to find a solution to Hartmann's non-existent problem, gifted men and women wasted years in fruitless effort, examining such tortuous propositions as the possibility that certain types of early experience resulted in 'drive neutralization' to permit the withdrawal of energy from the battlefield between the superego and the id so as to make it available to drive the ego's conflict-free activities, and so on. Because it became locked in issues of such Byzantine complexity, ego psychology has been side-lined by history. Though the notion of defence is still considered important by many contemporary analysts, new schools of psychoanalytic thought have emerged – such as interpersonal analysis, object relations theory, and self psychology – which, instead of focusing attention on the ego, study the impact of care givers on individual social development.

***

Following the absorption of Austria into Nazi Germany in 1938, Freud and his family (with the exception of four of his sisters) managed, with great difficulty and the assistance of loyal friends, to emigrate to England. The day after Hitler's triumphant arrival in Vienna, the Board of the Vienna Society had decided that everyone who could should flee the country and that the seat of the Society should be wherever Freud would settle. Freud commented: 'After the destruction of the Temple in Jerusalem by Titus, Rabbi Jochanan ben Sakkai asked for permission to open a school at Jabnet for the study of the Torah. We are going to do the same.' Freud's Jabnet was to be London, and by the time of the Freuds' arrival one-third of the members of the British Psycho-Analytic Society were immigrants from the continent. A number of these moved on to the United States where prospects were better, but this option was not open to Anna, for, being medically unqualified, she would not have been permitted to practice there. This was America's loss and Britain's gain, for she was to do valuable work in her country of adoption, particularly after her father's death in 1939, which liberated her from her demanding role as nurse as well as partially freeing her from thraldom to his intellectual influence.

In contrast to Freud's emphasis on the father's role in child development, Anna increasingly stressed the importance of the mother. This shift in emphasis, begun through her intimacy with the Burlinghams, was confirmed in England, where, after the outbreak of the Second World War, she became director of two nurseries in Hampstead, and another near Dunmow in Essex, for evacuees from badly bombed areas of London. In this work she received support and assistance from Dorothy Burlingham. Historically, her most important observation at this time was of the distress suffered by children on being separated from their mothers: they were much happier, Anna noted, sharing in the great physical dangers of the blitz, sleeping in air raid shelters or in the underground in close proximity to their mothers than they were in the relative safety of the Dunmow nursery many miles away from them. Though children separated from their families said they missed their fathers, their distress at being removed from their mothers was infinitely greater.

Anna became highly critical of the Government's failure to take account of the suffering inflicted on children by taking them away from their mothers' care. Sudden separation, without preparation, was most disturbing of all, and, when trying to comfort her bereft charges, she discovered they were particularly inconsolable if they experienced the separation as a rejection or punishment for 'bad' feelings or behaviour. Early or prolonged separations could result in serious disturbances such as temper tantrums, the loss of sphincter control, and worse.

Together with Dorothy Burlingham, Anna did her best to minimise the damage by providing care along the lines of a 'family grouping' or 'key worker' system, by which children were put together in groups of four, each group being cared for by a nursery 'mother'. This arrangement proved so successful that it was adopted by child care agencies in other parts of the world. For example, it was in operation at the Metera Babies Centre in Athens when I took up a research appointment there in 1966. In addition, Anna and Dorothy encouraged mothers whenever possible to visit the nurseries in which their children were placed and to spend as much time with them as they could. Children, they found, could cope better with their mothers' absences if they could keep with them a toy, doll, or piece of clothing that their mother had given to them. Wherever practicable mothers were actually employed as assistants at the nurseries where their children resided.

Anna gave lectures and published papers about these experiences, and these demonstrate the extent to which she was diverging from her father's position. She argued that child development, both normal and pathological, depended not so much on instinctual repression as on the nature and constancy of their attachment to the adults caring for them. She went on to develop the idea that the child's relationship with its mother influenced the success or failure of subsequent relationships. Thus, she anticipated Bowlby in calling attention to the vital importance of a continuing maternal presence throughout the early childhood years. However, she asserted her belief that a child became attached to its mother through a form of 'operant conditioning' reinforced by the mother's satisfaction of its basic physiological needs. This showed that her thinking was still powerfully influenced by her father's 'drive' theories. (She may have begun to move psychoanalysis in the direction of a more just appreciation of the profound psychological significance of the mother-child attachment bond, but it was John Bowlby who perceived its essentially instinctive nature.)

Whereas her father had insisted that the child's socialisation depended on the superego internalisation of paternal authority, Anna saw the mother-child bond as the crucial socialising influence. The mother, she said, was the 'first legislator', and, like a good child analyst, she functioned as the child's 'auxiliary ego'. Also in contrast to her father, and, incidentally, in contrast to Melanie Klein, she did not believe that untreated childhood neurosis inevitably resulted in adult neurosis, for she took an optimistic view of the child's endogenous capacity to triumph over environmental deficiencies and to achieve an adaptive adjustment in its own right. She did not systematise this view, however, by attempting to formulate – as Jung had done – a psychobiological concept of the self as equipped with innate capacities to meet environmental challenges.

Perhaps the most radical departure from normal psychoanalytic practice was Anna's use of careful observation of children and active participation in caring for them in a residential setting. Not only did this advance her theoretical understanding of critical issues for child development but it enabled her to make the practical recommendations that rendered her policies for child care so widely influential. As a consequence, greater emphasis came to be placed on supporting children in their own families, or, failing that, in foster families, rather than taking them into residential nurseries. One of the social workers in Anna's team was a conscientious objector, James Robertson, who later became well known for the research he did on maternal separation with John Bowlby and for the deeply affecting films he made showing the emotional sufferings of children in hospital separated from their mothers. It was these films, as much as Anna's and Bowlby's advocacy, that brought about radical changes in paediatric units which enabled mothers to be admitted with their children and stay with them during the course of their treatment, thus alleviating much of the misery involved.

After the war, at the Hampstead Clinic, which she ran from 1951, Anna developed the 'Hampstead Diagnostic Project' and together with Dorothy Burlingham organized the collection of observations on child development and treatment, indexing such factors as transference phenomena, reactions to psychoanalytic interpretations, acting out, and so on. These, and similar initiatives in the United States, such as the work of Rene Spitz, represented important beginnings in the application of research procedures to the study of psychoanalytic theory and practice.

While Anna's recommendations for child care proved widely acceptable, her ideas on child analysis were more controversial. And from no one did they meet more determined opposition than from that powerful though tragic figure, Melanie Klein.

***

One of the most difficult duties an experienced analyst has to perform is to interview people who present themselves for training. What criteria do you use to decide who will make a good analyst and who will make a bad one? If you err on the side of caution and reject a candidate you are doubtful about, how can you feel sure that you are not depriving humanity of a potentially distinguished therapist? All analysts establish their own priorities in this matter, and most professional bodies arrange for candidates to be interviewed by several members of a selection committee so as to achieve a consensus about their suitability for training. But everyone acknowledges that it is a pretty hit-or-miss affair.

When performing this task I am sure I am not alone in looking for possible areas of pathology in a candidate's background, trying to form an opinion of what the main complexes may be, and, above all, how the candidate has used insight in the course of his or her personal analysis (which most organizations require before candidates apply) to attain a certain objectivity about them. What one wants to guard against is the ever-present danger that future analysts will unconsciously project their own complexes, their own anxieties, despairs, inadequacies, and jealousies, into their patients and proceed to focus the analysis on what are, in effect, the analyst's neuroses rather than the patient's.

Testing myself, I sometimes wonder how some of the great names of psychoanalysis would have fared if, at the commencement of their professional lives, they had come before me as potential candidates. I don't think I would have had many doubts about passing the young Freud, Jung, Anna Freud, John Bowlby, or Donald Winnicott, but I fear I should have had grave doubts about Melanie Klein. Frankly, I believe I should have turned her down. I realize that many people would consider my decision to have been terribly misguided, arguing that I should have deprived psychoanalysis of one of its most original and innovative talents. But, on balance, I think I would have been right.

As Phyllis Grosskurth's exhaustively researched biography demonstrates (*Melanie Klein: Her World and Her Work*, 1986), Melanie Reizes, as she was born in 1882, came from a fraught and neurotic family background; had an intensely ambivalent relationship with her domineering and manipulative mother; felt neglected by her father who preferred her eldest sister (of whom Melanie was bitterly jealous); never succeeded in achieving a satisfactory emotional or sexual relationship with a man despite her marriage; experienced a series of traumatic bereavements, was an inadequate mother, who had to abandon her young children to her own mother's care. She was subject to recurrent bouts of depressive illness for which, on at least one occasion, she needed a long period in hospital, and stirred powerfully ambivalent feelings in practically everyone she met.

With this history, I would have felt strongly inclined to reject her: rightly or wrongly, I should have suspected that, however much analysis she received, she would remain preoccupied all her life with the dominant issues of unrequited love, anger, envy, anxiety, and despair. I would further predict that these preoccupations would determine her approach to her patients' material, so that she would be prone to evoke these issues in every analysis she conducted, at the expense of other human concerns. This I would consider unacceptable. For although I am in no doubt that we may all be a prey to the kinds of emotions that afflicted Melanie Klein during her formative years, there are more things in life than the torments of bereavement, anger, and unfulfilled longings for love. Patients coming into analysis have a right to expect that their analyst should be as much in touch with the experience of hope, joy, and emotional fulfilment as with their opposites. An analyst who is disinclined to value the positive and creative aspects of life while focusing on its negative and destructive aspects is likely to end up doing her patients more harm than good.

***

Melanie Reizes was born in Vienna the youngest of four children: her elder sister, Emily, was 6, brother Emanuel 5, and younger sister, Sedonie, 4. Her father, Moritz Reizes, was a doctor of Polish Jewish origin who could find work only as a dental assistant or as medical attendant at a vaudeville theatre, and the family was kept afloat through the formidable willpower of Melanie's mother, Libussa, who ran a shop selling reptiles, creatures that she loathed and detested. Libussa did not conceal from Melanie that her conception was unplanned and unwanted, and made it clear that of all her children she loved Emanuel the most. For his part, Moritz Reizes openly preferred his eldest daughter, Emily. Alone among her siblings, Melanie was not breast-fed and was farmed out to a wet nurse. In view of the crucial theoretical emphasis she was later to place on the developing child's relationship to its mother's breast, this fact is doubtless significant.

She was no stranger to feelings of rejection, anger, jealousy and envy from the start. Believing they were the emotionally underprivileged members of the family, Melanie and Sedonie became strongly attached to one another, a bond which intensified when Sedonie contracted tuberculosis and had long periods at home from school. She used the time to teach Melanie to read and write. Tragically, Sedonie died when Melanie was 4. It was the first of her bereavements, and her grief was so intense that it is possible that her vulnerability to depression began at that time. She seems to have overcome her grief by persevering in the development of the skills Sedonie had given her, and she proved to be an ambitious, hard-working schoolgirl, who won many prizes and distinctions. Thereafter, a schizoid withdrawal into hard, dedicated work seems to have been the way she always dealt with disasters in her personal relationships.

Having recovered from Sedonie's death, Melanie transferred her affection to her brother Emanuel, whom she came to regard as a literary genius and the most loyal and most loving friend she ever had. In fact, he was something of a waster, a free-rider who leant heavily on his mother to extract enough money to drift round Europe entertaining self-indulgent fantasies of achieving literary fame. Melanie colluded with him in this. Unfortunately for her, Emanuel had rheumatic fever when he was 12, suffered from heart disease, and contracted tuberculosis from which he eventually died in 1902 when she was 20. If anything, this second bereavement affected her more profoundly than the first.

Still grieving for Emanuel, she married one of his friends. This, as she afterwards acknowledged, was a bad mistake. Her husband, Arthur Klein, was a chemical engineer, and they had little in common. Their sex life revolted her from the start, and she could never bring herself to love him. Her biographer believes this could have been due to a sense that she had betrayed her love for Emanuel. 'I often wonder', she later mused, 'whether my brother, with whom I had such a deep and close connection, did not realize that I was doing the wrong thing, and whether he did not unconsciously know that I was going to make myself unhappy.' As it so happened, Arthur's work took him away frequently and they saw comparatively little of one another. Nevertheless, she was soon pregnant after their marriage and their daughter, Melitta, was born in January 1904. Melanie breast-fed her for 7 months and, apparently because she was depressed, left her with Libussa to go off for a rest cure in Italy and Yugoslavia.

In addition to Melitta, Melanie gave birth to two sons, Hans in March 1907 and Erich in July 1914. Whether she suffered from post-natal depressions or was just generally miserable because of her marriage, Melanie was certainly in a very low state throughout this period and not competent to care for her children. In her bossy, managerial way, Libussa moved in and took over the family, Moritz Reizes having died in 1900. Libussa sent Melanie off on countless holidays and 'cures' and did everything possible to take over her role in the Klein household, even to the extent of wearing Melanie's clothes and adopting her name! Melanie seems to have accepted her mother's interference and to have gone along with whatever she insisted was best. More than a hint of sadism is apparent in Libussa's letters. She wrote to Melanie to say how well she was getting on with Arthur and the children and how admirably they were all coping without her. Although Melanie's letters have not survived, it is clear from Libussa's that Melanie felt guilty at having abandoned her children. Libussa turned the knife in the wound by reporting that Hans often looked at the door and cried 'Mama, Mama!'

After a severe episode of depression in 1909 for which Melanie was treated for $2\frac{1}{2}$ months as an in-patient in a Swiss sanatorium, Arthur was appointed to a position in Budapest. Inevitably, it was Libussa who organized the move and continued to look after the children, while Melanie was sent off on trips with Arthur's sister-in-law, Klara Vago. Libussa insisted on keeping Arthur and Melanie apart, so that if they wished to meet they had to do so behind her back. It was during one of these clandestine meetings that their last child, Erich, was conceived. Four months after he was born, Libussa died, leaving Melanie once more grief-stricken, deeply depressed, and tormented by feelings of guilt, fear, and worthlessness.

Towards the end of her life Melanie wrote a brief autobiography in which she painted an idealized picture of her mother as a saintly figure dedicated to the well-being of her family. It was on this document that the Kleinian analyst Hanna Segal based her account of Klein's life. Phyllis Grosskurth was more thorough in researching her sources and discovered loose sheets of paper containing numerous versions of facts which had been re-worked for the autobiography 'until Klein had polished up a respectable family romance'. When she examined a hoard of family papers in Erich's possession, Grosskurth found the truth to be somewhat at variance with Melanie's version. 'Instead of the saintly figure Klein had depicted her mother as having been', commented Grosskurth in an article in the *Journal of Analytical Psychology* (1998), 'I found that she was domineering and controlling, instilling in her daughter the conviction that she was a hopeless depressive who was incapable of functioning without her mother. When first confronted with the reality of Libussa, Hanna Segal exclaimed to me, "When I think of the way she used to talk to me about her mother!" ' In her biography Grosskurth concludes, 'Libussa had assigned her the role of pampered baby, and Melanie had paid a terrible price for it. She could be given the world as long as she did exactly what her mother told her.

Libussa reinforced her infantile fear of abandonment by emphasizing that without her mother she was not viable, and this terror was confirmed by her mother's death' (p.65).

Not the least of Melanie's problems was the need to assume responsibility for her children, to replace the central role Libussa had played in their lives, and attempt to re-establish a continuous, intimate relationship with them. Reunions after separations between mothers and children are invariably fraught with difficulty, and with a mother in Melanie's demoralized state it must have been doubly so. Melitta was 10, Hans 7, and Erich 4 months old. How could she possibly cope? It was at this moment of major crisis that she discovered Freud. Giving up on the family, she retreated into a close reading of *The Interpretation of Dreams*, and it seemed to bring her a glimmer of hope. She approached Sandor Ferenzci, who had founded the Hungarian Psycho-Analytic Society in Budapest in 1913, and entered analysis with him.

Although he would not have used the term, Ferenzci seems to have become an early exponent of 'object relations' theory, for he believed that people became neurotic not through instinctual repression as Freud insisted but through lack of love. Rejecting Freud's cold, 'surgical' approach to analysis, Ferenzci permitted his patients to experience his warm, and compassionate personality. Melanie was evidently helped by him, not least in dealing with her difficulties relating to her children. Unfortunately, he seems to have given her the wrong idea. What her children needed was the abiding assurance of a mother's love. Instead, encouraged by Ferenzci, Melanie gave them 'analysis' – by which she meant a recurrent and intrusive examination of their sexual fantasies and fears.

Perceiving the sharp quality of her mind and her quick receptiveness to psychoanalytic ideas, Ferenzci encouraged Melanie to train as an analyst and to concentrate on the analysis of children – as yet a completely unexplored area of psychoanalytic practice. Since suitable patients were not available, she decided to extend her experiments on her children. Having, to her own satisfaction, made progress with them, she proceeded to present the material she gathered in the form of learned papers disguised as objective case studies of children other than her own. In this she was guilty of the same psychological felony as Freud was committing with Anna, and with even more disastrous consequences.

As her initial accounts make clear, Melanie attributed all her children's difficulties to a lack of sex education rather than to her own absences or her less than consistent and devoted mothering. Whereas Melitta and Hans had been brought up by Libussa, Melanie was able to concentrate on Erich's psychoanalytic education. She reported that his anxieties and his developmental retardation yielded dramatically to a programme of sexual enlightenment coupled with explanations designed to overcome his omnipotent feelings – e.g., telling him that there was no God, no magic, and no world of fairies – so as to promote his adjustment to reality. Deprived of such educational experiences, Melanie declared, Hans had become socially aloof and Melitta's keen intelligence was severely impaired because she would not allow her mother to tell her about sex.

Her childrens' schooling problems were analysed in the same way. Melitta's difficulty in adding together non-identical numbers, for example, was interpreted as being the result of anxiety about the sexual differences between males and females. Erich's school phobia – a common problem among insecurely attached children – was likewise attributed to sexual anxieties as yet unanalysed; while Hans's hatred of school games was attributed by his mother to castration anxiety induced by masturbation fantasies of playing football with girls and fondling their breasts. When Hans developed a tic, in which he threw his head backwards and sideways and then thrust it forwards, she came up with the usual Freudian chestnut that he must have witnessed the 'primal scene' at a time when he shared his parents' bedroom. The tic's first two movements represented an identification with his mother's passivity and the final forward thrust an identification with his father's penetration of her.

It is extraordinary that the advisability of a mother prying into her children's sexual fantasies was an issue that never seems to have troubled her. Clearly, she believed that it was for their own good and that such intrusiveness was therefore warranted. But had she tried this in these politically correct times her conduct would have attracted the attention of the social services and she would probably have been accused of child abuse or suspected of paedophilia.

***

Meanwhile, Melanie's marriage continued to deteriorate. After the war, Arthur went to work in Sweden, and in 1921 Melanie moved with the children to Berlin. There, in 1924, she entered analysis with Karl Abraham, rapidly becoming as attached to him as she had been to Ferenzci. Not only did Abraham encourage her to carry on her work with children but, like Ferenzci, he seems to have helped her to find a sense of personal security and greater self-esteem. It is possible that her relationship with these two men did something to heal the damage done by her father's neglect, but she was destined to suffer yet a further bereavement when a terminal illness struck Abraham and caused him to break off her analysis only 14 months after it had begun.

As a result of Karl Abraham's influence, her early preoccupation with the supposed sexual fantasies of young children gave way to an interest in depression and what Abraham considered to be its links with the oral stage of sexual development. From then onwards, the relationship between the infant and the feeding mother became the focal point of her psychoanalytic theorizing. On the basis of her imaginative and often fantastic assumptions about this primal relationship, the whole 'object relations' school of psychoanalysis was destined to arise.

Though she could depend on Abraham's backing as long as he was alive, she nevertheless found it a struggle to build up a practice in Berlin, for she was not popular with the other analysts there. Her Polish background meant that she ranked low in the Jewish social hierarchy in Germany. She also suffered from the disadvantage of being a woman – a flamboyant, tactless, comparatively uneducated, and, after 1926, a divorced woman at that. With the loss of Abraham she was bereft of a crucial professional support, as well as a loved and valued analyst. Again her life was in crisis.

This time, help came from an unexpected source. A number of foreign students were in Berlin studying at the Psycho-Analytic Training Institute established by Abraham in 1920. Among these were Edward Glover and Alix Strachey (wife of James Strachey, Freud's English translator) from Britain. They were much smitten by Melanie Klein and her work, and when Ernest Jones, the Director of the Psycho-Analytic Institute in London, came to Berlin on a visit he was so impressed by the originality of her approach that he invited her to London, ostensibly to analyse his wife and two children.

Jones's motives are not entirely clear. Did he feel sorry for Melanie on account of her difficult situation in Berlin? Did he genuinely see her as an outstanding analyst who would bring glory to the London Society? Or was his wife having such trouble with their two children that he believed only Melanie had the insight and the personality to take on the three of them and sort out their problems? Whatever his motives, Melanie seized the opportunity and moved to London with her youngest son Erich in 1927, leaving her other children to finish their education in Berlin.

She seems to have taken London by storm. Her radical ideas about the most primitive infantile experiences attracted considerable attention and generated much heat, rapidly polarizing opinion between those who were in favour of her views and those who were strongly opposed to them. This theoretical divide was to persist in British psychoanalytic circles for the rest of the century, hostility between the two groups reaching peak intensity during the war years, following the arrival of the Freuds in London in 1938. Backed by her ailing father, Anna Freud committed herself to the forces ranged against Melanie Klein and proceeded to establish her own brand of child analysis on English soil.

Though somewhat shy and diffident, Anna was also tough and determined. She was her father's daughter, and she would let no one forget it. When Freud died, Anna assumed his throne as head of the royal family of psychoanalysis. She had no intention of allowing herself to be deposed by an upstart like Klein.

The split between the Freudian and Kleinian factions thus had more to do with personalities than ideologies. The differences between them were not so great as to be irreconcilable: they were primarily about how early the Oedipus complex might be said to begin and the relative importance of aggression and frustrated sexual libido in the production of psychopathology. These were issues that intelligent adults should have been able to discuss and, if not resolve, agree to differ about them. Instead, the two groups, fuelled by the personal animosities of their leaders, were driven lastingly apart.

Throughout her career Klein maintained that, far from attempting anything subversive, she was merely validating and extending Freud's theories through direct observation and clinical work with children. That her theoretical revisions met with staunch opposition from Freudians of the ego psychology school both in Britain and the United States did not deter her, for she had an absolute conviction that she was right and that the future of psychoanalysis lay in her hands. So intense were her feelings on this matter that when Ernest Jones assisted in the rescue of Sigmund and Anna Freud from the Nazis and brought them to England, Melanie construed this as an act of treachery specifically directed against herself! With feelings running as high as this, it is not surprising that the war that now broke out within psychoanalytic circles in London was conducted with a ferocity of spirit not wholly incompatible with that about to be unleashed on the continent of Europe.

The 'death wish' postulated by Freud as a sequel to the First World War had been a source of embarrassment to the majority of psychoanalytic theorists who regarded it as a dubious and somewhat mystical speculation. Melanie Klein, on the other hand, had embraced it wholeheartedly and placed it at the very core of her theoretical system. Taking as her starting point Freud's view of the human personality as driven by erotic and destructive drives, which the ego seeks both to gratify and repress, she stressed the crucial developmental significance of the Oedipal phase, during which the young child is believed to struggle with powerful and dangerous incestuous desires. However, she put these Oedipal conflicts a good deal earlier than Freud, insisting that they emerged in infancy in much more primitive and terrifying forms than he envisaged.

Klein's picture of the psyche, in adults as well as children, was of a much more unstable and insecure structure than Freud's. In her opinion, there lurk beneath the level of consciousness deeply psychotic anxieties from which we all struggle to defend ourselves: we are tormented with two basic terrors – fear of abandonment (which she called 'depressive anxiety') and fear of annihilation ('paranoid anxiety'). It was the job of the analyst to detect these unconscious terrors through their manifestations in the transference and interpret them directly back to the patient, however young he or she might be. She insisted that deep interpretation of children's unconscious sexual anxieties was much more effective than working on the trivial conscious concerns which they were able to report. The material on which she based her highly coloured sexual interpretations was obtained by observing her young patients while they played with the toys which she provided. This was the essence of her technique. Such play, she argued, directly resembled the free associations and dream interpretations on which Freud based the psychoanalysis of adults.

A crucial aspect of the treatment she devised concerned the transference and the unequivocal manner in which she interpreted it to the child. Just as she had interpreted her own children's play behaviour as bearing a direct relationship to herself, she now insisted on interpreting the play of other peoples' children as also relating to her, the analyst, as *mother*. In particular, she insisted that it was essential to interpret any hostile or negative feelings that might arise in a child while it was in her custody. Failure to confront these feelings, she maintained, could jeopardize the entire analysis. This insistence on the wholehearted nature of the transference and the crucial significance of interpreting it back to the patient, in its negative as well as its positive manifestations, remains the hallmark of Kleinian analysis with both children and adults to this day.

Anna Freud disagreed with Melanie Klein in practically every respect. While she accepted that children were not capable of verbally producing free associations like adults, she decisively rejected Klein's assertion that children's play provided equivalent material for analysis. She thought Klein's practice of interpreting every aspect of the child's play as symbolizing sexual fantasies about the parents was unjustified and deprecated it as 'wild analysis': 'If the child overturns a lamppost or a toy figure', wrote Anna, 'she [Klein] interprets this action [to the child], e.g., as an aggressive impulse against the father [the lamppost or figure symbolizing his penis]; a deliberate collision between two cars as evidence of the child having observed sexual intercourse between the parents ...' But, Anna objected, 'the child who upsets a toy lamppost may have witnessed some such incident in the street the day before; the car collision may be reproducing a similar happening.'

It is noteworthy that, as good Freudians, Anna is at one with Melanie over the notion that the child's actions must have been *determined* by previous events – if only having 'witnessed some such incident in the street the day before'. Those who do not subscribe to Freud's doctrine of psychic determinism may, however, consider the possibility that the child knocked over the lamppost accidentally or bashed the cars together because he enjoyed the sensation. Melanie would have ridiculed such commonsensical suggestions as betraying a hopeless degree of psychological naivity, for, like Freud, she believed in the absolute validity of her own theories.

Anna Freud took issue with her over all these matters. What effect would Klein's impetuous interpretations of unconscious sexual fantasies have on the child? Would they not cause him to withdraw from the analytic encounter, or to 'act out' in an aggressive and destructive manner, thus overriding any positive transference feelings that might exist? Although she later came to accept that the interpretation of negative transference phenomena could actually help the analytic process, Anna felt that such interpretations had to be tactfully handled and that the child's co-operation must be carefully sustained, for children seldom came into treatment of their own accord. Once she had secured the child's involvement in the analytic relationship, Anna would begin to analyse his dreams, daydreams, and paintings, but only after tactful preparation.

Moreover, Anna completely rejected Klein's view that the child's relationship with the analyst was automatically a replica of its relationship with its mother. On the contrary, the analyst was experienced as a person in her own right as distinct from the mother, and the analytic relationship that emerged could actually be the obverse of that with the mother – for example, the more closely bonded to the mother, the more hostile the patient could be to the analyst, and vice versa. Certainly she did not accept that very young children internalized their relations to their mother and expressed them in the transference in the overt manner that Klein maintained. She suspected that Klein manufactured the transference artificially by continuously harping on it. Patients were understandably irritated when everything they did or said was instantly interpreted in terms of the transference, and it meant that negative feelings and aggressive behaviour were provoked and then became the focus of the analysis to the neglect of positive feelings involving love, sex, and attachment.

Nor did Anna accept Klein's claim that her form of play analysis could lead to 'discoveries' about the earliest pre-verbal stages of development. This she regarded as nonsensical, for she completely sided with her father's view that psychoanalysis was by definition a talking cure. She also rejected Klein's analytic fanaticism, disagreeing that all children could benefit from analysis, as Klein maintained, or that in an ideal world every child would be analysed. In view of how Klein's own children turned out, Anna was probably right. Another pioneer of child analysis, Dr Hermine Hugg-Hellmuth, who became Director of the Child Guidance Centre in Vienna, was murdered in September 1924 by her 18-year-old nephew, whom she had brought up and analysed.

Needless to say, Melanie dismissed all Anna's criticisms, using the same argument that Freud and Breuer had used to justify their treatment of Anna O. – *i.e.*, justification by results. The proof that her theoretical formulations were correct and her analytic approach entirely justified was that her patients' anxieties were reduced by her treatment. The obvious objection that this was no proof at all, and that the children's anxieties could have been reduced by a host of other factors having nothing to do with her interpretations, was not given a moment's consideration.

However, Melanie Klein's contribution to psychoanalysis was very considerable. In fact she made the mother and 'object relations' as central to psychoanalytic theorizing as Freud had made the father and sexual conflict. Freud had used the term 'object' to refer to a *target* for instinctual discharge. The object could be a person or a thing (e.g., a brassiere could be a target for instinctual discharge for an underwear fetishist). The object had no intrinsic value but it provided the means by which drive tensions were reduced. Thus, according to the Freudian scheme of things, a mother is not important in herself but only as a provider of gratification for her child's needs: the child has no primary desire to seek connection with her as a person in her own right. When he[1] eventually comes to conceive of her as the independent figure who gratifies his needs it is by a fortuitous process of association. Klein adopted a contrary view. She saw the object as actually built-in to the instinct itself. The object of love or hate was implicit in the experience of loving or hating. Moreover, in place of the continuous, integrated ego, conceived by Freud's structural model, dealing with distinct erotic or destructive impulses, Klein conceived of a discontinuous ego alternating between a loving orientation to lovable objects and a hating orientation towards hateful objects.

These polarized states, she insisted, are first experienced by the infant in relation to the breast. When hunger is satisfied by the bountiful presence of the warm breast full of nourishing milk it is experienced as 'good' and evokes loving feelings of gratitude and appreciation; when hunger attacks from within and the longed-for breast, for whatever reason, is not present, then it is experienced as 'bad' and evokes feelings of rage, together with retaliatory fantasies of mutilation and destruction. Since the 'good' breast cannot, in the natural order of things, be perennially present, it follows that the emotional equilibrium of the child must depend on its ability to distinguish the good breast from the bad.

Acquisition of the ability to make this distinction Klein equated with what she called the *paranoid-schizoid position*. By 'position' she did not imply a developmental stage like Freud's oral, anal, and genital stages, but a fundamental mode through which the individual organizes experience in relation to outer and inner objects. It is 'paranoid' because the child experiences the bad breast as persecutory; and it is 'schizoid' because the individual succeeds in splitting the good breast from the bad. This is a crucial defensive strategy. 'Splitting' is essential if the child is to deal with his fears that his destructive hatred of the bad breast could result in destruction of the good breast as well, thus fatally exposing him to the twin terrors of abandonment and annihilation.

The paranoid-schizoid position is thus an indispensable defence against feelings of persecutory anxiety which Klein believed were generated by Freud's 'death wish'. The infant is tormented with fears of imminent annihilation because of the destructive power of its own aggression turned against the self. This fundamental threat persists throughout life. Human beings have perpetually to defend themselves against paranoid fears that their very existence is profoundly at risk. It is not, it must be agreed, a particularly cheerful view of the human condition.

Klein believed that, with time, the infant begins to conceive of whole objects which are not intrinsically good or bad but which are sometimes good and sometimes bad. Good and bad breasts are no longer understood as independent of one another but as different aspects of the same object, namely, the mother. This results in a diminution of paranoid anxiety. But now, alas, a new form of misery arises. It is now the whole mother who disappoints, fails, or frustrates the child and who becomes the object of his vengeful fantasies, not just her bad breast. As a result, he becomes afflicted by the guilt and overwhelming terror of destroying the very person on whose nurturing goodwill his existence depends. The child's paranoid anxiety now gives way to depressive anxiety – a guilt-ridden mode of relationship to the loved and hated object which Klein called the *depressive position*.

In the paranoid-schizoid position the infant's innate destructiveness was projected onto the outer object, which was then experienced as persecutory or hostile. In the more integrated depressive position, the child suffers guilt because of the damage he fears his innate destructiveness will inflict on those whom he loves. After an episode of vengeful rage his mental-emotional state is one of deep remorse and of longing to make reparation. If all goes well, recurrent cycles of love, frustration, destruction, and reparation, encourage the child to believe that his reparative capacities can balance his destructiveness, and thus enable him to remain in relation to his mother without wholly destroying her.

But that does not let him or any of us off the hook, for, according to Klein, throughout life we all remain prone to fantasies of destructiveness, either consciously or unconsciously, against those whom we love whenever we experience them as frustrating or hurtful. These fantasies perpetually possess the power to stir up our depressive anxiety and feelings of guilt and induce in us an unending need to make reparation. However, there is an alternative solution to suffering the anguish of depressive anxiety and that is to adopt what Klein called the *manic defence*, by which one's need of the uniquely loved but frustrating person is magically denied.

Klein's conception of mental health is thus extremely dispiriting: far from being a happy state of contentment and fulfilment, health is a precarious condition which is perpetually lost and regained. Because we can never hope to escape the treadmill of love and hate, depressive anxiety is a life sentence, the never-ending calvary of human existence. The only refuge available to us at times of loss, rejection, frustration, or bereavement, is that taken by Klein herself on such occasions – namely, a retreat to the paranoid-schizoid position or the adoption of the manic defence. But, deny it if we will, each of us is doomed to a life of depressive anxiety, fearful of our own aggression, and terrified of what it might do to those we love.

Many found these ideas uncongenial but it was not possible to discuss them with her, for if you presumed to say that you did not experience life as the horrifying Grand Guignol she described, then she would counter that it was because you were 'in denial', repressing the reality of your situation, and keeping yourself unconscious of the truth. She made a habit of using her powerful, domineering, manipulative side to compensate for her depressive vulnerability. Like Freud she did not take kindly to criticism. She needed to be surrounded by loyal supporters in order to feel safe. You were either a devotee or an enemy. If you disagreed with her you were dropped, even if you had previously been very close to her, like her former analysands Paula Heimann, John Rickman, and Clifford Scott.

The ambivalent feelings which Melanie everywhere created are evident from what people said about her: 'I couldn't stand her', said R.D. Laing, who attended her seminars in the 1950s. 'I found her an absolutely detestable person.' In particular he recoiled from her 'adamantine dogmatism', and the way in which her followers were 'beaten down into complete submission'. In seminars he sat sullen and silent. He would not, he said, 'demean himself' by attempting to argue with her because he knew she would only tell him that he needed more analysis or that he was full of envy for her good breast. As far as her technique was concerned, Laing believed that by exaggerating the importance of her patients' anxiety, Klein intensified it and increased their dependence on her. It was, he thought, an excellent technique for a professional torturer. John Bowlby similarly complained of Melanie Klein's overweening self-righteousness and contrasted her unfavourably with Anna Freud. Neither of them, he said, had the remotest conception of scientific methodology, and both were in their own ways hostile to his introduction of ethology into psychology, but Bowlby distinguished carefully between what he called Anna's 'criticism' and Melanie's 'attack'. 'Anna Freud thought I was mistaken and made no bones about it. But Anna Freud was not destructive. The other group [*i.e.*, the Kleinians] were out to destroy.'

However, both Laing and Bowlby recognized the power of Klein's influence. Laing respected the 'sensibility' in her writings and the way in which she plunged headlong into deep and confused waters undeterred by the 'scorn and contempt' she invariably aroused in her critics. For his part, Bowlby acknowledged his Kleinian roots (he was analysed by Melanie's colleague Joan Rivière) and the importance of Melanie's emphasis on the early development of 'object relations'. But, to survive professionally, both Laing and Bowlby had to pursue their careers outside the Kleinian orbit and beyond Melanie's extensive reach.

By 1950 there were 75 psychoanalysts practicing in London and 'it was as plain as a pikestaff', says Bowlby, 'that it was advantageous to be a Kleinian.' He compared the Kleinians to a religious cult. Deviation from accepted doctrine carried the threat of lasting excommunication – a terrible fate for analysts without a medical qualification, for it meant that they would no longer have patients referred to them. It is a sombre thought that if Bowlby and Laing had not trained as doctors as well as psychoanalysts, their independent contributions might well have been stifled at birth.

***

A late arrival in the hellish pantheon conceived by Klein was envy, which she described as the most destructive of primitive mental processes. 'Envy is the angry feeling that another person possesses and enjoys something desirable – the envious impulse being to take it away or spoil it', she wrote. Envy was to become of immense interpretative importance to Klein and her followers, not least because it enabled them to explain those cases who displayed what Freud called *negative therapeutic reaction*: that is to say, the patient undergoing psychoanalysis not only failed to get better but actually got worse. The explanation she came up with amounted to another variation on the old Freudian game of 'blame the patient'.

According to Klein, patients experience the analytic situation entirely in terms of their primitive object relations. The analyst is sometimes identified with the good breast providing nurturance and succour and at other times identified with the bad breast, being frustrating, withholding, and destructive. People prone to envy, Klein mythologized, were innately endowed with an unusually powerful death instinct. As infants they were not only hostile to the bad breast but they were envious of the good one. Like the farmer who kills the goose that lays the golden eggs, the infant wants to possess and control and dominate the supremely valuable resource of the mother's nourishing breast. He cannot tolerate the fact that something so crucial to his existence should remain outside his control, and, as a consequence, it evokes intense feelings of envy. So unbearable is this envy that the only escape is to destroy the very source of goodness itself. To succumb to this strategy is a catastrophe, of course, because envy is not an attack on the bad breast but on the good one. Envy thus undoes 'splitting' and effectively destroys all love, security, and hope.

'Envious spoiling' thus provides a convenient explanation for those patients who fail to get better in analysis. Freud's explanation of 'negative therapeutic reaction' had been in terms of Oedipal guilt: such patients denied themselves the better life that analysis had to offer because, on account of their incestuous, patricidal longings, they felt they did not deserve it. Klein's explanation was in terms of 'envious spoiling' of the good breast with which the analyst is identified. The ability to offer these patients a positive way out of their difficulties is intolerable to them since it is the analyst's ability and not their own. So totally unacceptable is it that the analyst should possess something vitally important which is beyond their personal control that, rather than suffer unbearable feelings of envious helplessness, they wreck the analysis. With this Pyrrhic victory they are no longer at the mercy of what the analyst has to give.

These ideas were extended to the study of schizophrenia by another student and analysand of Klein's, Wilfred Bion (1879-1979). Bion posited the theory that when the child indulges in envious spoiling it is not just the good breast that it is attacking but parts of its own perceptual and cognitive apparatus that are connected to the object, thus destroying its own capacity to relate to reality. In this fantasized aetiology, the child's envy behaved in the manner of an autoimmune disease, the mind turning against and destroying itself. But Bion also had problems with Klein's autocratic insistence on theoretical conformity and managed to establish his independence only by escaping to Los Angeles.

As for the analytic situation, Klein accepted the Freudian description of the analyst's role as one who remains objective and distant, interpreting resistances and linking the patient's associations to the memories to be recovered (or reconstructed) on the basis of his or her analytic training and theoretical understanding. Many have verified that this was indeed her approach. Donald Winnicott's wife Clare, for example, was in analysis with Melanie Klein as part of her training to become an analyst, and very disagreeable she found the whole business. She disliked the impersonal atmosphere, the fact that Klein never greeted her or said goodbye, that she emphasized the destructive side of events, and interpreted positive actions as a disguise for hate. When Clare tried to break off the analysis, her husband advised her, 'If you give it up, she'll never let you qualify'. So she went back, albeit truculently. 'I have come back on your terms, Mrs Klein,' she said, 'not mine.'

With adult patients, as with children, Klein assumed that she could 'read' the stream of fantasy running in the unconscious and interpret it in her own peculiar brand of symbolic language, confined to the body and its most significant parts (breasts, genitals, orifices, belly, etc.) and to the erotic and destructive uses to which these parts were allegedly put in unconscious fantasy. Klein insisted that it is precisely because the analyst has depressive anxieties similar to those of the patient that she is able to interpret the patient's unconscious processes and projections with a high degree of accuracy. It does not seem to have troubled her that her own constellation of anxieties, conflicts, and needs may have been peculiar to herself or that she was generalizing from these in order to jump to conclusions about the human psyche as a whole.

Klein's peculiar brand of gonadocentric alchemy, whereby she projected her own fantasies into the children she was treating, is a highly dubious proceeding which was not confined to her own practice. To this day, trainee Kleinians are forced to emulate her example. Not only are they required to do regular periods of infant observation, but they have to record their own thoughts and feelings throughout each period of observation. If this were merely an exercise in self awareness so as to become conscious of their own counter-transference distortions, it could be of some value. But this is not the objective at all. Rather, Kleinians argue, the observer's emotional responses provide the most 'valid' indication of what is occurring in the child! Sometimes, of course, this may be so, but on many occasions it may not be. Who is to decide? The likelihood is that the records so obtained will tell us more about the psychological state of the observer than they will that of the child.

***

As a universal explanation of human psychology, Klein's theories are profoundly objectionable. While we all possess the capacity to be aggressive, destructive, depressed, paranoid, and envious, it is a grotesque travesty to depict these states as the fundamental issues of childhood development and of human life. In some unfortunate individuals, like Klein herself, they may be; but for most of us they are emotions that we may experience from time to time in response to some appropriate situation, not perennial torments which afflict us with such gothic intensity as Klein maintained. The drama of existence is infinitely richer and, for most of us, more agreeable than Klein's deeply depressive theorizing would allow.

If Jung's idea that every psychological system is imbued with the psychology of its originator is true, then it must apply more to Kleinian psychoanalysis than to any other form of psychotherapy. The way we are parented determines the way we treat our children and, less obviously, our patients. Libussa's efforts to manipulate and control Melanie were repeated in Melanie's attempts to manipulate and control her own daughter, Melitta. Like mother, like daughter, like granddaughter, the chain reaction worked through the generations. But whereas Melanie capitulated to Libussa, Melitta threw herself into an orgy of rebellion, malice, and 'envious spoiling' against Melanie, doing everything she could to wreck her mother's career.

Melitta's decision to become a psychoanalyst herself seems to have been motivated at least in part by a desire to settle a host of scores with her mother. Even before she was fully qualified, Melitta began what was to be a professional lifetime's assault on Melanie's work. Indeed, the paper she delivered at the Institute of Psycho-Analysis in 1933, on the basis of which she was elected to full membership in October that year, criticized her mother's exclusive emphasis on fantasies proceeding within the child, and insisted that the mother's own behaviour was equally important.

This first salvo was followed up by further attacks which became increasingly vindictive and personal, and Melitta mobilized powerful allies to join her in the fight. She infected her own analyst, Edward Glover, with her hostility to her mother, and he published a book which obliquely criticized Melanie as a 'self-aggrandizing, tyrannical and selfish' mother, who blithely overlooked the effect that such mothering could have on her children. Together with Glover and her husband, Walter Schmiderberg, Melitta hounded Melanie at every opportunity and did her utmost to get her thrown out of the British Psycho-Analytical Society. It was a vicious war of attrition conducted without a single truce. When Melanie died in 1960 Melitta did not attend her funeral, nor did she answer any of the letters of condolence she received, even from her brother Erich.

Melitta's public behaviour so soon after qualifying was embarrassing and painful enough, but in April 1934 Melanie suffered the most tragic blow of her life. Holidaying in the Tatra Mountains, her son Hans fell to his death. Melitta made no secret of her conviction that he had committed suicide and blamed her mother for her overpowering intrusiveness in the lives of her children. So devastated was Melanie by the death of Hans that she was unable to attend his funeral in Budapest or be seen at professional meetings in London. As on previous occasions of personal catastrophe, she sought solace in the 'manic defence' of hard work. It is surely not coincidental that it was at this time that she formulated her theory of the 'depressive position'.

With the loss of both Hans and Melitta, Melanie's patients increasingly became of emotional importance to her. In January 1935 she took into analysis Paula Heimann, a young refugee from Nazi Germany, who entirely replaced Melitta in her affections. This relationship lasted, with evident ambivalences, for twenty years. Then Paula also rebelled and it all ended in bitterness and recrimination. Needless to say, she received no further referrals of new patients.

Although Melanie Klein achieved undoubted eminence in psychoanalytic circles, hers was in many ways a tragic life – a long misery-go-round of ambivalent relationships, bereavements, persecutory anxieties, and depressions on the one hand, and the need to make reparation (which as often as not was enviously spoiled) on the other. That she was able to use this unhappy existence as the basis on which to create an entire school of psychoanalysis says much for the power of her personality, the ingenuity of her mind, and the strength of the human need for explanatory systems to be taken in by.

Note

[1] Here and later on, when discussing the mother-child bond, I use the masculine pronoun for the child. This is not because I believe girls are less important but because I wish to avoid confusion between the child ('him') and the mother ('her').

5

Object Relations Theory

Fairbairn, Winnicott, Balint and Guntrip

Very understandably, lay people are confused by psychoanalytic use of the term 'object'. In everyday life an object refers to a thing, but in psychoanalysis 'object' is used to refer to a person, or to part of a person, or to a symbol of one or the other. To Freud, an 'object' was what a subject needed in order to achieve instinctual gratification. But, with the emergence of object relations theory, interest in instinctual gratification was dropped in favour of the specifically social need of a subject to establish a relationship with an object (initially a mother-figure) and later with other significant people in the subject's life. It should also be remembered that in psychoanalytic parlance an 'object relationship' may be either external or internal – that is to say, it may be with an actual person in outer reality or with the mental representation of that person in the subject's psyche.

Freud's view of the human condition had overtones of Thomas Hobbes and Judeo-Christian 'original sin', as well as of Nietzsche, Fechner, Darwin, Haeckel, Jonathon Swift, and Lamarck. Each individual had to go through the biologically established pattern: the infant, with its bestial sexual and aggressive drives, developed into the human adult, possessing a psychic apparatus which permitted these instinctual demands to be curbed, and sublimated, in socially acceptable ways. Contrary to this early view, most contemporary psychoanalysts accept that the human infant is born better adapted to the social world than Freud believed. Historically, the analysts most responsible for promoting this shift of emphasis, were, as we have seen, Sandor Ferenzci, Anna Freud, Heinz Hartmann, and Melanie Klein.

Klein in particular prepared the path that led from Freudian ego-psychology to modern object relations theories (Gomez, 1997). Though she accepted that the infant was born with a more structured, better adapted psyche than Freud had proposed, she nevertheless failed to acknowledge that the task of childhood might well be to achieve a specifically social adaptation. To her, the child's primary objective was to preserve its sanity by dealing with the psychotic terrors by which it was afflicted. It was this 'Hammer Studios' portrayal of life that the British object relations theorists were to modify.

The main figures involved in these developments were Ronald Fairbairn, Donald Winnicott, Michael Balint, Harry Guntrip, and, most importantly in my view, John Bowlby, who went on to develop his own Attachment Theory, which we shall review in the next Chapter. Together they constituted what came to be known as the 'independent group' of psychoanalysts, who, thoroughly fed up with the implacable antagonism that raged between Kleinian and Freudian factions, had decided to go their own way in the spirit of 'a plague on both their houses'. Though each of them was to develop his own theoretical orientation, they were at one in rejecting Klein's nightmarish mythology of a conflict-ridden, destructive baby, tormented by its own 'death instinct'. Instead, they adopted a more benign position, perceiving the child as born with the necessary potential for forming social attachments, which would normally be healthy provided the child was cared for in an appropriately nurturing environment. Psychopathology would result, in their view, only if the child's natural development happened to be derailed by inadequate or inappropriate parenting.

This represented a crucial step towards a balanced, and ultimately verifiable, conception of human ontogeny, which was more compatible with scientific method than that hitherto embraced by the Freudians and Kleinians. However, the theoretical orientation, as well as the mode of practice, adopted by each of these innovators was profoundly dependent upon their own psychology (their personal equation). We will consider each in turn.

William Ronald Dodds Fairbairn (1889-1964)

As has already been indicated, original thinkers in the area of psychodynamic therapy are not strangers to the schizoid disposition. In none of them was this characteristic more apparent than in W.R.D. Fairbairn. Although he had important and original things to say, he was so retiring and introverted by nature that his influence had relatively little impact in his lifetime. Having trained as an analyst at a time when Melanie Klein's views prevailed, he nevertheless remained in his native Edinburgh, far away from the internecine warfare in the South, and unbuffeted by the main psychoanalytic currents of his time.

Fairbairn's parents were comfortably off, well-respected citizens of Edinburgh, his father a strict Scottish Calvinist, his mother a socially ambitious Englishwoman. An only child, he grew up to be a sensitive, high-minded, and emotionally detached young man. At Edinburgh University he read philosophy and later went on to London and Manchester to follow courses in theology and Hellenistic studies. He would probably have become a minister of religion had not the First World War intervened, and had he not developed a phobia about preaching. Encounters with soldiers suffering from 'shell shock' and with Dr W.H.R. Rivers who was to become famous through his treatment of the war poets, Siegfried Sassoon and Wilfred Owen, turned Fairbairn's interest to psychology, and, on Ernest Jones's advice, before entering analysis, he studied medicine, qualifying in 1923. He received no formal training as a psychoanalyst, but was analysed for two years by Ernest Connell, an Edinburgh psychiatrist, who had himself been analysed by Jones. On the strength of his medical degree and his personal analysis, Fairbairn began his own analytic practice in 1925.

Dedicated, hard-working, and with a strong social conscience, he took on as patients people suffering from a variety of conditions not normally treated in the privileged seclusion of the analytic consulting room. In addition to shell-shocked veterans, he worked with children who had been sexually and physically abused, people who were terminally ill, psychotic patients, and sexual offenders. He regularly worked a 10-hour day and spent his evenings reading and writing till midnight.

He did not marry until he was he was 37, and his wife, Mary, was not sympathetic to his work – presumably because it meant she saw so little of him. Between 1927 and 1933 they had 5 children, 2 of whom were twins who died at birth. Their marriage was not happy. Mary became an alcoholic and died in 1952. It is clear that Fairbairn had little time for family or friends: his energies were invested in his inner world of ideas and in his work. For many years he suffered from a neurotic symptom which he shared with his father – an inability to urinate when others were near enough to see or hear him. Like his phobia about preaching, this symbolized a fear of 'letting himself go' in the presence of other people, and it increased his professional and social isolation because it meant he was unable to travel or stay away from home.

As one might expect of an analyst with these characteristics, the schizoid state was the condition on which his theoretical interests were focused. His critical intellect, combined with his training in philosophy and his withdrawal from coercive outside influences, enabled him to detect flaws in Freud's theorizing long before other psychoanalysts became aware of them (Sutherland, 1989).

In particular, Fairbairn realized that Freud's basic scientific assumptions were out of date, and he questioned Freud's premise that libido is primarily pleasure-seeking. His philosophical training and Calvinistic upbringing had made him sceptical of any theory based on hedonism. Fairbairn argued that libido is not pleasure-seeking but object-seeking. Our basic need is for relationship and this takes precedence over other needs such as the desire for sexual gratification. Our greatest fears are about being separated from the people we love and on whom our physical and psychological well-being depends. His work with abused children showed him that they often remained powerfully attached to their abusive parents: the fact that they experienced pain and frustration from these parents, rather than pleasure and gratification, did little to weaken the bond. Since attachment-seeking was the child's primary motive, Fairbairn saw no place for an aggressive, destructive, 'death' instinct, arguing that a child will experience aggression only as a secondary reaction at moments when its attachment-seeking is frustrated. He also rejected the Freudian id concept, arguing that there is no need to postulate a 'seething cauldron' of unconscious energy if the libido necessary for attachment formation is a natural endowment of the ego.

One problem with Freud's pleasure principle and his notion of psychological hedonism is that they are hard to reconcile with the phenomenon of 'repetition compulsion', whereby people repeat the same self-defeating and maladaptive patterns of behaviour and experience. If people instinctively seek pleasure and avoid pain, why do so many persist in making themselves unhappy? Freud explained this in terms of the *adhesiveness* of libido: the libido tends to become stuck to the objects in which it was originally invested, even when these objects are either frustrating or inaccessible. It occurred to Fairbairn that this idea of libidinal adhesiveness might explain the strength of the bonds that a child forms with its parents. These bonds are made through the contacts that the parents provide, whether they be loving, dominating, or aggressive, and these kinds of contact determine the nature of the child's future patterns of relationship with others. If libido were merely pleasure-seeking, children would withdraw from abusive parents and seek attachments elsewhere, but they do not. They remain bonded to their abusers. It is rather like Konrad Lorenz's goslings who became firmly attached ('imprinted') to the first moving object they encountered on hatching, however inappropriate that object might be (e.g., Dr Lorenz himself).

Altogether, Fairbairn's papers reveal a shrewd mind capable of original insights, and his contribution to psychoanalytic theory and practice deserved greater acknowledgement than it received while he lived, even though it was constrained, as with most other 'depth' psychologists, by the nature of his 'personal equation'. Clearly, the central problem of his life was his schizoid personality: his longing for commitment to an intimate and lasting relationship on the one hand and his difficulty in achieving it on the other.

By exploring this dynamic in himself and in his patients Fairbairn advanced our understanding, but then, as did Klein, he committed the fallacy of generalizing what he had found out about himself to all humanity. The self, he maintained, is structured in all of us round the 'schizoid position': on the basis of this position personality development of whatever kind proceeds in everyone. Because none of us received parenting which was perfectly geared to our needs, we are unable to rejoice in a permanent sense of being loved unconditionally for who we are. There are inevitably times when a love object is inaccessible, neglectful, frustrating or downright rejecting, and this gives rise to feelings of not being loved and of not having one's love accepted. Since these feelings of rejection or abandonment are particularly intolerable early in life, every young child has to find ways of dealing with them. Children do this, Fairbairn affirmed, by 'splitting' – that is to say, by separating off the bad experience of the beloved object from the good. The bad experience is, nevertheless, introjected and repressed, so that the child may continue to enjoy relating to the external person to whom he is attached, without allowing damaged feelings to ruin it.

Thus, Fairbairn's object relations theory shares with Klein's the notion of internal objects and of 'splitting' between good and bad. But whereas Klein believed that internalized object relations were the very essence of all mental life, Fairbairn maintained that internalized objects of the sort Klein described only developed as the result of inadequate parenting. Though some degree of splitting is unavoidable healthy parenting, in his view, generates real bonds of attachment with real parental figures outside in the environment. Deficient parenting, which repeatedly fails to meet the child's 'dependency needs', causes him to retreat from a wholehearted relationship with the parental figure and withdraw into an internal realm of fantasied object relationships. A schizoid personality develops when the original splitting and repression are maintained to an extreme degree, which falls short of the complete psychotic fragmentation of schizophrenia.

Typically, the schizoid state is characterized by feelings of unreality, futility, deadness, and being cut off, as if separated from the world by a plate glass window. Many people may experience such feelings from time to time, but for the truly schizoid person they are the normal accompaniments of existence. Since their initial experience of a loving relationship was so intolerably painful, schizoid people tend to escape from such dangerous emotions into an inner world of fantasy and into the use of rational, intellectual areas of psychic functioning. Many philosophers, scientists and psychologists possess such a history, including Isaac Newton, René Descartes and Carl Gustav Jung. Fairbairn believed that Western child-rearing practices were particularly conducive to production of schizoid personalities because of the frequent periods of isolation that Western infants have to endure in every 24-hour period of their lives.*

* This would seem to tie in with Jung's diagnosis that people complaining of aimlessness and purposelessness were suffering from 'the neurosis of the age'.

Since as children we all relate to our parents through the characteristics they reveal to us, we absorb and reflect their character traits, whether they be adaptive or pathological, for these personal modes of expression represent the links of our mutual bonds of attachment. In this way we become like our parents, whether they be cheerful, loving and sociable, or depressed, hostile or anti-social, and this determines our characteristic mode of relating. If we have pathological parents, pathology becomes the means through which we relate to them and to others because non-pathological qualities are not available to us.

This becomes crucially relevant in the analytic situation. The patient enters analysis, says Fairbairn, in search of new and better modes of relationship, but inevitably brings to the transference all his old, problematic modes and expectations. The problem to be confronted is not, as Freud maintained, the release and sublimation of repressed infantile strivings, but to make conscious the neurotic patterns of relationship acquired in childhood. The neurosis consists of the only forms of relating the patient knows how to use. When resistance is encountered in the treatment, it is not because the patient is reluctant to own disreputable instinctual strivings, but because he fears to relinquish his old modes of adjustment, for if he does so he fears that he will be capable of no relationship at all and will be doomed to total abandonment and isolation.

The function of the analyst, in Fairbairn's view, was not so much to provide insight but to offer the patient a new model of relationship through the therapeutic alliance. The crucial factor that enabled the patient to change was not the transference relationship, as Freudians and Kleinians insisted, but the real relationship that developed between the patient and the analyst over time. When Fairbairn offered interpretations, it was less with the intention of granting insight than with demonstrating his commitment, and concern. Like Jung, he did away with the couch and declined to sit behind the patient out of sight because he felt this reactivated early traumas of feeling abandoned and rejected. However, unlike Jung, he took the precaution of separating himself from his patient by sitting behind a large desk! Presumably this represented a schizoid defence against too close an involvement with his patients.

Fairbairn did not spell out how transformation in the patient's condition could be achieved, but contemporary evidence would indicate that he was right to stress the provision of a dependable structure in the analytic situation and the necessary readiness of the therapist to be open and accepting in his attitude to the patient. But on the whole, Fairbairn's contribution to object relations was theoretical rather than practical. In the case of D.W. Winnicott it was the other way round.

Donald Woods Winnicott (1896-1971)

As far as I am aware, no carefully controlled studies have been done to establish the efficacy or otherwise of Kleinian analysis. Not having received a Kleinian analysis myself, it strikes me as doubtful that Kleinian theories could in themselves be particularly conducive to therapeutic success and possible that with many patients they could actually do more harm than good. On those occasions when a Kleinian analysis does result in positive outcome, I suspect it has less to do with the theoretical premises on which the procedure is based than with the personal qualities that both analyst and patient bring to the therapeutic alliance that is forged between them. One Kleinian analyst who clearly was able to help many thousands of patients was Donald Winnicott.

Winnicott was both a psychoanalyst and a paediatrician, and for most of his professional life he held appointments at Paddington Green Children's Hospital and The Queen Elizabeth Hospital for Children in London. It has been estimated that he must have seen somewhere in the region of 60,000 patients. Many people have recorded their appreciation of his warmth, kindness, humanity, and lack of dogmatism. It was through these qualities that he made his contribution to the practice of psychoanalysis rather than by producing any startling theoretical revisions. Evidently he possessed outstanding diplomatic skills, for he managed to steer his own professional course while remaining on good terms with Melanie Klein, who even entrusted him with the analysis of her son, Erich.

It is interesting that alone among the analysts we have considered so far, Donald Winnicott enjoyed an apparently happy, stress-free childhood. He was the only son of a Plymouth business man and grew up surrounded by loving females – his mother, sisters, nanny, governess, and aunt. The only discernible psychodynamic influences which may have helped to shape his future career are the qualities of feminine nurturance so apparent in both his background and his personality and a strong desire not to offend his kind but rather distant father.

A natural carer, he was strongly attracted by the medical profession. But initially he hesitated to commit himself to medical training for fear that it would disappoint his father, who wanted him to take over the family business. That he was eventually able to enrol in the medical school at Cambridge University was due to the support and mediation of a family friend. It is possible that this desire not to upset his father or lose the good opinion of the family matriarchy was instrumental in inhibiting him from launching any assault on the theoretical positions of Freud or Klein. He preferred to go his own way tactfully and without rocking the psychoanalytical boat.

Donald Winnicott was twice married but had no children of his own. His parental feelings were entirely sublimated in looking after the children in his care, sometimes taking the more needy of them into his home. His first marriage was to Alice Taylor in 1922. She is said to have had major psychological difficulties and Winnicott may have married her partly out of a desire to look after her. The marriage was not a success and they eventually separated in 1949, but not until Winnicott felt she could manage without him.

As far as his analytic training was concerned, Winnicott had a long experience of both the Freudian and the Kleinian traditions. His first analysis with James Strachey, Freud's translator, who had himself been analysed by Freud, lasted 10 years; and his second, with Joan Rivière, a leading Kleinian who also analysed John Bowlby, lasted 5 years. He was disappointed by both. He found Strachey a cold fish, who overemphasized the importance of interpretation and undervalued the significance of relationship both in personal development and the analytic situation; and he experienced Rivière as a dogmatic Kleinian, who was uninterested in his own ideas about child development and treatment. It is characteristic of him that he showed no signs of rebelling against either of these analytic regimes, but persisted in going along with them for no less than 15 years, only to emerge dissatisfied at the end. Again he seems to have been keeping 'the parents' happy, while quietly going his own way.

Privately, Winnicott differed from Freud in believing that relationship mattered more than instinctual drives, and from Klein in believing that environmental influences were every bit as important as inner constructs and unconscious fantasies. Like Anna Freud and Melanie Klein he carefully observed children, but he approached the task without dogmatic axes to grind, and, what is more, he observed children in relation to their mothers, noting how the kind of mothering a child receives may correlate with healthy or unhealthy development.

What he believed to be of critical importance was the mother's degree of responsiveness to the baby's needs, and this had more to do with the quality of the love she provided than with the capacity to feed and attend to her child physically. A mother who is loving and appropriately responsive – Winnicott referred to her as the 'good-enough mother' – provides the 'holding environment' within which the infant is able to discover its own subjectivity and emerge as a human being with a sense of its own reality and meaningfulness. Initially, the mother's 'primal maternal preoccupation' enables her to perceive and gratify every need of her child, thus generating in him the illusion of 'subjective omnipotence'. The final months of pregnancy, and the totally engaging miracle of giving birth, prepare the mother for the focused dedication that 'good-enough' mothering requires during the child's first weeks. Not only does she empathize with his inner state but she suspends her own subjectivity in service to the emerging subjectivity of the infant. This provides the indispensable matrix out of which the child's 'true self' can emerge, a spontaneous sense of natural being, of existing authentically in his own right in the world.

Then, very gradually, the mother's sense of her own subjectivity returns, and her maternal preoccupation becomes less intense. This brings home to the child the realization that he is not omnipotent but dependent on the goodwill of another human being. This is both painful and constructive, for it forces the child to broaden his sense of authentic subjectivity through a growing awareness of the subjective authenticity of another, who has needs and an existence of her own.

In this way, the child's 'subjective omnipotence' is integrated into an experience of 'objective reality'. This integration does not proceed directly but passes through a 'transitional' phase. In the state of subjective omnipotence, the child has the illusion of being able to create in the world everything that he needs. It is as if he is in possession of Aladdin's lamp: he has only to wish for something and it appears. The experience of objective reality comes with the realization that he has lost the lamp and can no longer command the world to do his bidding. He has to seek what he wants to find, acknowledge his separateness from the world, and acquire the ability to negotiate with it.

The transitional phase is intermediary between the child's '*participation mystique*' as Jung called it with his mother and his realization of his separateness from her. Typically, during this phase, the child becomes powerfully attached to a teddy bear, a woolly toy, a towel, blanket, or piece of rag. Winnicott was the first to draw attention to this universally apparent phenomenon in our culture and to offer a psychoanalytic explanation of its significance. The 'transitional object' (*i.e.*, the teddy bear, rag, etc.) enables the child to cope with his anxieties at being left alone: it renders the mother symbolically present when she is absent, and the child clings on to the object as a talisman which grants him sufficient security to acknowledge his own and his mother's separateness.

With time, the transitional object loses its importance, indicating that it has outlasted its psychological usefulness and that the child is capable of reconciling attachment with autonomy and taking both for granted. However, the transitional state between omnipotence and reality, between connection and separateness, between inner and outer, persists throughout life: it provides the psychic space in which play, the arts, and all cultural activities can thrive. The transitional state is thus indispensable to creativity.

Winnicott published his views in a series of theoretical papers. Up to 1960 these were written, very tactfully, as a reaction against the views of Melanie Klein, apparently in the forlorn hope of persuading her to change them. After her death he became more explicit, and the title of his second volume of collected papers, *The Maturational Process and the Facilitating Environment*, published in 1965, neatly summarized his understanding of human developmental psychology.

How then do psychiatric disorders occur? Development begins to go awry, according to Winnicott, if the mother, for whatever reason, is unable to provide the 'good-enough' environment necessary to establish the subjective experience of a 'true self' in the child. If he expresses his needs, and these needs are ignored, then he experiences himself as being at risk of annihilation. A spontaneous sense of authentic, effortless existence cannot emerge. It is supplanted by a struggle to survive in a hostile world, and the child is forced to come to terms with reality before he is ready to do so. Development of the true self then goes into abeyance, inhibited by premature engagement with the threatening demands of reality. This prepares the ground for psychiatric disorder.

Though he accepted the contribution that genetic factors can make to the aetiology of mental illness, these did not interest him. His primary concern was with what he called 'false self disorder', (essentially another term for 'schizoid disorder'), whereby the 'true self' fails to develop and is supplanted by a 'false self' which strives desperately to cope, while putting on a pretence of dealing competently with life in the outer world. If mental breakdown occurs, it happens when this pretence can no longer be kept up, and feelings of inner emptiness and inauthenticity become overwhelming.

How can analysis repair the damage once it has been done? In Winnicott's view, the task of analysis is to compensate for the 'not good-enough' mother by providing the necessary 'holding environment' to re-establish contact with the quiescent 'true self'. The analytic setting has to be truly 'transitional', enabling the patient to enter the psychic borderland where inner and outer worlds meet so as to 'play' with the different versions of reality which may emerge. When patients regressed to infantile stages of experience, this was necessary, in Winnicott's opinion, not to release incestuous wishes from repression, but to enable the ego to re-experience the legitimate needs of the growing self.

Unlike Klein, Winnicott possessed an optimistic faith in the endogenous regenerative powers of the human psyche: he believed that patients came into analysis actively seeking the experiences needed to revitalize the true self. It was the analyst's job to appreciate the nature of the patient's need and to provide the environmental qualities which were lacking in childhood. Whether in fact this admirable therapeutic objective can ever be satisfactorily achieved is a matter for dispute, but that Winnicott tried to practice what he preached is not to be doubted, and one must admire him for the generosity with which he devoted himself to his patients, as well as the apparently inexhaustible goodwill which enabled him to do it.

Michael Balint (1896-1970)

A Hungarian emigrant from Budapest, Balint was, like Melanie Klein, analysed by Sandor Ferenzci. A warm, ebullient personality, he is best remembered for the 'Balint groups' which he and his second wife conducted for general practitioners in London, and for developing the use of psychoanalytic concepts in brief psychotherapy on an individual basis as well as with groups and with couples. Being of a generous and affectionate nature, he readily extended Ferenzci's view that what patients were seeking in the analytic situation was not a cold, 'surgical' interpretation of their repressed infantile wishes but an experience of the unconditional, 'primary object love', which they had been denied in childhood. His clinical approach thus had much in common with that of Winnicott. He believed, like Fairbairn, that the capacity for object relations was present at birth and not derived from drives linked to the oral, anal, or genital erogenous zones. This view was also adopted by John Bowlby, who put Balint's 'primary object love' on a sound ethological basis.

Harry Guntrip (1901-1974)

Harry Guntrip was a Congregational minister whose pastoral work eventually led him into the practice of psychodynamic therapy. His mother and father were difficult, rigidly evangelical people, whose marriage was unhappy, and they were unlikely to have been very satisfactory parents. He was devoted to his younger brother, Percy, who died when Guntrip was 3. He was devastated by this loss and, maintaining that he never got over it, he attributed to it his life-long proneness to emotional distress and psychosomatic illnesses.

It was his personal unhappiness that took him into analysis rather than a desire for training. His first analysis, which lasted for 6 years, was with Hugh Chrichton-Miller, then Director of the Tavistock Clinic. After that, he spent 10 years in analysis with Ronald Fairbairn and finally a further 10 years with Donald Winnicott. His analyses with Fairbairn and Winnicott drew to an end only when each, in his turn, became too old and too ill to go on practising. Though he was appreciative of Winnicott, he was critical of Fairbairn, whom he did not feel had particularly helped him.

Guntrip himself believed his problems were due to not 'good-enough' mothering and protracted grief for his brother Percy's death. Fairbairn and Winnicott did not entirely agree: both believed that the emotional issue over Percy was jealous rage rather than grief and that this was compounded by the guilt he suffered when his murderous fantasies were realized. Whether or not this was so, his 26 years of treatment, which were a heavy drain on his family's resources (he was married with one daughter), do not provide a very good advertisement for the efficacy of analysis. Guntrip's biographer, Jeremy Hazell, who was also one of his analysands, believes that Guntrip's analysis with Winnicott did enable him to become more peaceful and less compulsively hyperactive (a symptom which was attributed to his 'non-existent sense of basic being').

Having himself suffered the destructive consequences of early emotional deprivation and gone through a protracted and equivocal experience of analysis, Guntrip, more than any other object relations theorist, stressed the necessity for the analyst to act as the good parent, whom the patient lacked, so as to provide 'replacement therapy' within the context of the analysis. Only if the analytic relationship is truly nurturing on a highly personal basis, Guntrip maintained, could it be the means to a satisfactory outcome (Mitchell and Black, 1995).

Like Winnicott, he was a good, kind-hearted man, and he evidently strove to radiate loving warmth to his patients. His approach remained essentially psychoanalytic, however, because he believed that the regressed, split-off, and isolated ego could only be reached through the analytic relationship after years of slow, painstaking analysis of the patient's defences. A cynic might comment that after investing so heavily in 26 years of analysis he would have a powerful incentive to believe that it was not all in vain. However, patients who have suffered inappropriate mothering and who have experienced rejection in childhood inevitably fear entering into a close, trusting relationship with their analyst, and this can be a formidable obstacle to progress. The kind of warm acceptance provided by analysts like Winnicott and Guntrip is necessary if such patients are to recover some of their lost feeling, and that takes time.

What is more, to reach that point is only the beginning, for once these patients start to have real feelings for the analyst, fears arise that he is going to treat them as they were treated by their parents. The old dread of rejection and abandonment recurs, and they become angry and resentful at times when they suspect their analyst is going to desert them. Not infrequently, they will abuse and reject him, as they were abused and rejected themselves, and, if the analyst is not very careful, the analysis gets bogged down in the same kind of sterile interactions that the patients experienced as children in relation to their parents. It is not surprising, therefore, that the analysis of such patients can be a long and arduous business, and positive outcome is by no means assured. One can but admire the dedication of analysts who are willing, nevertheless, to try.

But, whether an analyst, however warm and loving, can ever, on a professional basis, provide the kind of replacement therapy that Guntrip craved and which Winnicott sought to provide, seems extremely doubtful. Certainly, if it is possible, it is not something that can be learned from the systematic 'manuals' that different schools of psychotherapy are producing in increasing numbers at the present time. It is hard to escape the conclusion that to provide the kind of analytic ambience prescribed by Winnicott and Guntrip would require such limitless resources of love as only a saint could provide. There doubtless exist many generous and good-hearted analysts who are devoted to the welfare of their patients, but practitioners possessing these suprahuman capacities must, in the natural order of things, be rather thin on the ground.

***

Object relations theory made an important contribution to our understanding of the development of human relationships: it provided insights into how these relationships may go wrong, and advanced techniques for treating them when they do. However, it suffered from two serious deficiencies: it was unduly narrow in its focus and almost entirely lacking in links with biological science. Like the Freudian drive theories which it sought to supplant, it constructed an elaborate theoretical edifice; but it was built on epistemological sand.

Jock Sutherland (1980) put his finger on a crucial point when he said that, as a group, the object relations theorists had stopped short of any systematic conceptualization of the self. They provided no explanation of how the self originated or on what principles it developed. 'Why the center of the person should have been so long in becoming the center of our theoretical concern is itself a fascinating question', he wrote. He blamed the Cartesian split between the body and the mind for the reluctance of psychoanalysts to enter the forbidden arena of innate possibilities. This is unfortunate, Sutherland argued, because the study of biological systems tells us that 'every system has to have an organizing principle' and that the environment is integral to the system. But having said so much, he then immediately backtracks: 'To imagine an organzing principle at work in the self', he hurriedly reassures his readers, 'does not necessarily take us into innate forms ...' His conclusion is frank: 'The British group does not presume to have made anything like an adequate conceptual map for the development of the psyche.' Thus, although they accepted that infants were endowed with an inherent imperative to form a relationship with a mother figure, their acceptance of any biological contribution to the process stopped at that point. The idea that future development should occur on the basis of an evolutionarily created blueprint does not seem to have entered their thinking.

It is characteristic of psychoanalytic writing that at no time in his paper does Sutherland acknowledge that these conceptual issues had all been addressed by Jung, who had long since postulated an 'organizing principle' in the form of the Self and had provided the beginnings of a 'conceptual map for the development of the psyche' in his 'stages of life'. Both Sutherland and the object relations theorists were constrained not merely by the barriers of their Cartesian inheritance but by vestiges of the Freudian thought police which continued to control scientific rectitude. Consequently, object relations theory, though in many ways ingenious, is ultimately disappointing because it provides a jerry-built conceptual structure devoid of evolutionary foundations: the personal history of the patient is considered as proceeding in a biological vacuum, utterly dislocated from the natural history of the species. It is this fatal weakness that Bowlby's Attachment Theory was intended to correct.

6

Attachment Theory

John Bowlby (1907-1990)

With John Bowlby's arrival on the scene, the hitherto sluggish, meandering course of psychoanalytic history begins to quicken into a broad, fast-moving stream, offering glimpses of the charted seas and wide horizons of a humane science. The nautical metaphor is not inappropriate, as Bowlby was destined for a naval career, and was spared for psychoanalysis only when he rebelled against the intellectual restrictions of Dartmouth Royal Naval College and persuaded his father to buy him out of the service. But there was always a residual element of the naval officer about him. As I was to discover, if you arrived unexpectedly to see him, there was a moment when he looked at you like a surprised Admiral, wondering what on earth you were doing on his quarterdeck, before his gentle courtesy intervened and you were made welcome.

Bowlby was one of the most creative and influential psychiatrists produced by any nation in the twentieth century. Not only did he revolutionize psychoanalytic theory and transform our understanding of psychopathology, but he provided a scientific basis for the practice of psychotherapy and improved the lot of children in hospitals and institutions throughout the world.

He was born in 1907, the second son of a distinguished but psychologically remote father, Major-General Sir Anthony Bowlby, Bart (1855-1929), surgeon to King Edward VII and King George V. His mother was an emotionally fickle, rather self-centred woman, who, like many mothers of her class, was content to leave the care and upbringing of her children to the family servants. John had three sisters (Winnie, 7 years older, Marion, 4 years older, and Evelyn, 4 years younger) and two brothers (Tony, 13 months older, and Jim, 2 years younger than himself). As children, they saw relatively little of their parents, except for long family holidays in Scotland, which were occasions of great happiness for them all. Bowlby retained a deep affection for Scotland, especially the Isle of Skye, where he died in 1990. Never closely bonded to his mother, he became specially attached to a much-loved nursemaid,

Minnie. But she left the family when he was only 4, and his grief must have been intense. In addition, he suffered the major trauma, shared by all male members of his class and time, of being sent away from home at the age of 7 to endure the harsh and unloving regime of an English preparatory boarding school.

In his invaluable *John Bowlby and Attachment Theory* (1993), Jeremy Holmes compares Bowlby with Charles Darwin, whose biography Bowlby wrote at the end of his life. 'Like Darwin', writes Holmes, 'Bowlby had a strong and successful medical father; both seem to have aroused in their sons a rebelliousness hedged about with caution ... Apparently bolder than Darwin, Bowlby kept his vulnerability well hidden. But in his rebelliousness we see perhaps the protest of the child who has been hurt and neglected. In his application and indefatigability we find the attempt to make good the unthinking damage the adult world so often does to children' (pp.34-35).

This rings very true; and it is likely that Bowlby's preoccupation with attachment, separation, and loss, which he saw as the key issues for psychotherapy and psychiatry, was indeed a direct out-growth of his own life experience. 'In his concept of maternal deprivation', comments Holmes, 'it is as though Bowlby was simultaneously reproving and idealizing his neglectful mother'. A close friend and colleague, Jock Sutherland, whose family shared a home for many years with the Bowlbys, believed Bowlby's sensitive understanding of the maternally deprived 'affectionless character' was based on his personal empathy with the condition. 'John's slightly formal and detached manner struck many people on first knowing him', he wrote, and considered his 'protective shell of not showing his feelings' was due to emotional inhibition in early childhood. Nevertheless, he possessed 'a deep and powerful fund of affection – the source of his intensely caring concern for those who worked for him.' This same concern extended to all children who lacked the loving intimacy which he knew to be indispensable to their secure, happy, and healthy development.

Having left Dartmouth in 1925, he entered Trinity College, Cambridge, to study pre-clinical medicine and psychology. Before transferring to London to do his clinical training, he took a year out to work in a progressive school for delinquent children which had been inspired by the reforming educationalist, A.S. Neill. There he discovered he had a talent for getting on with these children and was intrigued that their delinquent behaviour could often be directly traced to serious disturbances in their early history and family background. His father having recently died, he felt free to choose whichever medical specialty he pleased, and he had no hesitation in opting for psychiatry and psychoanalysis. Accordingly, having begun his clinical studies at University College, London, in 1929 at the age of 22, he entered analysis with Joan Rivière, a close colleague of Melanie Klein. Like Clare Winnicott he became stuck in this Kleinian analysis and wanted to change to a non-Kleinian, but, also like her, he was forced to toe the party line. Being of an independent spirit, this can only have reinforced his intention to steer his own course once he was free to do so.

After medical qualification in 1933, he worked at the Maudsley Hospital, where Sir Aubrey Lewis ruled, and completed his psychoanalytic training under the supervision of Melanie Klein and Ella Freeman Sharpe. Of the two, he much preferred the latter, who was a supporter of Anna Freud. He described her as 'a warm-hearted middle-aged woman who had a good understanding of human nature and a sense of humour.' This was very different from the humourless intensity of Klein and the Kleinians. Writing in October 1955 to the renegade Freudian, Wilhelm Reich, A.S. Neill, the progressive headmaster of Summerhill, described a wedding he had attended which was packed with the followers of Melanie Klein. 'Interesting to hear their talk', he wrote. 'I mentioned your name as a test; their faces clouded with disapproval which amused me. They can't laugh; Melanie has evidently shown them humour is a complex which no normal man should have … *Gott*, they were a dull crowd … rather like talking to communists with a blank curtain that you couldn't penetrate.'

Once qualified, Bowlby joined the staff of the London Child Guidance Clinic in 1937 where he rapidly began to develop his own ideas in contradistinction to those of Melanie Klein. The following year he married Ursula Longstaff. They were to remain happily married for life and they had four children. From the outset he was openly critical of the state of psychoanalysis. He saw that its biological assumptions were hopelessly out of date and he was appalled by the wilful ignorance displayed by psychoanalysts of current scientific thinking. In their preoccupation with inner fantasies and conflicts they attached too little importance to real events impacting on a child's psychological development from the outer environment. 'It was regarded as almost outside the proper interest of an analyst to give systematic attention to a person's real experiences', he wrote (1988). 'Almost by definition it was assumed that anyone interested in the external world could not be interested in the internal world, indeed was almost certainly running away from it.' While he accepted that the practice of analysis was an art, he maintained that its concepts should rest on a body of systematically validated knowledge.

Bowlby's ambition was to place psychoanalysis on a sound scientific basis and to build links between it and other scientific disciplines. At first he hoped that collaboration would be possible with the Kleinians to collate their imaginative formulations of internal processes with objective observations of external events so as to produce a more factually based discipline. But the Kleinians made it clear that they regarded his efforts to be misguided, presumptuous, and unwelcome. Undaunted, he proceeded to study a series of children in whom stealing was a problem, and published *Forty-Four Juvenile Thieves: Their Characters and Home Life*. He reported that a significantly large number of these children (who came to be known as 'Ali Bowlby's 40 thieves') had suffered maternal loss or separation in their earliest years. This provided the theme which was to engage him for the rest of his life.

During the Second World War he served as an army psychiatrist and ended up with the rank of Lieutenant-Colonel. On demobilization he became a consultant at the Tavistock Clinic, where he remained until his retirement in 1972, serving as Chairman of the Department of Children and Parents from 1946 to 1968. The most significant opportunity of his career came in 1950 when he was appointed as a consultant to the Mental Health Section of the World Health Organization. This gave him time to read the literature on the ill effects of institutional care and maternal deprivation on personality development and to meet researchers on both sides of the Atlantic. On the strength of this he published in 1951 his widely influential WHO monograph *Maternal Care and Mental Health*, in which he called attention to the distress of young children when they are separated from those whom they love, and made clear recommendations of how best to mitigate the consequences of such separations. *Maternal Care* was translated into 12 different languages and in its abridged paperback English edition sold 450,000 copies.

Researching the material for his monograph convinced Bowlby that the mother-child bond is a *primary* phenomenon, irreducible to any other source, such as feeding or the reduction of physiological drives. 'It is as if', he wrote, in a vividly memorable phrase, 'maternal care were as necessary for the proper development of personality as vitamin D for the proper development of bones.'

Over the next six years, together with James Robertson and Christopher Heinicke, he continued to collect data on children separated from their mothers, and, in 1958, he published his classic paper on 'The Nature of the Child's Tie to His Mother', in which he drew on ethological as well as psychological sources to support his view that the mother-infant attachment bond was based not on 'operant conditioning', as the academic learning theorists insisted and as the psychoanalysts agreed, but on instinct. Infants became bonded to their mothers because they were innately programmed to do so from birth. Learning plays an important role in the process, but it proceeds on an instinctual basis.

This proposal proved extremely controversial, for it demanded a radical revision in both behavioural and psychoanalytic theory. Bowlby conceived attachment behaviour as operating through a system quite separate from eating or sexual behaviour and maintained that it proceeded on similar lines to attachment behaviour in other mammals. In other words, the formation of the mother-infant attachment bond is a direct expression of the genetic heritage of our species. This outraged too many cherished assumptions for it to be received with enthusiasm.

In the first place, the term 'instinct' had become unacceptable to academic psychologists, who insisted that innate factors played little or no part in the behaviour of human beings. They also objected to the readiness with which Bowlby drew parallels between human attachment behaviour and that observed among mammals and birds, maintaining that human psychology was quite different from that of lesser breeds. But Bowlby was adamant that such comparisons were biologically justified and he was able to cite examples of strong infant-mother bonds that had been formed through mechanisms bearing no relation to feeding gratification and which developed in the absence of any conventional rewards such as those postulated by academic and psychoanalytic theorists.

Bowlby pointed out how much of Freud's thinking had been formulated under the influence of the discredited theories of Lamarck and that the basic assumptions of psychoanalysis required urgent revision if the discipline were to fulfil Freud's intention of remaining consistent with developments in biology. Accordingly, in place of Freud's theory of development based on libidinal phases and on the fixation and regression of libido, he proposed a theory of developmental pathways akin to C.H. Waddington's theory of epigenesis, which by then had been adopted by developmental biology. For Bowlby, psychoanalysis should never content itself with being a mere branch of hermeneutics (the art of interpretation), for it had to be rooted in science. When analysts abandoned science they deprived themselves of all objective means of settling theoretical conflicts between them. Hence the never ending battles between the Kleinians and the Freudians. He resolved that in framing his own hypotheses he would always do so in a manner which rendered them scientifically testable.

Although he devoted a third of his time to clinical practice, his heart was primarily in research. In addition to James Robertson and Christopher Heinicke, the main figures with whom he developed his developmental theory were Mary Ainsworth, Mary Boston, Dorothy Heard, and Colin Murray Parkes. In its final form attachment theory was to bring together psychoanalysis, developmental psychology, cybernetics (systems theory) and ethology. His lucid, eloquently written books are models of good sense, shrewd observation, and scientific fact, and *Maternal Care* together with his monumental trilogy *Attachment and Loss*, published between 1969 and 1980, have had more impact on the study of psychopathology than books by any writer since Freud or

Jung. The concentrated focus of his interest on bonding persisted to the end of his life, when he published the biography of his hero, Charles Darwin, tracing the great biologist's ill health and hypochrondria to repressed grief and chronic anxiety associated with the death of his mother when he was eight.

While the majority of psychoanalysts acknowledge a fundamental allegiance to Freud, it was Darwin who always held a central place in Bowlby's thinking, especially the stress Darwin placed on the *adaptive* nature of animal and human behaviour. Instead of the 'seething cauldron' of instincts in the id, requiring disciplined vigilance from the ego and superego, as envisaged by Freud, Bowlby conceived instincts to be *pre-adapted* to the environment in which we evolved – the so-called 'environment of evolutionary adaptedness'. This was an extremely important idea, and, as we shall see, it was to become the basic concept of the newly emerging discipline of evolutionary psychiatry.

Many objected violently, however, arguing that since human behaviour is so variable from person to person and from culture to culture it could not be described as instinctive in any respect. But this extreme position is no longer tenable and Bowlby was right to reject it: 'Man's behaviour is very variable, it is true, but not infinitely so,' he wrote, 'and, though cultural differences are great, certain commonalities can be discerned. For example, despite obvious variability, the patterns of behaviour, often very intensely motivated, that result in mating, in the care of babies and young children, and in the attachment of young to parents are found in almost all members of the human race and seem best considered as expressions of *some common plan* and, since they are of obvious survival value, as instances of instinctive behaviour' (Bowlby, 1969; italics added).

Bowlby was surprised when I pointed out to him soon after it was published that this passage could have been written by Jung and that his 'some common plan' had already been defined by Jung forty years earlier as an 'archetype'. 'You'll be writing about the collective unconscious next!' I ribbed him. 'I think not', he said firmly, with his Admiral's look. But there was an unmistakable twinkle in his eye. It is characteristic that after this episode he invited me to present a paper at one of his monthly attachment seminars, which I regularly attended in the '70s and early '80s, comparing and contrasting his views with Jung's. He listened with close attention and was evidently intrigued: 'So that's what he was getting at!' he exclaimed; 'I had no idea.' This openness to other people's views was in complete contrast to the attitude of Freud and Klein, and it was one of his most endearing qualities. When I eventually published my linkage of Bowlbian and Jungian insights in my *Archetype: A Natural History of the Self* (1982), his response was one of the warmest and most appreciative I received. But it was characteristic of all members of the 'independent' group of psychoanalysts, as indeed it was of committed Freudians and Kleinians, that they never read Jung or attempted to understand him. In this regard, as in many others, John Bowlby was an exception.

The only other psychoanalyst to have stressed the adaptive nature of psychic functions was, as we have seen, the ego psychologist, Heinz Hartmann. But whereas Hartmann confined himself to the cognitive and perceptual functions of the ego, Bowlby concentrated on behaviour that was observable, filmable, and comparable to that of other species. In addition to bond formation, he focused on other readily apparent features of every child's developing repertoire of behaviours – especially separation protest, stranger anxiety, and exploratory activities. He noted how, from the very beginning, infants are powerfully motivated to seek physical contact with their mothers and not to relinquish contact once it has been obtained. Physical contact, he concluded, was something which went beyond mere sexuality. It is apparent in all mammals – especially mammalian infants – as a primary *appetitive* need and is the very essence of the attachment bond. The purpose of this fundamental 'behavioural system', argued Bowlby, was abundantly clear: *survival*.

In the 'environment of evolutionary adaptedness' human mothers and infants spent as much time in close physical contact as do gorillas and chimpanzees. This has been observed in hunter-gatherer societies which have survived into the present century: babies are not kept in a cradle or a pram as with us but, as with monkeys and apes, are carried about piggyback fashion. Although human infants are less able to hang on to their mothers than infant primates – they are not so strong and their mothers lack a natural easy-grip fur coat – nevertheless all human babies have vestigial grasp reflexes strong enough to support their own weight. The primary need to be cuddled, when fully satisfied, forms the foundation of what Erik Erikson called the child's 'basic trust', and it is a need which persists into adult life. When held, one experiences security, protection, and comfort: holding is a gesture which has enormous therapeutic potency in the treatment of pain or despair. Perhaps the most destructive aspect of loneliness is that one lacks access to such effective reassurance. As Professor George Brown and his colleagues of the Social Research Unit in London have shown, individuals who can depend on the physical and verbal expression of attachment from an intimate companion enjoy a vital social asset which protects them from depression and neurotic distress.

The child's physical orientation to its mother is soon augmented by sound and sight. Within hours of birth, babies begin to single out the human voice – particularly the higher pitched human voice – from other sounds in the environment. They will, for example, quieten and reduce spontaneous movements more reliably in response to the sound of female speech than to other auditory stimuli of like intensity. Similarly, the visual apparatus appears to be programmed to respond to the 'faceness' of stimuli, so that some crude representation of two eyes, a nose and a mouth will be attended to more readily than visual stimuli presenting other configurations. Most effective of all in quietening a new-born infant are the combined stimuli of human face, human voice, and the physical stimuli of being rocked and held. These observations all support Bowlby's (and Jung's) contention that the child is prepared by its genetic endowment to interact appropriately with the world.

The most potent social assets with which the human infant is endowed are its innate ability to cry and to smile. As Bowlby pointed out, the baby's cry is analogous to the 'lost call' of young mammals and ground-nesting birds which has the effect of releasing retrieval behaviour in the parents. It is no accident that few sounds are more disturbing to a human being than the sound of a baby crying. Some inner imperative tells one it must not be allowed to continue: something must be done to stop it. The appropriate maternal response of gathering up the protesting infant while speaking soothingly usually does the trick.

Smiling has a no less potent effect on maternal responsiveness. At first, smiling is apparently indiscriminate – little more than a reflex which can be elicited by rocking or the sound of a gentle female voice. In the earliest months of life the infant does not seem to mind who looks after him as long as he is fed, kept warm and dry, and cuddled. It is only very slowly that he manages to form a conception of his mother as a special person in her own right and to show the beginnings of a personalized bond to her. The earliest sign that this is starting to happen occurs at about the fourth week when he is prone to spend time staring up at his mother's face; and this can have a profound emotional impact on her, especially if he happens to smile at the same time.

Such interactions go to make up the complex behavioural chain of mutual responsiveness through which each individual mother and child work out their own variations on the ancient biological theme of mother-infant bonding. As Bowlby repeatedly stressed, the first and most essential requirement of the mother figure is that she should be there – and lastingly there. For the provision of consistent and appropriate mothering confers upon the child the priceless experience of living in a predictably reliable world. It is this experience which is the essence of Erikson's 'basic trust' – the feeling that life, people, and society can be relied upon, and that they are worthy of trust and positive collaboration. In fulfilling this function, the mother-child bond has deep social and political implications: it is the nucleus round which all human communities have formed.

Gradually, as the child becomes capable of locomotion, he uses the mother as a 'secure base' from which he begins to make exploratory forays into the environment. As he does so he continues to keep her in sight as if constantly reassuring himself as to her continued existence. At times of real or imagined danger he scuttles back to her as to a bolt hole. Such behaviour is to be observed in all young mammals. 'Probably for all', wrote Bowlby, 'the haven of safety which terminates escape responses and brings a sense of security is the proximity of mother.'

The primal strength of the mother-child bond is never more apparent than when a young animal or child is forcibly separated from its mother. The loud protest and dreadful despair which such separations induce are, Bowlby maintained, *primary responses* not reducible to any other cause: they are due directly to the *a priori* nature of the attachment bond. The extent of the infant's suffering and the damage caused is broadly related to the duration of the separation: brief separations are bad enough; long ones can be quite devastating. Almost unbearable evidence of the trauma children suffer when separated from their mother, home, and family, comes from the films made by Bowlby's colleagues, James and Joyce Robertson, of children admitted to hospital for treatment of infectious illnesses 'in isolation' (to prevent cross-infection). The children were between 15 and 30 months of age: all had formed secure attachments to their mothers and had never been separated from them before. From the very first moment of separation, a predictable sequence of behaviour was set in train. Bowlby detected three stages in the sequence which he called *protest*, *despair*, and *detachment*. His description is as graphic as the films:

> The initial phase, that of protest, may begin immediately or may be delayed; it lasts from a few hours to a week or more. During it the young child appears acutely distressed at having lost his mother and seeks to recapture her by the full exercise of his limited resources. He will often cry loudly, shake his cot, throw himself about, and look eagerly towards any sight or sound which might prove to be his missing mother. All his behaviour suggests strong expectation that she will return. Meantime he is apt to reject all alternative figures who offer to do things for him, though some children will cling desperately to a nurse.
>
> During the phase of despair, which succeeds protest, the child's preoccupation with his missing mother is still evident, though his behaviour suggests increasing hopelessness. The active physical movements diminish or come to an end, and he may cry monotonously or intermittently. He is withdrawn and inactive, makes no demands on people in the environment, and appears to be in a state of deep mourning. This is a quiet stage, and sometimes, clearly erroneously, is presumed to indicate a diminution of distress.
>
> Because the child shows more interest in his surroundings, the phase of detachment, which sooner or later succeeds protest and despair, is often

welcomed as a sign of recovery. The child no longer rejects the nurses; he accepts their care and the food and toys they bring, and may even smile and be sociable. To some this change seems satisfactory. When his mother visits, however, it can be seen that all is not well, for there is a striking absence of the behaviour characteristic of the strong attachment normal at this age. So far from greeting his mother he may remain remote and apathetic; instead of tears there is a listless turning away. He seems to have lost all interest in her.

Should his stay in hospital or residential nursery be prolonged and should he, as is usual, have the experience of becoming transiently attached to a series of nurses, each of whom leaves and so repeats for him the experience of the original loss of his mother, he will in time act as if neither mothering nor contact with humans has much significance for him. After a series of upsets at losing several mother-figures to whom in turn he has given some trust and affection, he will gradually commit himself less and less to succeeding figures and in time will stop altogether attaching himself to anyone. He will become increasingly self-centred and, instead of directing his desires and feelings towards people, will become preoccupied with material things such as sweets, toys, and food. A child living in an institution or hospital who has reached this stage will no longer be upset when nurses change or leave. He will cease to show feelings when his parents come and go on visiting day; and it may cause them pain when they realize that, although he has an avid interest in the presents they bring, he has little interest in them as special people. He will appear cheerful and adapted to his unusual situation and apparently unafraid of anyone. But this sociability is superficial: he appears no longer to care for anyone (1969, pp.27-28).

As this classic but deeply distressing description indicates, the depressive reaction of the second stage acts as a means by which a terrible loss becomes acknowledged and accepted and through which the child becomes detached from the most precious asset in his world: his mother. It is possible that Bowlby's description offers a model of all depressive reactions to loss and that to achieve detachment from the lost asset is the primary goal of depression. We shall return to this theme in a later Chapter. Suffice it to say here that each of the three phases of response to separation is related to a central issue of psychoanalytic theory: protest raises all the issues relating to 'separation anxiety'; despair those of grief and mourning, and detachment those of defence. Bowlby argued convincingly that attachment theory is able to give a more coherent account of these phenomena than conventional psychoanalysis.

It is interesting that when Bowlby showed the film *A Two-Year-Old Goes to Hospital* which he made with James Robertson, to the Psycho-Analytic Society in the early '50s, Anna Freud was impressed, but not so the Kleinians. They considered that the little girl's distress, so evident in the film, had nothing to do with separation from her mother but was attributable to her unconscious destructive fantasies against the unborn baby in her mother's womb!

***

With Bowlby true scientific procedures were introduced into psychoanalysis for the first time. In this he was ably assisted by Mary Ainsworth, who went on to achieve distinction with her experimental work in Baltimore, Maryland. Working together and independently they were not only able to make specific correlations between certain mother-child interactions and later patterns of health or pathology but were also able to make accurate predictions as to future outcomes. Never in the annals of psychotherapeutic practice had this been possible before.

Mary Ainsworth's 'strange situation' experiment is a shining example of how experimental and developmental psychology can be brought to bear on psychoanalytic theory to yield reproducible results. The 'strange situation' is an unfamiliar playroom with a one-way mirror through which observations can be made. The subjects of the experiment are a mother and her one-year-old baby, who enter the room with an experimenter. Time is allowed for the child to settle down and begin to examine or play with the toys. Then the mother is asked to go out of the room, leaving the child with the experimenter. After 3 minutes she returns and is reunited with the child. Then both mother and experimenter go out of the room, leaving the child on its own for a further 3 minutes. Finally mother and child are once more reunited. The whole drama is videotaped and the child's behaviour on each separation and reunion carefully scored and rated so as to yield a measure of the strength and security of the child's attachment to its mother.

Analysing the results of several hundred such experiments, Ainsworth detected four characteristic patterns of response, ranging from secure to insecure attachment, and she described how each pattern was related to the mother's behaviour with the child. *Securely attached* infants were usually distressed by the separation and needed to be comforted when their mothers returned, but were then able to settle down to explore the room or play with the toys. Less securely attached children, Ainsworth classified into three groups which she called 'avoidant', 'ambivalent', and 'disorganized'. *Insecure-avoidant* children showed little distress on separation and tended to ignore their mother on reunion, but they were inhibited in their play. *Insecure-ambivalent* children were highly distressed by the separation and could not be readily comforted on reunion. They approached their mother and sought contact with her, but then squirmed away from her, struck her, or pushed away proffered toys. As Holmes comments, it is as if the child is saying to the mother 'Don't you dare do that again!' but clinging on to her at the same time since he knows from experience that she will. These children were also unable to play. Lastly, children in the small group of *insecure-disorganized* subjects were most disturbed of all. They displayed a bizarre range of behaviours, involving chaotic, repetitive, or stereotyped movements, and were prone to 'freeze' on reunion with their mothers.

Before putting them through the strange situation experiment, Ainsworth and her team had visited the mothers and their infants in their homes for regular periods of observation during the whole of each child's first year of life. They found that the experimental results correlated highly with the quality of the mother-child relationship which they observed during the previous 12 months. Thus, mothers of the secure group of children had been rated as essentially responsive to their babies; mothers of the insecure-avoidant group were unresponsive; mothers of the insecure-ambivalent group were inconsistently responsive; and children in the insecure-disorganized group were found to come from extremely disturbed homes, where they had been abused or seriously neglected.

Each of these groups can therefore be understood as representing a strategy which the child has adopted in relation to its mother's behaviour. The avoidant child keeps his distance, keeping a wary eye on the mother whom he needs yet knows will frustrate and disappoint him; the ambivalent child clings helplessly to the mother who will either fulfil or frustrate his needs as the whim takes her; while the disorganized child gives up, unable to make any sense of the overwhelming and disorganized world in which he has to live.

Ainsworth's findings have been amply confirmed by subsequent studies, and they support Bowlby's repeated assertions in the teeth of psychoanalytic opposition that environmental influences are critical for a child's healthy development. But even more important from the scientific standpoint is Ainsworth's achievement of making accurate predictions about the future development of one-year-old children on the strength of the strange situation experiment. Follow-up studies of these children have established that on the basis of this experiment it is possible to predict how they will approach a new person or tackle a new task when they have reached the age of $4\frac{1}{2}$ to 6 years and are attending nursery school.

Children judged securely attached at one year will have a longer attention span, be more skilful at handling conflict with their peers, and be more confident and more resilient than children who were insecurely attached. Here again, the findings support Bowlby's view that during the early years a child builds up an 'internal working model' of itself as being worthy of receiving and giving love, provided it has been securely attached to a mother who is responsive to its needs. The insecure-avoidant child, however, will form an internal working model of itself as being not worthy of love and will have to conceal its anger and despair at its mother's uncaring rejection if it is not to drive her away altogether. The insecure-ambivalent child also has a working model of itself as unlovable, but conceives of its unpredictable mother as one who has to be coerced into granting affection. 'Human infants', Bowlby wrote, 'we can safely conclude, like infants of other species, are programmed to develop in a socially co-operative way; whether they do so or not turns in high degree on how they are treated' (1988, p.9).

Summarizing his position, Bowlby (1979) wrote: 'The key point of my thesis is that there is a strong causal relationship between an individual's experiences with his parents and his later capacity to make affectional bonds and that certain common variations in that capacity, manifesting themselves in marital problems and trouble with children as well as in neurotic symptoms and personality disorders, can be attributed to certain common variations in the ways in which parents perform their roles.' He was able to define a number of the 'common variations' which constitute pathogenic parenting. For example, parents may abandon their children altogether, leaving them to the social services to deal with, or if they remain with them they may prove persistently unresponsive to their care-eliciting behaviour. They may make a practice of threatening to withdraw love, abandon the family, commit suicide, or even to kill the spouse or child; they may subject the child to excessive criticism inducing feelings of being bad and unwanted; and a parent (usually the mother) may display 'anxious attachment' to her child, exerting pressure on it to be the primary care-giver in their relationship, thus inverting the normal pattern. Any one of these forms of parental frustration of a child's basic attachment needs can result in anxious, insecure individuals who report themselves to be lacking in confidence, shy, inadequate, or unable to cope. They often have difficulty in forming and maintaining lasting relationships, and under stress they are prone to develop neurotic symptoms such as phobias, persistent anxiety, and depression.

In addition, the emotional state of the parents, as well as their predominant mode of personality adjustment, has a direct impact on their children. The mother is particularly influential in this regard, for she mediates the world, in all its ambiguity, to the child. In this crucially significant role as mediator, an extremely anxious mother will tend to induce defensive arousal and fear in her children, while a depressed mother will have difficulty in responding to their needs in such a way as to foster their development of 'basic trust'. The world for such children will necessarily remain ambiguous, uncertain, and potentially threatening. Such findings are in accordance with one of Bowlby's most important formulations: that of 'cycles of deprivation', whereby 'the neglected child becomes the neglectful parent' and a self-perpetuating vicious circle is established. Numerous studies have confirmed this view. Adequate parenting tends to produce adequate parents, whereas people who have received pathogenic parenting of the kind described above are more likely to be delinquent, become teenage mothers, physically abuse their children, and have unhappy marriages ending in divorce.

The idea that maternal deprivation was a cause of delinquency and mental illness was, when Bowlby proposed it, a revolutionary concept. That we are no longer surprised by it, and, indeed, accept it as a truism, is a measure of Bowlby's achievement. However, Professor Michael Rutter, one of the sternest and steadiest of Bowlby's critics, has made much intellectual mileage out of the fact that some children from such a background do not become neurotic and go on to make a success of life. Bowlby never denied this. But, as he often pointed out, only 1 per cent of people who contracted polio were permanently crippled by it, yet this was never advanced as a reason not to devote medical resources to the eradication of the disease. However, Rutter is right to suggest that antisocial behaviour is not due solely to maternal deprivation but is more closely linked to the disruption that divorcing families undergo, which may also be associated with temporary or lasting separations from the mother. Whereas children who have lost their mothers through death have a normal delinquency rate, those who lose them through divorce are more likely to become delinquent. Consequently, it seems likely that rather than being the sole causal factor, maternal deprivation acts as a 'general vulnerability' factor which increases a child's susceptibility to later emotional and social disturbance. Rutter is also right to point out that Bowlby's phrase 'maternal deprivation' is a misnomer, since many of the children he studied suffered *privation* (they had been denied maternal care altogether) rather than *de-privation* (the loss of already established maternal care). This distinction is important because it has become clear that complete maternal privation is more reliably and lastingly damaging than maternal deprivation.

The past decade of research into attachment theory has reaffirmed the extent to which relationship patterns established in the first year of life powerfully influence the child's self-concept and subsequent behaviour as well as its capacity for self-reflection. Jeremy Holmes has drawn particular attention to the ability to give a coherent narrative of past relationships ('autobiographical competence') as an index of secure attachment. People who have a history of insecure attachments experience far greater difficulty in narrating their past. Holmes suggests that an important task of psychotherapy is to assist patients to piece together a coherent account of their emotional history. Initially, patients pour out a story that is often disjointed and full of gaps and uncertainties. As the details are worked over collaboratively in the analytic situation a more coherent narrative begins to emerge. 'Out of the narrative comes meaning', Holmes asserts, 'the "broken line" of insecure attachment is replaced by a sense of continuity.' Holmes stresses that the narrative is not just the patient's case history but also becomes the history of the therapeutic relationship itself.

***

When it came to the practice of psychotherapy, Bowlby's approach was derived from a direct application of attachment theory. Like Jung many years before him, Bowlby stressed that the therapeutic relationship should be equal and collaborative instead of based on 'the doctor's authority'. Like Jung, too, he emphasized the patient's endogenous powers of growth and development: 'The human psyche', he wrote, 'like human bones, is strongly inclined towards self-healing. The psychotherapist's job, like that of the orthopaedic surgeon's, is to provide the conditions in which self-healing can best take place.' Because attachment is indispensable to psychic well-being, it is the therapeutic *alliance* that is critical for success rather than an obsessive focus on the transference and its implications. Here again, he is at one with Jung. What Bowlby provides is not a new form of psychotherapy but an endorsement of basic principles which are common to all forms. These stress the importance of relationship with the therapist, leading to the formation of a bond and a secure base from which problems can be explored, the working out of a coherent explanation of how these problems came about, and the provision of a method for overcoming them.

Just as a distressed or frightened toddler will seek out its mother, so a distressed or frightened adult will seek out an attachment figure to provide relief. Once this 'secure base' has been found, then attachment behaviour is 'switched off' and exploratory behaviour begins. This provides a parallel to the patient entering therapy, the exploratory behaviour being directed towards an examination of the cause of the distress and the 'inner working model' which underlies it. A crucial factor determining outcome is whether the patient perceives the therapist as an appropriate attachment figure and whether the analytic situation is experienced as a secure base.

Assuming that the therapist is caring and empathic, this should, in theory, occur, but difficulty may arise in patients who in the past have exhibited avoidant, ambivalent, or disorganized patterns of attachment, and have had difficulty in finding a secure base anywhere. The therapist has to be acutely sensitive to these possibilities and by being responsive and attuned to the patient's feelings, use skill in interpreting his projections and anticipations so as to enable the treatment to proceed. The object is then to examine the history of attachments to all significant figures from the mother up to the present, and to monitor the patient's mode of relating to the therapist. When this has been clearly conceptualized it becomes possible to modify those patterns of relating which are clearly neurotic or self-defeating. Inevitably, the therapist gets cast in the parental role, but the therapeutic endeavour is less gigantic than that advocated by Winnicott or Guntrip. The therapist's task is not to give the love that the patient's mother failed to give, but to provide a secure, reliable, and consistent source of support and understanding in an effort to help the patient revise his internal working model and improve the quality of his relationships. This is a more realizable, if less heroic, objective than seeking to provide the 'emotional reparation' of Winnicottian therapy. The intention of Bowlbian therapy is that through the transformative experience of the analysis, patients will be able to form less anxious attachments in the outer world and feel more securely based in themselves.

Bowlby's interest in 'circular reactions' between generations, the process by which 'insecure parents create insecure children' inevitably led to the application of his insights to families as a whole. It was on his initiative that families began to be seen together at the Tavistock Clinic, and it is to him, as well as to Gregory Bateson in Palo Alto, California, that the credit for originating family therapy must go. This work has been ably developed in Britain by Dorothy Heard, Robin Skynner, and John Byng-Hall. Dorothy Heard, together with her partner Brian Lake, has stressed the importance of 'companionable interaction', a form of warm affiliation, in the therapeutic relationship, a notion which is alien to traditional Freudian or Kleinian teaching; while Robin Skynner has sought to correct the maternal bias in Bowlby's thinking by highlighting the role of the father in family attachment behaviour. At first the father is needed to protect and feed the mother-child pair so as to permit the mother's 'primary maternal preoccupation' to flourish. Later on, by intruding on their intimacy and forming his own attachment bond to the child, the father facilitates its separation from the mother and promotes its growing sense of autonomy.

The father's presence also cushions the intensity of the mother-child interactions and helps to prevent the mother becoming worn out or overwrought by the child's constant demands. As a result of his presence, the mother is less likely to issue threats of rejection or abandonment at times when the child becomes too much for her and is less likely to induce anxious attachment in him as a result. The truth, or otherwise, of this insight will become apparent as more and more women rear children on their own, without the benefit of a husband's support. It is quite possible that father/husband deprivation will become as serious a problem in the future as mother deprivation has been in the past and growing populations of mothers, stretched to their emotional and economic limits, will find it extremely hard to provide their progeny with the continuous, loving intimacy and the secure base that every child requires. The social consequences of this have not begun to be imagined, let alone anticipated or prepared for.

With an achievement as significant and well recognized as Bowlby's, it is not surprising that many critics have striven to point out its limitations. In the first place, Bowlby's commitment to scientific parsimony encouraged him to seek a simple underlying theory to account for the enormous complexity of human behaviour and psychopathology. As a result, he confined his attention specifically to the mother-child bond and attempted to derive all modes of relationship from it. While his formulations possess the great virtue of being precise, and verifiable, it has since become clear that the phenomena he sought to explain are more complex than he realized. His exclusive emphasis on the destructive consequences of maternal deprivation and threats of abandonment did not give sufficient weight to other potentially damaging factors; and he lacked the overall view of the life cycle as one long developmental process (such as that adopted by Jung and by evolutionary psychology). Consequently, his theory is not able to account adequately for those resilient children who seem to survive appallingly traumatic childhoods without displaying signs of major damage. Moreover, Bowlby's work fosters a view of neurosis as a form of passive suffering inflicted by unsatisfactory circumstances. This leaves out the idea of *agency*. It is not just the fact of deprivation, loss or separation, but the way in which the individual *deals* with them that counts.

The criticism of Bowlby most commonly voiced by psychoanalysts is that he betrayed the essential spirit of their discipline, which is concerned with the unconscious fantasy life of the individual, not a quantifiable approach to behaviour. It is true that there is little interest in fantasy, dreams, and the power of the imagination in Bowlby's work. He was so preoccupied with establishing psychoanalysis on sound scientific principles that he had little time for the inner symbolic life. On the whole he was happy to leave that to others. Perhaps there is some truth in the assertion, repeated by the Kleinians, that he was avoiding the inner life and overemphasizing the outer. If so, it was a necessary correction, a much needed counter-swing of the theoretical pendulum. In any coherent psychotherapeutic discipline there has to be room for both the symbolic and the behavioural, the inner and the outer, the hermeneutic as well as the scientific. The greatness of Bowlby's contribution is that he brought such a synthesis closer within our reach than it had ever been before.

7

Jung Revisited

Since I have stressed the importance of personal factors in shaping what psychoanalysts write, it is only fair that I should say something about my own 'personal equation'. Experience has taught me that the most crucial decisions in peoples' lives are often taken in a remarkably haphazard manner. My own decision to become an analyst was no exception. It was made late one evening when I was 16 years old. I was alone and already in bed when I turned on my radio tuned to the BBC Third Programme. A play was just beginning. To the sound of waves crashing against rocks, a narrator announced that we were at Elsinore and that the recently crowned King Claudius is worried by the odd behaviour of his nephew, Hamlet. Accordingly Claudius has sent to Paris for a celebrated doctor, a specialist in distempers of the mind, and invited him to Denmark so that he may study the Prince and discover what ails him. Shakespeare's play begins, and at critical moments the doctor is heard making sotto voce interpretations of Hamlet's state of mind. Like some psychological Sherlock Holmes, he picks up clues which enable him to diagnose the essence of Hamlet's problem: Hamlet is incestuously tied to his mother, Gertrude, and cannot obey the command he has received from his father's ghost to kill his uncle Claudius, because *Claudius has done precisely what Hamlet himself unconsciously wished to do* – namely murder the old king (Hamlet's father) and take possession of Gertrude (his mother). Locked in this unconscious predicament, Hamlet's will is paralysed, which explains his incorrigible procrastination. This play greatly excited me: it seemed to give me a clear image of what to do with my life. As the play ended, I knew with absolute certainty that *I must become that doctor*.

Of course, I later came to realize that the play (which, incidentally, was based on a paper by Ernest Jones) moved me so deeply because it touched on my own family situation – an only child with an adorable mother and a kind but very introverted father, who was frequently away on business, leaving me to fill the emotional vacuum in my mother's life. The sort of understanding possessed by the doctor offered a way out of my own predicament: how to escape entanglement in my parents' marriage and establish a life of my own, with, one hoped, less tragic consequences than befell Hamlet and his entire family. So much became clear when I entered analysis at the age of 23.

I was particularly fortunate in my analyst, Irene Champernowne (1901-1976). Even allowing for an inevitable degree of idealization on my part, she was one of the shrewdest and most impressive women I have ever met. She was widely experienced and well read in the major analytic traditions of her time. Having had a Freudian analysis at the Tavistock Clinic in the late 1920s, she spent half of each year during the early '30s working with Alfred Adler in Vienna and later analysing with Adler's colleague, Leonard Seif, in Munich, before moving on to Zurich to analyse with Jung and Toni Wolff. Though she came from an intensely religious family (her father was a missionary), she had elected to read for a science degree at Birkbeck College and went on to become a lecturer in biology at Gypsy Hill Teachers' Training College in London. She was an inspired teacher and found that students in personal difficulties gravitated to her as an untrained but natural counsellor. The course of her life changed in her mid-twenties when she suffered a religious crisis, became seriously depressed, and got herself into analysis. When she eventually reached Zurich she had a profound sense of spiritual homecoming, for Jung's approach drew together the three primary interests of her life: psychology, religion, and biological science. It struck her that Jung had reconciled the highest achievements of the human spirit with the base materials out of which that spirit had evolved.

Irene said that it was as if Jung had succeeded in building a bridge between Darwin and God! The theory of archetypes provided 'the missing link between psyche and nature'. As she told me on one memorable occasion, archetypes could be conceived as biological entities which had evolved by natural selection: they achieved their highest expression in the production of culture and the organization of human consciousness. This hit me with the force of a revelation. It was a tremendous statement, and it seemed to me that in making it Irene had struck the bedrock of psychology as a biological science. It is an insight that has much influenced my thinking ever since.

When my analysis began I was in my preliminary year as a medical student at Oxford. Before going to Oxford I had spent three years at Reading University where I obtained a BA honours degree in psychology. At that time, psychology departments were still in the grip of behaviourism, and students were required to study the huge literature on learning experiments performed on rats running in mazes. This was as dispiriting for the students as it must have been for the rats. Fortunately, the professor of psychology at Reading, Carolus Oldfield, though a behaviourist, had sufficient vision to look ahead to a time when psychology should be established as a science compatible with Darwinism. To this end he had in his department a physiologist with a particular interest in animal behaviour called, appropriately enough, Dr Voles, and it was from Dr Voles that I first learned about ethology and the work of Niko Tinbergen and Konrad Lorenz. As a result, the experimental work I did as the basis for my degree thesis was not on rats, or for that matter on human beings, but on 'Colour and Brightness Discrimination in the Three-Spined Stickleback'. This, I will be the first to admit, was no great contribution to the sum total of human knowledge, but it taught me the rudiments of scientific method and experimental design, which was to come in handy later on.

At Reading I had the luck to be the only psychology student in my year, and this meant that I was able to enjoy a closer relationship with my lecturers than would otherwise have been the case. My tutor in psychopathology was a colourful character called David Stafford-Clark, author of a best selling Penguin *Psychiatry Today*, who later became a television celebrity. A consultant at Guy's Hospital, he arranged for me to spend a day each week with him, seeing patients and attending case conferences. This experience confirmed in me a conviction that I must become a psychiatrist as well as an analyst and a psychologist.

A curious fact of life at Oxford was that medicine was not considered a subject worthy of an honours degree and one was required to spend an added year doing anatomy or physiology, which, for some reason known only to the university authorities, were acknowledged as honours subjects. It was also possible to do an honours degree in psychology, philosophy and physiology (known as 'PPP'), but that took 2 years. By a happy coincidence, Carolus Oldfield was appointed to the chair of psychology at Oxford soon after I had enrolled there as a medical student, and as I already had one degree in psychology Carolus arranged for me to do the PPP course in one year instead of two. This, as it turned out, was not a waste of time, for it enabled me to extend my knowledge of ethology and physiology, and to learn more about the intricacies of planning research.

My analysis with Irene continued with brief interruptions for nearly 5 years and was the most important event of my life. It ignited creative sparks in me which, touch wood, have so far shown few signs of being dimmed. Her greatest gift was the ability to bring to life unlived potential that I had no idea I possessed. To her, the collective unconscious was not just a scientific theory but an empirical fact, a vital, continuously present 'companion of the way'. Though having good friends of my own age, I had, before my analysis, felt isolated in my personal cocoon, painfully different from everyone else. But Irene's understanding of the archetypal symbolism emerging in my dreams and paintings drew me into a recognition of my identity as a fully paid-up member of the human race.

That, combined with the overflowing warmth of her personality, was profoundly healing, and it stood me in good stead for the rest of my life. There can be no doubt that for me Jungian analysis worked. Whether this was because of Irene's ability as a therapist or because of the effectiveness of analytical psychology itself I was not at the time sure, but that my horizons widened, that my capacity to understand myself and others grew, that my ability to share love deepened, that I felt personally enriched, was as evident to me as it was to my nearest and dearest.

By the time I was medically qualified my analysis was over and I had fallen in love with Greece. This began on the island of Samos, where I was the guest of an Oxford friend who had rented a cottage for three months. The blight of mass tourism still lay in the future and we were virtually the only foreigners on that idyllic island. We were treated with immense kindness by the locals and, my mind being hyperactive after medical finals, I rapidly learned Modern Greek. On my way back to England to start my first intern 'house job' I lingered in Athens, where I was introduced to Spyros Doxiadis, a professor of paediatrics and medical director of a progressive orphanage for unwanted children called the Metera Babies' Centre. Impressed by my background in psychology, he offered me a research fellowship in infant behaviour at the Metera to be taken up when my pre-registration house jobs were completed.

I have described my time at the Metera in *Archetype: A Natural History of the Self* (1982) and so I will repeat here only what is germane to my development as an analyst. What was remarkable about the Metera was that Spyros Doxiadis and his staff had taken Bowlby's findings very much to heart, with the result that their policy was to provide every child, for as long as the Metera was its home, with a substitute mother with whom it might share that warm, intimate, continuous relationship which Bowlby regarded as indispensable to normal human development. When I took up my research appointment there in the spring of 1966, 96 nurses were employed to look after as many infants. The soulless anonymity of traditional institutions was avoided by splitting up the community of nurses and children into small, relatively autonomous groups, each centred on one of 8 separate pavilions. Each pavilion contained 12 children, and, in accordance with the 'family grouping' or 'key worker' system devised by Anna Freud and Dorothy Burlingham, their cots were arranged in 4 compartments, with 3 nurses allocated to each. As a result, both medical and senior nursing staff appeared satisfied that every child was receiving intensive care from a small number of women – much as a normal family-reared Greek child might be looked after by its mother, grandmother and eldest sister.

It seemed an admirable arrangement. But within days of beginning my research it became clear to me that the only occasion on which this system worked satisfactorily was when the matron made her rounds. As soon as she departed the nurses and the youngest children interacted to an extraordinary degree, so that in the course of a few hours each nurse came into contact with practically every child in the pavilion. A form of maternal communism reigned in which caretaking was shared – from each according to her ability, to each according to his need. This was an exciting discovery. For I realized that I had fallen into a situation which was perfectly set up to test the two rival theories of infant attachment formation which were then the subject of unresolved controversy. On the one hand was the theory, supported by Anna Freud as well as the behaviourists, that infant attachment was learned through a form of operant conditioning, associated with natural rewards and punishments, and on the other hand was Bowlby's theory that it was instinctive. As Anna Freud (1946) put it: 'When its powers of perception permit the child to form a conception of the person through whose agency it is fed, its love is transferred to the provider of the food.' This theory, known as the 'cupboard love theory' still had the greater number of adherents, though Bowlby's 'ethological' theory was gaining ground. The Metera offered a perfect milieu in which to test the relative validity of these two theoretical positions.

My reasoning ran like this: if the cupboard love theory were valid it must follow that children receiving care from such a large number of mother figures would become attached to all the nurses who regularly cared for them. Moreover, the nurses to whom a child became attached would necessarily be arranged in a hierarchy of preference, the nurses at the top of the hierarchy being those who fed him the most.

If, on the other hand, Bowlby's theory were valid, the outcome would be very different. In the environment in which our species evolved (the 'environment of evolutionary adaptedness'), the women responsible for an infant's care would be few in number (usually the mother and perhaps a close relative), and the innate mechanism controlling the development of attachment would tend to focus only on one or two figures. The tendency for an innately determined behavioural system to take as its goal a particular individual or a small group of individuals Bowlby believed to be a biological characteristic of our species. He called this *monotropy*. If Bowlby were right, therefore, a Metera child would not become attached to the majority of its caretakers as the cupboard love theory would predict, but would come to demonstrate clear preference for one nurse above all the rest.

It was almost too good to be true. All I had to do was select a group of infants and make regular observations of their social progress. Quickly I chose 24 unattached children aged 3 months and above, and, with two assistants, began recording their interactions with their nurses. Within six months I had collected enough data to establish beyond doubt that far from becoming attached to all their nurses, 75 per cent of the children became specifically attached to one nurse, who was preferred way above all the rest. Even by the strictest statistical criteria, allowing for the small size of the sample, Bowlby's monotropic principle was confirmed. The 25 per cent who did not display attachment had left the Metera for adoption before the age at which specific attachment becomes apparent.

What effectively did for the cupboard love theory was my finding that no less than one-third of the children became attached to nurses who had done little or nothing in the way of routine caretaking of the child before the attachment bond had been formed. The crucial factors leading up to the paring off of a particular nurse with a particular child were not so much linked with routine feeding as with play, physical contact, and social interaction; the whole process was more akin to falling in love through mutual delight and attraction than to 'operant conditioning'.

Having established this much in direct observational terms, I began a detailed study of the typescripts of tape-recorded interviews I had personally conducted with each of the nurses to whom the children in my sample had become attached. As I did so, I began to feel uneasy. Although Bowlby was undoubtedly right, it seemed to me that his theory did not pay adequate attention to certain aspects of the attachment phenomenon which I came to see as possessing great significance.

In the course of these interviews I had asked each nurse what she thought it was that had motivated her and her infant to become attached to one another. Without exception, they all replied that it was 'love'. My attempts to probe what they understood by this elusive concept indicated that they used 'love' to describe the subjective emotion of fondness, solicitude and delight which accompanied caresses, kisses, tender words, eye-to-eye contacts, smiles, songs and tickling games. They spoke freely of their child's personal attractiveness, popularity, charm, and evident need for themselves. Although their statements often betrayed their lack of psychological sophistication, much of what the Metera nurses said had a fresh, original quality which possessed the virtue of being uninfluenced by psychoanalytic dogma and second hand beliefs. Their observations provided me with a timely reminder that attachment is the synonym of love.

***

These thoughts compelled me to acknowledge that there are serious limitations to the application of the ethological approach to human psychology. The Metera nurses had taught me, in their innocence, that if we are not very careful, we could allow ethology to lead us into the same reductive trap as had imprisoned the behaviourists, the Freudians, and the Kleinians. Preoccupation with the detailed investigation of behavioural systems, fascinating though such studies can be, might well yield not a unified science of humanity so much as an arid technology which seeks to boil down the infinitely rich phenomena of life to the last 'innate psychological mechanism'.

In particular, the difference in emphasis between the Metera nurses' reports and the observational data presented me with a problem. How was one to bring all aspects of the attachment phenomenon within the ambit of a single theoretical formulation which honoured the subtle complexities involved? What I needed was a comprehensive theory capable of embracing both the behavioural manifestations of attachment and the inner psychic experiences occurring in consciousness in the form of symbols, images, feelings, and words. The more I thought about it the more clear it became to me that the theory I was attempting to formulate already existed in the form of Jung's theory of archetypes.

Jung's original insights into the archetypal processes underlying the mother-child relationship were developed by his Israeli colleague, Erich Neumann in two books, *The Great Mother: An Analysis of the Archetype* (1955) and *The Child: Structure and Dynamics of the Nascent Personality* (1973). Both these works suffer from the disadvantage that Neumann's biology was even shakier than Jung's and much more subject to Haeckelian and Lamarckian influences. However, when shorn of these unfortunate accretions, the Jungian position is impressive. It must be remembered that when Jungians speak of a mother archetype they are not referring to an innate image but to an inner dynamic at work in the phylogenetic psyche. Symbolic expressions of this dynamic are found in the myths and artistic creations of humanity. As Mother Nature and Earth Mother, the archetypal mother is celebrated as goddess of fertility and dispenser of nourishment; as water or sea, she represents the origins of life as well as a symbol of the unconscious, the fount of all psychic creativity; as Moon Goddess, she exemplifies the essential periodicity of womanhood. She also takes the form of divine animals: the bear (jealous guardian of her children), the celestial cow, who nourishes the earth with milky rain.

Like all archetypes, the Great Mother possesses both positive and negative attributes. On the one hand, she is creative and loving; on the other, she is destructive and hateful. This paradox on the mythological plane corresponds to the observation shared by all schools of analysis that children are deeply ambivalent in their feelings and behaviour towards their mothers. Where the schools differ is in their explanation of how the 'good' and 'bad' images of the mother are formed. As we have seen, the object relations school sees these as 'introjected' internal objects based on the child's actual experiences of the personal mother.

Jungians, however, see them as symbolic actualizations of the Good Great Mother and the Terrible Mother archetypes respectively. In other words, the child is phylogenetically 'forewarned' of the mother's inevitably dual nature: she who caresses also slaps, she who gives also withholds, she who grants life may also take it away. Whereas the Good Mother's symbols are the flowing breast, the abundant cornucopia, the fruitful womb, the Terrible Mother is the bloodstained goddess of death and destruction: she is Kali dancing on the hapless form of Shiva, she is Rangda with slobbering mouth and great lolling tongue who steals and devours children, she is the Gorgon with writhing snakes hissing about her head, so hideous that she turns men to stone when they look at her. The animal forms that she most characteristically adopts are the dragon and the devouring sea serpent, with whom the heroes of countless mythologies have grappled down the aeons of time.

Both 'Good' and 'Terrible' aspects of the mother archetype condition the behaviour of mother and child at a predominantly unconscious level of psychic activity. Activation of either aspect results in what Neumann calls 'a state of biopsychical seizure', a compelling state of possession which drives the behaviour of the subject and is associated with powerful emotional accompaniments. When the Good Mother rules, all is peace and contentment; but should the Terrible Mother be activated pandemonium is the result: inconsolable screaming in the child (often rationalized as 'teething', 'colic' or 'wind'), fury, even battering in the mother (who, in retrospect, may find her own behaviour incredible and deeply shaming when the 'biopsychical seizure' has passed). Clearly, it is important for the stability of the attachment bond and the health of the child that the mother should succeed overall in constellating the Good rather than the Terrible Mother. When one appreciates the symbolic power of the archetypes involved, the truth of this statement becomes very apparent, yet, in his neglect of the archetypal psychic background to the attachment bond, Bowlby excluded a dimension of enormous prognostic significance. What matters from the point of view of healthy psychic development is not always the actual behaviour and personality of the mother as Bowlby supposed, but the *archetypal experiences actualized by her* in the child.

The critical factor for psychopathology, in the Jungian view, is not so much the actual mother but the mother complex which is formed within the individual's psyche. This complex is no inner reproduction or 'video-recording' of the personal mother-out-there, but a product of her interaction with specific phylogenetic components in the child's maturing psyche.

This fact, with all its implications, has to be grasped if success is to be achieved in the psychotherapy of people with dysfunctional parental complexes. For those archetypal components that the personal parents succeed in actualizing in their child may not be as crucial for his individual destiny as those that they *fail* to actualize. As children, we all begin by experiencing our parents as infallible, vividly numinous embodiments of the Mother and Father archetypes; only later, as we attain years of discretion, do we recognize them as fallible human beings with their own personal limitations.

Theoretically, every archetype possesses a totality. Individual parents, however, being human and not gods, are by their very nature imperfect and incomplete: consequently, they can never hope to embody in their own lives all the attributes of a parental archetype. All that any parent can realistically aim to be is 'good enough', to use Winnicott's phrase, to provide the key that opens the archetypal lock and, in doing so, realize that the parental archetype so released will profoundly influence the child's expectations. As we ourselves discover when we grow up, children always expect more of us than we have to give them, and when we disappoint them, they go off to seek what they want elsewhere. It would be cruel and ungrateful were it not that each generation repays what it owes to the last by giving to the next.

Repeatedly it is found in practice that whatever archetypal characteristics parents may have failed to activate nevertheless persist as *potential* in the child's unconscious psyche and they continue to seek actualization in reality. Indeed, it is this need to actualize unlived potential that brings patients to therapy in the first place. The extent of this unactualized potential is inversely proportional to the parents' effectiveness: the more incompetent they are, the greater the archetypal potential seeking fulfilment and the greater the 'parental hunger' manifested by the child (hence, for example, the 'clinging' children one encounters in institutions).

This Jungian conception of innate archetypal potential available to be activated to a greater or lesser extent by appropriate figures in the environment is a major theoretical advance beyond object relations and attachment theories. Not only does it provide a unitary explanation of both outer behaviour and inner experience but it also counts for some of the commonest and most impressive findings in clinical practice. I was later to publish reports of a number of cases to illustrate this point, but the person who sticks most vividly in my memory is a woman who came to me with a father complex that had blighted much of her life. Her personal father had been a tyrant, who insisted always on having his own way and made terrifying scenes whenever he was thwarted. As a result, the father archetype had been activated in her psyche, but only in the most partial and destructive manner: only the law-giving, authoritarian aspects of the father archetype were built into her father complex, while the loving, protective aspects of the archetype remained in the unconscious as unactivated potential. The result was that throughout her life this woman seemed fated to be drawn into the orbit of bullying, self-righteous men, whom she felt she had no alternative but to placate, appease, and obey. At the same time, there persisted in her an unfulfilled longing for the man who would do none of these things to her but, on the contrary, would give her love, support, and protection. Unfortunately, she could never seem to find him, for she could never get into a relationship with such a man: he was too alien, too essentially unfamiliar to her, and she did not possess the emotional vocabulary necessary to share such love.

In the initial stages of her analysis, her father complex inevitably got into the transference: unconsciously she would project the 'imago' of the tyrannical father on to me, as became clear when she misinterpreted my words or gestures as signs that I was becoming furious with her for not being a better patient! At other times, her dreams, fantasies and behaviour revealed how much she longed for me to bring into living reality the positive father potential that remained unactualized in her unconscious. This, I realized was another aspect of the transference that none of the object relations analysts had detected because their thinking lacked the archetypal dimension. There was in the transference not only the father she had, but also the father she never had but longed for.

As the analysis progressed, she was able to become conscious of the destructive influence of her father complex, to find the strength to stand up to the men who bullied and exploited her, and to distance herself from them, integrating some of their authority in her own personality. Gradually, a warm, trusting relationship, freed of negative projections, developed between us, and this resulted in activation of enough positive father potential for a much healthier and more supportive father complex to form in her psyche. As a consequence, the capacity to relate to decent men, who were kindly disposed to her, began to improve.

This analysis, which was one of the first I conducted under Irene's guidance, brought home to me the fact that the more unconscious a complex the more readily it is projected onto figures in the environment who correspond in certain ways to essential characteristics of the complex. So it was that my patient projected her complex on to men possessing qualities reminiscent of her father and then proceeded to become, much against her will, the victim of their sadistic power. The advantage of Jung's insight into the nature of archetypes and their mode of actualization in the form of complexes provided me with both an understanding of her condition and the means to help her grow beyond it. The result was that her individuation, which had hitherto been blocked, was now freed to proceed on its way.

***

My training as an analyst was something of an anachronism. It resembled that of all analysts, both Freudian and Jungian, before official training institutes came into existence. In those days one had a personal analysis with Freud or Jung, or one of their associates, attended their meetings or seminars when they conducted them, read intensively, and then started to see patients. The idea of performing 'control' analyses under supervision was a comparatively late innovation. For example, when Max Eitingen, a Swiss psychiatrist from the Burghölzli, came to Vienna in 1907, Freud analysed him as they strolled through the streets and parks. Neither Freud nor Jung had any formal analysis, except on their journey to and from the United States in 1909, when they analysed each other's dreams – an activity which ended in stalemate, since Freud censured his associations rather than compromise his authority. (When he did that, commented Jung, he lost it anyway!).

Describing how he became a psychoanalyst in the early 1920s, Freud's translator, James Strachey, recalled that he had 'no medical qualifications, no knowledge of the physical sciences, no experience of anything except third-rate journalism. The only thing in my favour,' he said, 'was that at the age of thirty I wrote a letter out of the blue to Freud, asking if he would take me on as a student. For some reason, he replied, almost by return of post, that he would, and I spent a couple of years in Vienna.' When Strachey returned to London he was at once elected an associate member of the British Psycho-Analytical Society. 'So there I was, launched on the treatment of patients, with no experience, with no supervision, with nothing to help me but some two-years of analysis with Freud.' As we have seen, the training received by Anna Freud, Melanie Klein, Ronald Fairbairn, Donald Winnicott (who was himself analysed by James Strachey) and Harry Guntrip was very similar.

Irene's training had been somewhat more systematic. After her initial analyses with Jung and Toni Wolff in Zurich, she returned to London and continued to analyse with Jung's chief lieutenant in England, Godwin Baynes. They got on so well that in 1938, her analysis concluded, Baynes invited her to share in his analytic practice, giving her the use of a consulting room in his house in Mansfield Street. This arrangement continued until they were driven out of London by the blitz in 1941. It was through working as Baynes's colleague that Irene learned her craft, rather in the manner of a medieval apprentice. They popped in and out of each other's rooms for impromptu case conferences between patients and regularly had working lunches at the Bolivar Restaurant round the corner. Irene always believed this was the best way for analysts to learn their job, and it was the way that I, eight years after my analysis with her had ended, and after a further two years with another woman analyst, began to learn what skills I possess as a therapist from Irene.

By then my research project in Athens had finished and I was working as a psychiatric registrar at Horton Hospital, Epsom, while preparing to sit examinations for the Diploma of Psychological Medicine, a necessary *rite de passage* to full psychiatric qualification in the days before the Royal College of Psychiatrists had been founded. At Horton fate was again kind to me. My immediate boss was the eminent forensic psychiatrist, Henry Rollin, who was then deputy physician superintendent of the hospital. Henry and I quickly became, and have remained, firm friends. A brilliant diagnostician and patient teacher, he gave me a secure grounding in general psychiatry and passed on to me the expertise necessary to understand and treat the most disturbed and challenging of patients. His lively personality and rich sense of humour meant that working at Horton was great fun as well as highly instructive. It was the sort of experience I could wish for any budding psychotherapist as a practical means to knowing the terrible extremes to which human nature can be pushed.

From 1968 until her death in 1976, Irene and I shared consulting rooms in London and, as she had done with Godwin Baynes, had regular discussions about the patients we were treating. During this period I was also analysing the mountains of data I had brought back with me from Greece and had embarked on an intensive reading of Jung's *Collected Works*. I obtained my DPM in 1969 and in the following year withdrew from the NHS into private practice. Though I continued to do some general psychiatry, and provided Irene and some other lay analysts with their psychiatric 'cover', I committed myself increasingly to my first love, analysis.

Of all that I learned during that apprenticeship, the most valuable was the realization that beneath the personal intelligence of everyone there is a deeper intelligence at work which is the *evolved* intelligence of humankind. Through Irene I learned that the most effective way of mobilizing this intelligence is working with dreams. Though analysis of the transference is important, it is only part of the process, and can be anti-therapeutic when it is made the primary focus of treatment. What is of crucial importance is the quality of the therapeutic alliance and collaborative work with the unconscious as manifested in dreams. I have gone on doing my best to work in this way up to the present time, and I attempted to condense this experience in my book, *Private Myths: Dreams and Dreaming* (1995).

When Irene went to work with Godwin Baynes, he was writing *Mythology of the Soul*, and they spent many hours discussing the paintings and dreams of a physician on whose analysis the first half of the book is based. The physician concerned was to have a powerful impact on the development of Jungian psychology in England and, eventually, in the United States. His name was Michael Fordham (1905-1995). A decisive event in Michael Fordham's history, in Baynes's view, was the death of his mother when he was 12. This trauma, combined with the personality of his detached, intellectually erratic father (who devoted himself to Fabian enthusiasms and the arts and crafts movement rather than to the emotional needs of his bereft son) resulted in a one-sided, inhibited development, which Baynes did not hesitate to diagnose as schizoid. Fordham later confirmed this opinion in the autobiography he wrote towards the end of his life: 'School life began well, but after my mother's death and the disintegration of family life, it changed. I did not realize why at the time but I knew later that I had split and that my emotional life had gone underground ...' (Fordham, 1993, p.46). Baynes described him as proceeding through life like an automaton among automata: 'He saw that experiences which moved other men meant nothing to him. Instead of being fluid and adaptable, his feeling was withdrawn and unready. From the time of his mother's death there seems to have been a certain withdrawal or inversion of personal feeling. Charm of manner made him acceptable, but psychologically, he lived in chilly isolation.'

Coming from an ancient clan of East Anglian farmers, Fordham was educated at Gresham's School, Holt (where he was a contemporary of W.H. Auden and the embarrassed recipient of a love poem from him), and Trinity College, Cambridge. He studied medicine at St Bartholomew's Hospital, and would have become a neurologist were it not for his early marriage to Molly Swaby when he was 23. Shortage of money forced him to accept an appointment as a junior medical officer at Long Grove Hospital, a mental hospital close to Horton, where I was to be employed more than thirty years later. There he began reading Jung.

At first sceptical about Jung's theory of the collective unconscious, Fordham nevertheless decided to put it to the test. One of his Long Grove patients believed himself to be 'the devil's disciple'. The evil which had him in its power was rotting away his internal organs, and his eventual death, he declared, would take away the sins of humanity. If Jung was right, Fordham reasoned, then this unfortunate patient was in the grip of some scapegoat myth and he should be able to find comparable details in Frazer's *The Golden Bough*. Sure enough, the themes apparent in the patient's delusions were all there.

Fordham's experience of mental hospital work does not seem to have been as happy or rewarding as mine. He was not an easy man to get on with, and, having fallen out with his colleagues and his physician superintendent Dr F.G.L. Barnes, he left Long Grove to work at the London Child Guidance Clinic. Although, as he himself acknowledged,

Fordham had 'no special liking for children', he found the clinical work interesting. At first he understood the behaviour disorders and neuroses of his patients to be a function of unconscious conflicts in their parents. Such an approach accorded with Jung's view that child analysis could achieve little and could do actual harm if the parents' problems were left untreated. As he gained experience, however, Fordham felt a need to intervene more actively in his work with children whose psyche he came to see less as a passive reflection of parental influences and more as a dynamic entity with its own priorities and agendas. Adapting some features of his own analysis with Baynes, he encouraged children to recount their dreams, draw and paint their inner images, and take pleasure in fairy tales. As a result of this imaginative approach, he began to build up a reputation for the treatment of severely disturbed children.

Feeling a need for more extensive psychological understanding, Fordham went (on Baynes's suggestion) to Zurich to seek an analytic training with Jung. He wrote to Jung explaining that his financial resources were low and that he would have to support himself by finding work in Switzerland. He drew all his funds out of the bank to pay for the journey and his hotel. When he presented himself in Zurich, however, he was told by Jung that the Swiss authorities, fearing a massive influx of refugees, had made it virtually impossible for foreigners to work there. 'As I went back to England I became very angry', wrote Fordham in his memoir *The Making of an Analyst* (1993). 'How could he drag me out to Zurich when he knew that my proposition was impossible; he must be seriously out of touch with human requirements or feelings!' Fordham was to remain ambivalent about Jung for the rest of his life. According to Vera von der Heydt, Irene, and several other members of the generation who knew Jung well, it was an ambivalence which Jung reciprocated, though he was later to propose Fordham as one of the three editors of the English translation of his *Collected Works*.

On his return to England after this fruitless journey, Fordham resumed his analysis with Baynes and his work in child guidance. It was then that he turned to the work of Melanie Klein. He read *The Psychoanalysis of Children*, he tells us, 'with amazement and emotional shock.' He was particularly impressed by Klein's use of play as a means of communication, by her belief in the basic role of fantasy in a child's development, and by her insistence that children invariably develop a transference to their therapist. He became particularly interested in the transference phenomenon and this made him critical of Baynes's handling of his own analysis. Moreover, he had started an extra-marital affair, which Baynes encouraged him to continue as a means to making a conscious relationship with his anima. Fordham blamed him for this: 'his support contributed to the undermining of my marriage.' He also began to feel trapped in the analysis. Because he could not afford to pay fees, Baynes had agreed to accept Fordham's analytical material as payment, for inclusion in *Mythology of the Soul*. 'One disadvantage of this', commented Fordham, 'was that I felt obliged to keep on producing pictures to keep up payments!' As his relationship with his wife deteriorated, he convinced himself that it was due to the absence of transference analysis in his work with Baynes.

Uncertain what to do, he asked to see Jung when he was next on a lecturing visit to London. It was characteristic of Jung's easy informality that he received him in his bedroom where he was dressing for dinner. When Fordham told him that he was finding it difficult with Baynes, Fordham thought he heard Jung mutter, 'Yes, I bet it is!' Then he said clearly: 'I saw at once that [Baynes] was identified with your material and if you want to do so you had better get out.'

Fordham followed Jung's advice, acknowledging, nevertheless, that his work with Baynes had been far from unproductive. It had released his imaginative powers, convinced him of the reality of unconscious processes, and inspired him to go his own way in seeking his own professional destiny.

For a while he analysed with another Jungian, Hilde Kirsch, to whom he felt powerfully attracted, but he thought she also ducked the erotic nature of his transference and failed in her duty to him by declining to analyse it. Since, in his view, neither Baynes nor Kirsch knew how to analyse his childhood or understood how to work with transference, he felt impelled to make these two aspects of analysis his particular concern.

During the war, having divorced Molly and married Frieda Hoyle (with whom he declared he found the sort of love he had had for his mother), Fordham was appointed to a consultant post created to help evacuee children in Nottinghamshire who had not been able to settle in billets. He seized this as a further opportunity to extend Jungian theory into childhood. Since his charges had been removed from their homes, their parents were not available for treatment and Fordham had, *faute de mieux*, to work on their internal representatives in the children's psyches through the medium of the transference. On the basis of this experience, he published his first book, *The Life of Childhood*, in 1944. He reaffirmed that the Self, in the Jungian sense, was an active factor in child development and rejected the idea that disturbed children could only be treated indirectly. Children showed a remarkable capacity to overcome their difficulties if given sympathetic understanding and support.

Godwin Baynes died of a cerebral tumour in 1943 and Fordham was to assume his mantle as the leading British Jungian for the next fifty years, founding with others the Society of Analytical Psychology (SAP) in 1946, the *Journal of Analytical Psychology* in 1955, and, together with Gerhard Adler, Herbert Read, and William McGuire, producing the English edition of the *Collected Works of C.G. Jung*. In addition, he wrote numerous articles and published eight books. Though his contributions gave rise to much controversy and dissent, Fordham has to be acknowledged as one of the last analysts in the twentieth century who, by the force of his own personality, was able to influence the course of analytic theory and practice. He saw himself as an innovator who corrected deficiencies in Jung's theoretical legacy by laying stress on the importance of transference and counter-transference interactions between analyst and patient and on the influence of infantile wishes and defences on the later development of the personality. Pursuing this line, he advocated a rapprochement between Jungian theories and those of the neo-Freudian, Kleinian, and object relations schools of analysis. For these innovations he was applauded by some but condemned by others, who accused him of leading a regression to Freud's couch-oriented, reductive analytic techniques and of betraying the creative-symbolic approach to personal development at the heart of classical Jungian practice.

To many who wished to train as analytical psychologists in England, Fordham's amalgam of Jungian and Kleinian theories, augmented by his own observations and formulations concerning psychological development in infancy and childhood, were to prove attractive. By enshrining these principles in the training programme offered by the SAP Fordham exerted an influence over the practice of Jungian psychology not only in Britain but also in the United States.

However, these developments did not meet with unqualified acclaim. In the 1950s, a growing number of critics complained that Fordham's theoretical revisions had contributed to a crisis of identity among members of the SAP, who began to question whether they could describe themselves as Jungian analysts at all. Gerhard Adler, one of Fordham's co-editors of the *Collected Works*, who was analysed by Jung in the 1930s, felt so strongly that Fordham had deviated from the original spirit of Jung's work that, together with other analysts trained in Zurich, he set up an 'alternative training' within the SAP. The conflict which ensued between these two theoretical orientations proved too intense for them to be contained within the same organization, and the 'orthodox' Zurich-oriented analysts eventually seceded to form their own Association of Jungian Analysts (AJA). This was itself to give birth to another 'classical' group, with even closer ties to Zurich, the Independent Group of Analytical Psychologists (IGAP). The British Association of Psychotherapists (BAP) has also arisen, which offers both a Freudian and a Jungian (though SAP biased) training.

There are those who maintain that the existence of no less than four

Jungian training groups in London is due to Fordham's revision of Jungian psychology and his attempt to put a neo-Kleinian stamp on it. However, it is in the nature of analytic groups, of whatever school, to split on doctrinal grounds, and there is justice in Fordham's argument that analytical techniques, if they are to gain wide acquiescence, should be based on empirical observation. Accordingly, on Fordham's insistence, the training programme of the SAP encourages candidates training as adult analysts (and requires all those training as child analysts) to devote time to the systematic observation of infants and young children. The SAP has continued to flourish and is now one of the largest and most influential Jungian societies in the world.

Fordham regarded the original split between Freud and Jung in 1913 as 'a disaster from which analytical psychology and psychoanalysis both suffer and will continue to suffer until the damage is repaired.' He devoted his life to attempting to effect this repair but in the process succeeded in generating further splits which resembled in their intensity and animosity that between the Freudians and the Kleinians.

The problem about reconciling differences between groups embracing differing ideologies is that people become so deeply wedded to their belief systems as to feel wholly identified with them. As a result, any attempt to persuade them to relinquish or modify their beliefs is experienced as an assault on their personal security. Their response is to band together with like-minded colleagues and look to their defences. Moreover, as studies of religious cults reveal, the more irrational the belief system and the more it lacks empirical foundation, the more loyal its adherents, and the more hostile they become to those who hold contrary opinions. In analytic societies this loyalty to group beliefs is intensified by the training analysis, whose purpose is to ensure that candidates do not merely learn their theories and techniques but integrate them as indispensable components of their own personality.

One may respect Fordham's efforts to extend analytic understanding of the role played by the Self in early childhood development but, with hindsight, we can see that in carrying Jungian psychology in a Kleinian direction he had taken a wrong turning. It would have been scientifically more productive and theoretically more compatible with the corpus of Jungian theory if instead he had turned towards Bowlby and attachment theory. Fordham sometimes wrote as if he were the only analyst to hold that the child was no *tabula rasa* but an intact individual full of innate human potential, who influenced and moulded the environment as much as the environment influenced and moulded her or him. But, as we saw in the last Chapter, this position was proposed and developed to much more systematic and influential effect by Bowlby and Mary Ainsworth, whose carefully framed hypotheses concerning child development have given rise to much valuable research and many therapeutic initiatives throughout the world. Yet, in his books, Fordham omitted all mention of Bowlby and the important consequences of his work.

Not surprisingly, attempts to bring the four individual Jungian groups in London under a general 'Umbrella Group' have so far failed to heal the split between the Fordhamite and classical wings. What, then, is the split about, and what are the main characteristics of the two approaches? In his book *Jung and the Post-Jungians*, (1985), Andrew Samuels summarized these differences under four headings: use of the couch, frequency of sessions, the use of reductive interpretations as opposed to amplification, and the more passive versus the more active participation of the analyst in the analytic relationship.

Whereas Jung abandoned the couch to facilitate mutuality between analyst and patient, Fordham reverted to its use. Classical Jungians find this reversion unacceptable because they say the couch gets in the way of the therapeutic alliance, emphasizes the patient's passivity, and encourages a retreat from the real world into a regressive infantile state of dependency. Fordham's supporters counter that the couch stresses the fact that the analysand is a patient, that analysis is a formal procedure, and that it facilitates the recovery of infantile fantasies which provide vital analytic material.

With regard to the frequency of sessions, Fordham's followers insist that at least four sessions a week are necessary if the procedure is to be called 'analysis'. Any fewer sessions must be regarded as mere 'psychotherapy'. However, this is a circular definition of analysis which completely leaves out of account what goes on in an 'analytic' session. Jung's position on this was quite clear: 'In my experience', he wrote, 'the absolute period of cure is not shortened by too many sittings. It lasts a fair time in all cases requiring thorough treatment' (*CW* 17, para.43). Contemporary outcome studies provide no evidence to contradict him. Classical Jungians contend that analysis essentially consists of working with unconscious material, whether in dreams, fantasies, symbols, or transference phenomena, irrespective of the number of sessions per week. Most 'classical' practitioners see their patients once or twice a week.

The third major difference between the two camps is one of emphasis, the Fordhamites indulging more in reductive interpretations of their patient's material, whereas the classical Jungians make greater use of amplification (*i.e.*, educing mythic, historical, and cultural parallels to 'amplify' the material, enabling patients to reach beyond their purely personal associations so as to relate them to a wider human context). In part, this distinction reflects Freud's pessimism as opposed to Jung's therapeutic optimism: the reductive view sees the glass half empty whereas the synthetic view sees the glass half full. Jung again:

'The analytical reductive view asserts that interest ("libido") streams back regressively to infantile reminiscences and there "fixates" – if indeed it has ever freed itself from them. The synthetic or anagogic view, on the contrary, asserts that certain parts of the personality which are capable of development are in an infantile state, as though still in the womb. Both interpretations can be shown to be correct. We might almost say that they amount virtually to the same thing. But it makes an enormous difference in practice whether we interpret something regressively or progressively' (*CW* 17, para.9). A further important distinction arises here: whereas Fordham stated that 'interpretation is the cornerstone of analytic technique', classical Jungians find the very notion of 'technique' or 'interpretation' objectionable for a number of reasons: it puts the analyst in a position of power, encouraging him to impose his dogmatic preconceptions on the patient, it inhibits the autonomous flow of psychic images and the honouring of new symbols as they emerge, and it negates Jung's conception of analysis as an art.

Finally, the fourth difference concerns the analyst's conduct: whereas Fordham advocated the Freudian model of reticence, waiting for the patient to produce material to which the analyst may or may not respond, the classical analyst is more willing to contribute to the dialogue and draw on his own knowledge of symbolism to amplify the patient's material. Since, for the classical Jungian, a session is a social occasion as well as a therapeutic encounter, more emphasis is placed on the therapeutic alliance than on the use of transference and counter-transference. Not only does there exist good empirical evidence in support of this emphasis but some psychoanalysts are coming round to a similar position. For example, Heinz Kohut, with his stress on the importance of empathy, has abandoned the neutral 'reticent and reserved' model: 'To remain silent when one is asked a question', he says, 'is not neutral but rude.'

In view of the radical differences that exist between these two positions it would be extraordinary if the Umbrella Group had succeeded in transcending them. Its work has not been made any easier by the formal creation of two much bigger official bodies, whose function is to regulate the psychotherapeutic profession in such a way as to prepare its members for legal registration. These are the United Kingdom Council for Psychotherapy (UKCP), consisting of over 3,000 members, and the smaller and more recently formed British Confederation of Psychotherapists (BCP), which split off from the UKCP in 1992. Whereas the UKCP incorporates members from a host of different psychotherapeutic bodies, the BCP is an exclusive club restricted to eight member organizations drawn from psychoanalysis, psychoanalytic psychotherapy, and analytical psychology. Psychoanalysts make up the majority of BCP members, and it was these neo-Freudians and

Kleinians who led the move to establish their own Athenaeum out of a distaste for having to rub shoulders with the great unwashed of the UKCP. This has caused further friction between the four Jungian groups, for whereas the two Fordhamite groups have been permitted to join the BCP the two 'classical' groups have not (mainly because they are regarded as 'unsound' on the issues of frequency of sessions and analysis of the transference, Casement, 1995).

The main preoccupation of the BCP is with 'standards'. This is understandable. When a group embraces a system of belief and practice which is not empirically based or verifiable, it necessarily becomes rigid over the matter of rules and regulations. Thus, the BCP has become obsessional about the number of analytic sessions per week conducted by analysts, trainees, and trainees working with clinical patients, insisting on an absolute minimum of three-times-a-week. So far, no controlled study has established that 'three-times-a-week' is necessary for positive outcome in treatment. And there is good reason to suppose that, with the decline in psychoanalytic repute, practitioners who insist on 'three-times-a-week' will price themselves out of a dwindling market.

Thus, the whole question of frequency of sessions may well become less a matter of ideology than of economics. Increasingly, analysts on both sides of the Atlantic are experiencing difficulty in finding enough patients willing to pay for more than one or two sessions a week for a treatment that is by no means certain of producing the profound and lasting therapeutic results they would wish for. I suspect that psychoanalysts and Fordhamite analysts will, sooner or later, have to compromise and become increasingly flexible on this issue.

***

The battles which raged throughout the 1970s between the different Jungian groups left me unaffected because I did not belong to any of them. As a qualified psychiatrist and medical practitioner, I was free to treat my patients as I wished, using whatever procedures I considered best suited to their needs. Every week I spent three days in London and four days at my home in Devon. Though I continued to do some general psychiatry, my practice was predominantly analytic. In cheerful accordance with Jung's advice (having carefully prepared my patients beforehand), I took long breaks every year, usually in Samos or Crete, where it was possible to rent a seaside cottage for about £3 a week. There for three glorious months I would enjoy a sense of total freedom – to read, ponder, and write, swim and walk in the mountains, enjoy the delights of Greek food and retsina, and, best of all, the company of Greek friends.

Intellectually, the '70s were a challenging and creative time for me. Irene died of cancer in 1975, leaving me her library which contained all the volumes so far published of Jung's *Collected Works*. I grieved for her and was professionally very much on my own. But, largely thanks to her, I had a flourishing practice and was finding my feet as an analyst in a way that Jung would probably have approved. For he resisted the foundation of an Institute of Analytical Psychology until almost the end of his life, and only agreed to it then because, as he said, 'They'll only set up one up between my death and my funeral', and he felt it might be as well if he had a hand in the form that it took. The last thing he wanted was to shackle his followers with the bureaucracy and the kind of doctrinal orthodoxy imposed by Freud on the Freudians.

As Freud's reputation has declined, the authoritarian grip exerted by psychoanalytic institutes has, if anything, tightened, as is well described by Stephen Frosh, Reader in Psychoanalytical Psychology at Birkbeck College and a consultant at the Tavistock Clinic. In his book *For and Against Psychoanalysis*, (1998), Frosh describes how training to become a psychoanalyst in the British Psycho-Analytical Society consists of passing time under the critical scrutiny of authority figures and several years of five-times-a-week personal analysis, plus the management of two five-times-a-week cases under weekly supervision. 'Given the enormous investment of time and money in the training – particularly the personal analysis', Frosh writes, 'plus the exposure of one's own secret longings, impulses and failures to the scrutiny of someone who, until the very last minute, is in a position to refuse a trainee entry into the professional society, it would not be surprising if what was produced were dogmatic, conformist and scared neophytes unable to challenge any of the received wisdom to which they have been exposed.' This is the kind of tyranny that is prone to occur when a society coheres round a corpus of doctrine and belief not susceptible to empirical verification: it employs the well-tested processes of indoctrination characteristic of a totalitarian state rather than the non-coercive give-and-take one would hope to find in an association of enlightened professionals.

I am thankful that my own peculiar development as an analyst enabled me to escape such intellectual subjugation, though I am naturally aware that analysts who have put themselves through such initiatory torments will regard me as hopelessly untrained – not least because my 'training cases' were supervised by the person who had been my analyst, a practice which is nowadays considered distinctly bad form. However, not having to stick to an official curriculum, I was free to read widely in ethology, mythology, anthropology, Freudian psychology and object relations theory, as well as Jung's *Collected Works*, which, like Shakespeare's plays or Beethoven's quartets, yield greater rewards every time one returns to them.

Intrigued by the striking parallels between Jung and the ethologists,

I began writing my first book, *Archetypes: A Natural History of the Self*, which was eventually published in 1982. This was an attempt to bring together all the strands of my experience up to that point so as to integrate the analyst in me with the psychiatrist and the experimental psychologist. Standing outside the professional organizations, with their political agendas and mutual hostilities, and unhampered by any doctrinal allegiances, I felt free to explore the evolutionary implications of archetypal theory in such fundamental areas as the formation of attachment bonds between adults and between parents and children, the development of the personality through the course of the life cycle, the role of religious practices and initiation rites in incorporating individuals within their community, the role of the shadow personality in causing hostility between individuals, groups, and nations, the pathological consequences of thwarting archetypal needs or intentions, and so on. As I wrote it, there developed in me the desire to share in the creation of a humane science of human nature which would embrace psychology, anthropology, psychoanalysis, psychiatry and medicine within the ambit of evolutionary theory. Such an achievement could ultimately transcend the doctrinal differences between warring analytic factions by opening up their formulations and practices to empirical investigation and putting them on a sound epistemological base.

Though the book sold well in Britain and the United States, and many Jungians expressed polite appreciation, few appeared to share my enthusiasm for the biological aspects of Jung's thinking, ostensibly because such concerns seemed irrelevant to what they did in their consulting rooms. Jungian psychology had done pretty well without an interest in evolution up to now, so what was the point? What was more hurtful was that some also accused me of being 'reductive', of trying to turn Jung into some kind of Darwinian fundamentalist. These criticisms have resurfaced in reviews of *Evolutionary Psychiatry: A New Beginning* (1996) which I wrote with the evolutionary psychiatrist, John Price. I will respond to these suggestions in the Chapter 9, but at this juncture I would make the point that what I am truly concerned about is the survival of what I perceive to be of greatest value in Jung's achievement, and for this reason my primary concern has been with epistemology – the foundations of psychological knowledge. Why do we believe what we believe about human psychology, and how do we know that it is true? This has become the crucial issue as the first century of psychoanalysis draws to a close.

The two widely acclaimed books by Richard Noll have sought to establish that Jungian psychology is a mere religious cult geared to an exploitative capitalist enterprise and that Jungian theory is without any basis or value. Noll alleges that the evidence Jung advanced in support of the theory of archetypes is entirely fraudulent and wholly incompatible with biological science. Judging from the enthusiasm with which these books have been received in the press – the first won the 'Best Book of the Year' award of the American Association of Publishers – this is what a large number of people want to hear.

So why do Jungians hold to the principles, theories, beliefs and practices that they do? The public, no less than the academics, are going to require evidence. The justification, 'Dr Jung said it was so', will no longer be sufficient. This is why epistemology is the essential issue for analytical psychology at this time in its history, and why it is important, when evolutionary theory is beginning to play a central role in psychological and psychiatric thinking, to examine the biological implications of archetypal theory. Jung corrected, deepened and extended Freud's intention to make psychoanalysis a science compatible with biology. Instead of conceiving the psyche as the product of postulated drives and conflicts, Jung saw it as a richly adaptive consequence of the evolution of the human species. He may have had some curious notions about how precisely that evolution occurred, but his commitment to the ideas of evolution, metamorphosis, growth and development was apparent in nearly everything he wrote.

What is most profoundly important is Jung's concept of the Self as the central organizing principle of the personality, maintaining a state of homeostatic balance between conscious and unconscious forces, guiding the individual through the stages of life from the cradle to the grave. It is infinitely richer in its implications than the self postulated by neo-Freudians like Donald Winnicott and Heinz Kohut who view the self as something created in the course of personal development and not as an archetypal 'given' rooted in the evolutionary history of the species, which itself guides and influences the course of ontogeny.

Much psychoanalytic theory-building is imaginatively architectural. But the structures so erected are generally castles in the air, spectral concretizations of their creators' personal fantasies. Too often the theoretical bricks used in their construction are reified and treated as if they were real. The purpose of the training analysis then becomes to sustain the illusion through succeeding generations of practitioners. Many intelligent lay persons, outside the analytic fraternities, have always suspected this. Public scepticism about the value of analysis, combined with reluctance on the part of governments, hospital trusts, and medical insurance companies to pay for such an expensive, open-ended, and uncertain treatment, is going to mean that analytical theories and procedures will increasingly come under critical scrutiny. This may well result in the different analytic traditions having to agree on the basic principles that they all share and rendering their activities more accountable to systematic evaluation. However, each therapeutic approach develops its own value system or 'culture', which is attractive to some people and repellent to others. It would be a misfortune if these cultural differences were lost under the grey imposition of bureaucratic uniformity. Psychotherapy is such an intimate procedure, and the personality, attitudes, and values of the therapist so decisive as to outcome, that there will always be a place for different philosophical traditions, however much scientific agreement may emerge about the basic characteristics of human nature. Often, in the actual therapeutic encounter, wisdom becomes more important than science. While the theories on which analysis is based should be scientifically grounded, the practice of analysis is, and will always remain, an art.

At the present state of knowledge, therefore, the kind of therapy one chooses to submit to as a prospective patient, or the analytic association one seeks to join as a trainee analyst, must be a matter of taste rather than scientific reasoning. Given the nature of my own 'personal equation', it is understandable that, by and large, my sympathies should lie with the classical Jungians; and when, in the mid-'80s, the Independent Group of Analytical Psychologists kindly invited me to join them, I was pleased to accept, not least because of my awareness that, given my idiosyncratic background, they were probably the only group that would have me: unlike Groucho Marx, I was *glad* to join a club that would have me as a member! This in no way reflects adversely on the other members of IGAP, who include some of the most distinguished analysts in Britain; but that they are willing to tolerate me is in accordance with their thoroughly independent philosophy.

Personally, I believe that Jung's contribution to the world of analysis has been of incalculable importance because of his open-mindedness, his broad humanity, and his profound insight into the human condition. His temperamental antipathy to reductionism, institutionalism, and the imposition of rigid orthodoxy is deeply attractive, and in stressing the evolutionary implications of his thought I have no desire to reverse what George Hogenson has called Jung's 'radical empiricism' in order to implicate him in some form of Darwinian fundamentalism. As Jung himself put it: 'We keep forgetting that we are primates and that we have to make allowances for these primitive layers in our psyche … Individuation is not only an upward but also a downward process. Without any body, there is no mind and therefore no individuation' (McGuire, 1977). For Jung, the psyche was primary, more important than anything else, since it was only through the psyche that we could know anything or feel anything at all. However much we may come to know about how the brain works and how genes influence our behaviour, it is in our psyches, that we shall continue to live.

It was in teaching the art of mobilizing psychic potential that Jung was an unsurpassed master. Most important is his emphasis on the supremely personal nature of analysis and the need for the analyst to go on growing: 'The analyst must go on learning endlessly,' he wrote, 'and never forget that each new case brings problems to light and thus gives rise to unconscious assumptions that have never before been constellated. We could say, without too much exaggeration, that a good half of every treatment that probes at all deeply consists in the doctor's examining himself, for only what he can put right in himself can he hope to put right in the patient. It is no loss, either, if he feels that the patient it hitting him, or even scoring off him: it is his own hurt that gives the measure of his power to heal. This, and nothing else, is the meaning of the Greek myth of the wounded physician' (*CW* 16, para.239). As a new science of evolutionary psychotherapy begins to emerge, it will need to be practised in this quintessentially Jungian spirit if it is to be truly humane.

8

Research

It has to be acknowledged that not an awful lot is understood about how or why therapy works, when it works, and whom it works for. Whatever therapists may say about what they do or why they do it, the fact of the matter is that the origins of their therapeutic beliefs and practices are derived, ultimately, from magic. As in the remote past, patients come to therapists in search of a miraculous cure. This is why the most successful schools have grown up round a charismatic founder of impressive personal authority. From Father Gassner's exorcism in public of hysterical nuns in 1775, Anton Mesmer's therapeutic successes in Vienna and Paris in the 1780s, Justinus Kerner's treatment of the Seeress of Prevorst (and the immensely successful book he wrote about it – the first detailed study of one psychiatric patient and the first systematic record of the extraordinary myth-making capacities of the unconscious), to Charcot's dramatic induction and removal of hysterical paralyses at the Salpêtrière using hypnosis, and Breuer and Freud's (spurious) cure of Anna O. through the talking treatment. All this grew out of the ancient theory and practice of exorcism. The notion of unconscious motivation, the use of free association, the interpretation of dreams, and the analysis of the transference, are modern attempts to apply these principles in a rational manner, but we are still largely ignorant of the underlying processes involved.

That the different schools of therapy, founded on the assumptions of their charismatic leaders, have developed into exclusive 'sects' is because these assumptions have largely escaped objective verification. In the absence of sound empirical foundations, each school has attempted to make good the deficiency by establishing strictly 'professional' credentials, with strict rules and regulations of varying degrees of practical relevance about how therapy should be done. These regulations have, as we have noted, sometimes attained obsessive-compulsive rigidity: the number of times a week patients must be seen, whether or not they should be greeted, touched, or helped on with their coats, whether they should continue to pay for their sessions when they or their analysts are on holiday, and so on. The furious arguments that have characterized the proceedings of the United Kingdom Council for

Psychotherapy have largely centred round such arcane details, and the impasse that results is attributable to the lack of reliable evidence concerning the relative success or failure of these different therapeutic approaches. If a way is to be found out of this confusion, then well conducted research could provide the key.

For the first half of the century no systematic attempt was made to assess the outcome of psychoanalytic treatment. But then in 1952, Hans Eysenck, Professor of Psychology at London University, caused a sensation by producing statistics that seemed to demonstrate that psychoanalysis did no good whatsoever. His initial onslaught was followed by a further attack in 1965. Quoting more statistics, Eysenck tried to show that neurotic patients who received psychoanalysis were no better off after two years of treatment than comparable patients who received no treatment at all. However, in the bitter controversies that ensued, doubt was thrown on Eysenck's interpretation of the data available to him. More rigorous research followed, the results broadly supporting the claim of psychodynamic therapists that their efforts were effective. In 1970, Meltzoff and Kornreich published a careful and much quoted survey of one hundred research projects and concluded that the benefits of psychotherapy were established beyond all reasonable doubt.

But Eysenck remained unconvinced. The only valid form of treatment in his view was behaviour therapy, because it was based on the scientifically verifiable principles of Pavlovian conditioning. This assertion caused a further row, this time between the psychoanalysts and the behaviourists, which engendered some interesting research designed to compare the results of these two methods of treatment. One such investigation was that of R. Sloane and his colleagues, published in 1975. They studied three groups consisting of 30 neurotics in each group: one group received psychodynamic therapy, another received behaviour therapy, and the third group was kept on the waiting list. The members of all three groups were thoroughly assessed at the beginning of the programme, again after 4 months and again 1 year later. A number of individuals improved or recovered in all three groups, although the people who received treatment in the two treated groups did significantly better than those in the control group, who languished in limbo on the waiting list and received no treatment at all. An interesting finding, not well received by the analysts, was the absence of any significant difference between the improvements displayed by the group that had had behaviour therapy and the group treated by psychodynamic therapy. Later research yielded similar findings. Predictably, the psychoanalysts explained the success of the behaviourists in terms of the transference, while the behaviourists explained the psychoanalytic successes in terms of their own learning theories.

But having established that some form of psychotherapy was better than no therapy at all, researchers turned their attention to what precisely it was that contributed to psychotherapeutic success. Fairly general agreement emerged that, contrary to the assertions of Freudians and Kleinians, lengthy analysis of the transference and detailed unravelling of Oedipal and castration anxieties were not indispensable to favourable outcome. The latest research findings are in tune with these conclusions. The present decade has seen publication of a number of authoritative, not to say 'magisterial', reviews such as *Psychodynamic Treatment Research* edited by N.E. Miller and colleagues (1993), *Handbook of Psychotherapy and Behavioural Change*, edited by Allen E. Bergin and Sol L. Garfield (1994), *Research Foundations for Psychotherapy Practice* edited by Mark Aveline and David Shapiro (1995), and *What Works for Whom: A Critical Review of Psychotherapy Research* by Anthony Roth and Peter Fonagy (1996). The latter is of particular interest because of its scrupulous objectivity, written as it is by a cognitive therapist (Roth) and a professor of psychoanalysis (Fonagy). Reviewing the evidence for the efficacy of psychotherapy in the treatment of common psychiatric disorders such as depression, anxiety, eating disorders, personality disorders, sexual dysfunction, and so on, they divide the different therapies available into those which have been demonstrated to be effective and those which have either proved to be promising or have received only limited support for their efficacy. On the whole, cognitive behavioural therapies fare best, while evidential support for psychodynamic therapies is harder to come by, though the authors repeatedly stress that lack of evidence does not necessarily mean that psychodynamic therapies are ineffective.

In his Foreword to Roth and Fonagy's book, David Shapiro, Professor of Clinical Psychology at the University of Leeds, declares that the beliefs and claims of psychotherapists have been more critically and searchingly challenged than those of any other practitioners and that there is now more and better scientific evidence to support the effectiveness of psychotherapy than many other interventions in health care at the present time. However, he too acknowledges that there has been relatively little progress in developing an evidence base for longer-term psychodynamic therapies. Moreover, the extensive research of recent years has still failed to establish beyond doubt that one form of therapy is more effective than others across a range of different psychological disorders. This persistent finding has come to be known as the 'Dodo bird verdict' (after the Dodo bird in *Alice in Wonderland*, who, judging the outcome of a race, gave his verdict that, 'Everyone has won and all must have prizes.').

Several explanations have been offered to account for this. One possibility is that the essential factors contributing to positive outcome may be common to all therapies, including psychoanalysis. Patients who have reported they benefited from therapy have attributed their improved condition to such factors as the reassuring comfort derived from forming a bond to a warm, accepting psychotherapist, the reduction in anxiety or despair afforded by the expectation of being helped, the gaining of some understanding of the nature of their problems, the acquisition of better adjusted patterns of behaviour, and the influence of the therapist's personality. A further crucial factor may well be the provision of a plausible system of explanation enabling patients to make sense of their situation.

Satisfaction of the need for explanations might indeed serve to explain the extraordinary cultural success of the entire therapeutic enterprise. The need for explanatory systems is apparent in all human societies, and accounts for the ubiquitous occurrence of mythic and religious explanations of the origins and nature of human existence. In our own culture Christianity is one example of such a system: Darwinism, Marxism, and Freudianism are others. Up to the time of the Ancient Greeks explanatory systems had been essentially mythic or magico-religious, expressed in terms of occult powers. In modern times, scientific explanations have banished hidden 'powers', replacing them with naturally occurring 'energy'. Freud's explanatory system fell somewhere between the mythic and the scientific, for he still clung to the notion of occult 'drives' operating in 'the unconscious'.

Both Freud and Jung have been accused not only of founding 'cults' but of seeking to replace Judeo-Christianity with quasi-religious systems of their own devising. There is an element of truth in this, since the cultural vacuum left by the demise of Judeo-Christianity was demanding to be filled with something. In the last decade of the twentieth century it has become apparent that Freudianism has failed as a satisfactory explanation in the West as Marxism has in the East. Both have retreated, leaving monetarism and scientific materialism as the primary explanatory systems which rule our cultural lives. For many people this is not enough. The explanatory vacuum remains. It is in this vacuum that psychotherapists continue to do their work.

Freud's constantly repeated claim that psychoanalysis was a science has not withstood the attacks of philosophers of science like Ernest Nagel, Sidney Hook, and Karl Popper, who have demonstrated that psychoanalytic theory does not satisfy the most basic requirements of a true science, since the bungie-like flexibility of its postulates does not permit of their falsification. Given the most exhaustive case history, highly qualified and experienced psychoanalysts can produce conflicting but equally plausible interpretations of the same material, and no systematic method exists for establishing the validity of their alternative formulations; nor are they able to make accurate predications about the patient's future mental state.

The scientific credibility of psychoanalysis stands or falls on Freud's 'tally argument'. The tally argument holds that a patient's condition will only improve if the interpretations offered by the analyst tally with the actual processes occurring within the patient. But, as Grünbaum pointed out in an influential book, published in 1984, Freud's tally argument rests on the conjunction of two causally necessary conditions: that psychoanalysis *alone* can provide valid insights into the unconscious conflicts responsible for a neurosis, and that these insights are *indispensable* to cure of the neurosis. Since, as recent research has demonstrated, unique validity cannot be attributed to psychoanalytic insights and unique effectiveness cannot be claimed for psychoanalytic treatment, it follows, Grünbaum argues, that psychoanalysis must surrender its 'epistemic warrant' to scientific credibility.

As early as the 1960s, 'independent' psychoanalysts, such as Charles Rycroft, were arguing that psychoanalysis should cease to think of itself as a scientific discipline, but rather as a branch of the humanities, like literary criticism or biblical exegesis (from which the term hermeneutics is derived). Understandably, this 'hermeneutic perspective' has grown in popularity among psychoanalysts, since it would allow them to escape with some dignity from the uncomfortable realization that their work has no basis in science. Laying the issue of scientific proof on one side, the hermeneutic approach holds that the value of a formulation can be derived from its coherence, consistency, and narrative intelligibility, considered within the whole context of the patient's history in conjunction with data derived from the analytic situation. This rather begs the issue of who makes the judgement of coherence, consistency, and intelligibility, and what determines the grounds for assessing the criteria on which the judgement is based.

A straight answer to the question 'Does psychoanalysis work in the way that psychoanalysts say is does?' is 'No, it doesn't.' Five-times-a-week treatment analysing the transference and counter-transference over a period of several years at a cost of about £7,500 a year does not necessarily produce any greater improvement than once a week 'supportive' therapy with a sympathetic nurse on the National Health. 'All that time and money', exclaims Stephen Frosh, 'all those complicated words and painful silences – and it does not even work.'

The research leading to this uncomfortable conclusion is not inconsiderable. One of the most impressive psychoanalytic studies was conducted by the Menninger Foundation which followed up patients over a period of up to 30 years (Wallerstein, 1986). Patients were given either psychoanalytic psychotherapy or supportive psychotherapy. They were seen by their therapists for as long as necessary: this varied between 6 months and 12 years from their initial assessment in the 1950s. All patients were followed up 2 or 3 years after termination of their treatment, and many remained in contact with the researchers for 12 to 24 years longer. Some were still receiving treatment 30 years later! The most striking finding of what Frosh calls 'this remarkable and honourable study', was that it provided no evidence of any superior effect of psychoanalytic psychotherapy over supportive therapy. In fact, the outcome of psychoanalytic psychotherapy was worse, while that of supportive psychotherapy was better than the investigators expected.

Other studies have produced similar results. In a review of outcome research in psychoanalysis published in 1995, Judy Kantrovitz summarized the results of six 'systematic clinical-quantitative studies of terminated analyses' which had been conducted over the previous decades. Altogether these involved 550 patients in four or five-times-a-week psychoanalysis conducted by supervised trainees at four psychoanalytic institutes. The findings of each of these studies were strikingly similar: while all patients received some therapeutic benefit for their neurotic difficulties, their improvement was not directly attributable to the specifically psychoanalytic aspects of their treatment.

These negative findings are all the more impressive when it is realized that the studies were mostly conducted by researchers well disposed to psychoanalysis, many being psychoanalysts themselves, and were therefore likely to be biased in the direction of producing positive results. It says much for their integrity that they reported their findings with such commendable objectivity. 'Still', comments Frosh, 'the point is that despite the failure of researchers wedded to psychoanalysis to demonstrate its effectiveness, the profession grinds on, its fees charged and paid, its training institutes still in demand.'

Some psychoanalysts have followed Charles Rycroft in responding to these negative findings by insisting that since theirs is an interpretative or hermeneutic discipline unrelated to the physical sciences and logically distinct from them, their work cannot be subjected to scientific evaluation. However, this ingenuous argument completely overlooks the fact that psychoanalysts make the kind of statements about the pathological consequences of certain childhood events and about the positive outcomes of psychoanalytic treatment which *are* susceptible to scientific validation or refutation. The only escape from such scrutiny would be for psychoanalysis to give up all claims to therapeutic effectiveness and psychopathological explanation and become a branch of 'cultural studies'.

In an excellent paper on research methodology, Chess Denman (herself an analyst as well as a researcher) has listed the enormous difficulties involved in setting up effective studies into long term therapy: these include the heterogeneity of the disorders treated, uncertainty about the natural history of each of these conditions (which of them is likely to improve spontaneously with time?), the inability to control extra-analytic, real life events which can impact on the patient and alter his or her psychological status, the problem of establishing clear criteria for studies of outcome, variations in style and therapeutic procedures between different institutes and schools of analysis, and so on – to say nothing of the huge costs which any long-term study must incur.

One way of reducing the cost factor has been developed by Wolfram Keller and his colleagues of the Free University of Berlin, who approached 111 former patients, who had received long-term Jungian analysis (*i.e.*, more than 100 sessions), six years after their treatment was completed. Objective estimates of improvement or deterioration were provided by health insurance claims made by the subjects five years before and five years after their analysis. Between 70 and 94 per cent of the subjects reported substantial and lasting improvement in such areas as their mental state, their general satisfaction with life, their performance at work, and their personal relationships. This corresponded with assessments independently provided by their former therapists and also with a reduction in the number of days spent off work for sickness or for treatment in hospital, as well as the number of out-patient visits to a doctor and prescriptions received for drugs. Since these strongly positive findings are at variance with those derived from other long-term outcome studies, they will require confirmation from other sources. A more ambitious 'prospective' study into the efficacy of Jungian analysis is being conducted by Wolfram Keller in association with G. Rudolf of Heidelberg University. The results of this study must, of necessity, lie some time in the future.

A major difficulty confronted by those organizing such studies is the fact that many analysts remain consistently hostile to the entire notion of research into what they do. They argue that the procedures involved (taping sessions, interviewing patients during treatment, etc.) interfere with the therapeutic process and that research focusing on symptom-removal and other behavioural measures completely overlooks the very stuff of analysis which is concerned with the inner life of the patient. Moreover, their entrenched scepticism of research means that when findings conflict with their theories, these analysts invariably question the research methodology rather than the value of the theory. They argue that the studies so far completed have been conducted on poorly selected patients, who may not always have been appropriate for psychoanalytic treatment, and that the practitioners providing the treatment were usually trainees rather than experienced analysts. But, as Chess Denman has said, there are limits to the length of time that a form of treatment can claim to be considered 'promising' but 'insufficiently researched'. Psychoanalysts have had 100 years to prove what they do is valuable and so far they have conspicuously failed to do so.

It is precisely because funding decisions are based increasingly on outcome studies and 'clinical audits', that it is unlikely that government agencies or insurance companies will be willing to finance psychoanalytic treatment in the future and that this expensive, long term treatment may be confined to patients who are rich, undiscriminating, and not particularly ill. Psychoanalysts have always claimed that their form of intensive therapy is indispensable to bringing about any radical improvement in people with deep-seated personality disorders. But, here again, the evidence is against them. Such disorders are extremely difficult to treat by whatever methods have been tried and psychoanalysis has no greater success to its credit than any other therapeutic approach. If anything, it has been shown to be less effective than cognitive behaviour therapy in this regard.

So, what is left? Should psychoanalysis see itself no longer as a means of treatment for psychiatric disorders and more as a mode of cultural education designed to enrich the personality and enhance the quality of life of those who have the time and money to devote to it? This is, perhaps, the more honest position for psychoanalysts to adopt. At least with psychoanalysis in its present form, with its present postulates and procedures.

In the absence of clear evidence that psychoanalysis is indeed more effective in the treatment of neurotic and personality disorders than briefer, less expensive forms of treatment, it should relinquish its claims to be a superior 'treatment of choice' for these conditions. Rather it should accept that what therapeutic achievements it can claim are based on principles common to all other forms of psychotherapy and be clear about what it is, if anything, that psychoanalysis may add to them. Otherwise, it will disappear, like so many other mythologies, in to the mists of history.

What, then, has research demonstrated the active ingredients of psychotherapy to be? From their extensive reviews of such research, David Orlinsky of Chicago University and his colleagues have been able to define definite links between the processes involved in psychotherapy and their positive outcome for patients. Overwhelmingly, this research points to the crucial importance of the therapeutic bond or alliance. It is essential that this alliance should be experienced as positive and supportive and that it should be based on a 'collaborative sharing of responsibility', as both participants focus on the patient's feelings, experiences, and difficulties. It is also important that the therapist should be perceived as skilful as well as sympathetic and that the patient should be open, non-defensive, and actively committed to the therapeutic process. There is also some evidence that longer treatment duration (rather than greater number of sessions) is associated with a more lasting positive outcome, but this has to be confirmed.

All these factors apply to the practice of psychoanalysis as well as other therapies. What psychoanalysis would claim to add to them specifically is the transference and its interpretation. Is there evidence to support the psychoanalytic contention that this procedure is crucial for long term success? In order to answer this William Henry and Hans Strupp of Vanderbilt University and their colleagues undertook a detailed review of empirical studies of transference interpretations and their outcome. They concluded that far from contributing to positive therapeutic results, 'several studies have linked greater frequency of transference interpretations to poorer outcomes'. What is more, 'transference interpretations do not necessarily repair poor alliances and may damage the existing alliance.' Transference interpretations do not deepen the intensity of the analytic experience in comparison with non-transference interventions, and they are 'more likely to elicit defensive responding than any other types of interventions.' Since there is universal agreement that the decisive factor for positive outcome in psychotherapy is the establishment of a good, close working alliance between the patient and the therapist, it would seem that, on the basis of William Henry's and Hans Strupp's findings, the emphasis placed on transference analysis by Freudian, Kleinian, and Fordhamite Jungians adds little to what is provided by other schools of psychotherapy and, indeed, may be anti-therapeutic.

However, what all these forms of research fail to reveal is the quality of the exchanges which occur in the analytic session, the way in which the significant meanings that dominate a patient's life are recovered, experienced, formulated, and 'reconstructed', and what this means in terms of the patient's aesthetic of living. Here it may be that the intensive dialectic of the analytic situation has the edge on other forms of therapy, but, again, the quality of both analyst and patient as people as well as the richness of their exchanges will be decisive. Such factors, however, are difficult, if not impossible, to measure.

It is at this point that the line between science and art grows hazy, and where therapy becomes more a matter of culture and philosophy than of scientific empiricism. What is clear is that the old certainties are crumbling. The iron curtain separating the Freudians from the Kleinians, and the great wall separating both from the Jungians, are beginning to disintegrate. But as Thomas Kuhn has shown, old paradigms do not yield directly to scientific disproof but only to a new, more attractive paradigm when it emerges to take its place. It is possible that this new paradigm is already upon us and it is time that we examined its characteristics to determine what it may have to offer.

9

Evolutionary Psychotherapy

The New Paradigm

A central concern for all schools of psychotherapy is the question what has gone wrong for the patient in the first place? The major schools have come up with different answers to the same question and different solutions as to how the problem may be put right. To the classical Freudian the problem is the repressed urges and memories of childhood which need to be made conscious; to the object relations theorist it is the formation of a false self at the expense of the real self which the analytic relationship must undo and correct; to the attachment theorist it is the pathological development of an internal working model of the self as incapable of receiving and giving love that needs to be readjusted; to the Jungian it is the frustrated archetypal intent which needs to be liberated so that the patient can achieve his or her full potential; to the microbiological psychiatrist it is the absence or excessive presence of some biochemical substance which needs to be corrected; while to the clinical psychiatrist it is the presence of some pathological process or disease which needs to be diagnosed and treated with pills or electric shocks. What, if anything, can the evolutionary perspective add to this already crowded playground of aetiological and therapeutic ideas?

The solution which evolutionary psychiatry proposes is elegantly simple. Through the process of natural selection, specific patterns of behaviour emerged which effectively solved the problems of survival during the hunter-gatherer stage of human development. These patterns, or archetypes, became encoded in our genetic make-up, and they continue to affect how people behave in contemporary situations. Far from being a blank slate, the human mind possesses a large repertoire of genetically encoded psychological mechanisms which enable us to respond adaptively to the social and physical eventualities that the environment creates from moment to moment. How, then, do psychiatric disorders arise? Evolutionary psychiatry takes the view that the symptoms that cause people to seek treatment – depression, anxiety, phobias, mania, delusions, hallucinations, obsessive-compulsive phenomena, etc. – are not signs of 'disease' but natural responses with which all members of our species are equipped. These responses become troublesome in certain people when they are exaggerated or distorted, or occur in inappropriate situations. According to this view, the development of a child into an adult may be broadly compared to the development of an acorn. The acorn will become the best oak tree it can, given the kind of soil, the condition of the climate, the proximity and height of the surrounding trees, and so on. Deficiencies in any of these environmental conditions will result in stunting or distorted growth.

The meaning of anxiety and depression

That mental symptoms could have a biological basis is not a new idea. In his essay, 'A Phylogenetic Fantasy', Freud suggested that certain states of mind, such as paranoia and anxiety, were remnants of responses which were biologically adaptive in human beings up to the time of the Ice Age. Jung also believed that such states possessed an evolutionary basis which predated the family conflicts which figure so extensively in the psychoanalytic literature. Unfortunately, by insisting that anxiety is a classifiable 'illness', psychiatrists have given the impression that anxiety is a 'neurotic' condition that no well-adjusted person should ever experience. Viewed in the evolutionary perspective, however, the capacity to experience anxiety is *indispensable to survival*, for an animal incapable of fear is a dead animal. The dodo died because it had always inhabited an environment without predators and knew no fear. But when humans arrived, bringing predators with them, this tame, fearless creature rapidly succumbed to them and became extinct.

In clinical practice, psychiatrists distinguish between patients who suffer from 'free-floating anxiety' (which can be triggered by anything and everything) and those who suffer from 'phobic anxiety' (which is triggered by specific objects or situations). However, the actual physical, emotional, and psychological components of anxiety, fear, and panic are broadly similar whatever the triggering factor may be, and their biological function is to promote survival by facilitating an appropriate response, whether this be violence, escape, submission, or 'freezing'. Thus, predators promote flight, weak challengers promote attack, strong challengers stimulate submission, and high places cause freezing.

Specific phobic anxieties are thus often linked to specific forms of response. Fear of heights (acrophobia) promotes *freezing* rather than escape because it renders one less likely to fall; fear of blood (haemophobia) causes *fainting* with its associated slowing of the heart rate and lowering of blood pressure (thus rendering one less likely to bleed to death). Fear of open or public spaces (agoraphobia) causes one to stay at home (thus rendering one less likely to be mugged or raped); while fear of flying (aerophobia) keeps one on the ground (thus making it impossible to be killed in an air crash). Naturally enough, these links are not always specific. After all, fear of spiders, fear of snakes, and fear of animals in general results in avoidance, freezing, escape or attack according to one's appraisal of the situation. When it comes to responding to anxiety it is one's appraisal of precisely what is happening that is the crucial factor. To misquote Kipling, If you can keep your head when all about you are losing theirs, it's just possible that you haven't grasped the situation!

To be seized by an attack of phobic anxiety is to experience the power of what Jung called 'an autonomous complex' operating at an ancient and unconscious level of the brain. You may realize how absurdly irrational it is to be terrified of a little spider in the bath, but your higher, recently evolved cerebral capacities are incapable of doing anything to control it. You have to withdraw and leave somebody else to deal with the spider. This, as it happens, is the usual way of coping with a phobia: one does everything possible to avoid proximity to the source of the fear. Being quite unable to control it, one has no option but to keep away from everything associated with it. This is the biological 'purpose' of the fear concerned. It is 'designed' to keep one out of harm's way. That is why it evolved and why it has remained as part of our behavioural repertoire.

Evidently, situations are assessed at different levels of the brain, and conflicts can arise between these levels as to what strategy one should adopt. At the conscious level, you may tell yourself not to be silly, that it's only a harmless little spider, and that you should swat it with the loofah and stop making a fuss. Instead, you find yourself running out of the bathroom, screaming for help. Clearly, you have been taken over by a defensive response, which is beyond voluntary control because it is located beyond the reach of consciousness in a part of the old mammalian brain (which is incorporated within the human brain) known as the limbic system.

Anxiety disorders are of considerable interest, therefore, because they provide an example of an archetype entering the personal psyche as a complex. When the various phobias suffered by modern men and women are examined in detail, there is, in fact, little that is modern about them. They are all exaggerated fears of objects, animals, or situations that were potentially life threatening in the environment in which our species evolved and in which we are adapted to live. This vital point is invariably overlooked in textbooks of psychiatry and it represents the key insight of the evolutionary approach to human psychopathology.

Anxiety and fear are adaptive responses to the kinds of dangers humans have been exposed to in the course of their evolution. This is why we fear ancient dangers such as snakes, spiders, high or open places, and not modern dangers such as cars, guns, cigarettes, whisky, and saturated fats, which kill off our contemporaries in infinitely greater numbers. Modern phobias, such as going to school, going out to do the shopping, going to the dentist, or contracting AIDS, are contemporary versions of adaptive fears of going off the home range, getting hurt, or becoming diseased. Some modern phobias are composites of ancestral fears: for example, fear of flying is made up of biologically appropriate fears of the primordial dangers represented by heights, falling, loud noise, and being trapped in small, enclosed spaces from which there is no exit.

Another major group of psychiatric conditions which is yielding to evolutionary insights is made up of the affective or mood disorders, commonly known as manic-depression. That both depressive and manic reactions are adaptive is indicated by their universal occurrence throughout human communities in response to certain characteristic life events. The subjective sense of misery, the inability to take pleasure in anything, the complete loss of energy and drive, the feelings of anxiety, tension and worthlessness are *core* symptoms of depression, which are recognized and diagnosed in different terminologies in all human societies throughout the world. It was my friend and colleague, John Price, who made the original observation that depression in human beings has features in common with the state that many different kinds of animals get into when they are defeated in conflicts for territory, mates, or status within the rank hierarchy of their group. He realized that both mania and depression have an extremely long evolutionary history. Three hundred million years ago our ancestors competed for resources such as food, territory, and mates, on an *individual* basis – as many vertebrates continue to do to this day. Then as group living became established and territory began to be shared, individuals stopped competing directly for territory and instead began to compete for rank. Once acquired, high rank brought with it access to the resources that were desired.

Competition for rank took the form of threat displays and physical duels or tournaments. Very early on, animals evolved the capacity to assess their own strengths in comparison with an adversary and to make good guesses as to the probable outcome of being involved in a fight. On the basis of this guess, they attack, run away, or submit. This kind of behaviour is particularly apparent among reptiles, and the capacity for evaluating success or failure, as well as the patterns of behaviour involved, must reside in the reptilian brain, vestiges of which persist in the oldest parts of our own brains.

Repeated successes in duels result in high self-assessment on the part of the animal, while defeats result in a lower self-assessment, which causes the animal to indulge in what behavioural biologists call the 'yielding subroutine'. What John Price recognized was that this defeated state, together with the proneness to make use of the 'yielding subroutine', provides the basis of the depressive reaction in human patients. The reason why the depressed state evolved, he argued, is because it provides a means of adapting to loss – whether it be loss of rank, or loss of a loved person. In other words, the adaptive function of the depression is to facilitate losing and to promote accommodation to the fact that one has lost. This has the effect of preventing the loser from suffering further injury and of preserving the stability and competitive efficiency of the group, which would otherwise be disrupted by constant battles for status and for sexual partners.

The typical life events which trigger either a depressive or a manic reaction, therefore, are the perception of one of two possible outcomes: loss or gain. What is lost or gained may be a spouse or a child, a job or financial security, health or reputation. But what the particular loss or gain amounts to in the long term scale of ultimate biological objectives is a decrease or increase in the resources needed for reproductive success and getting one's genes into the next generation.

The evolutionary approach provides similar insights into such conditions as eating disorders, obsessive-compulsive phenomena, and a variety of personality disorders. Readers wishing to follow up these leads will find them discussed in *Evolutionary Psychiatry: A New Beginning*, which I wrote in collaboration with John Price and published in 1996.

Attachment, rank, and two modes of being

The immediate cause of many psychiatric conditions may be understood as a subjective prediction on the part of the patient that he or she will fail in competing for two highly valued social resources: attachment and rank. We all need to feel that we are loved and worthy of love. We also need to feel that we have status in the eyes of others because this determines the level of our self-esteem. If we feel unworthy of love and lacking in status, the result in especially vulnerable people is neurosis or psychosis, or any one of a number of personality disorders.

Interest in the evolutionary history of competitiveness for rank and resources has, understandably, proved controversial. The commitment of social scientists to ideas of cultural relativity and behavioural plasticity (together with a tendency to idealise the apparently egalitarian spirit of surviving hunter-gatherer communities) has meant that the importance universally attributed to rank and status in human societies has been largely overlooked. Recent acknowledgement of this oversight has resulted in the discovery that hunter-gatherer societies are in fact less egalitarian than they seemed. Not only is the propensity to form social hierarchies a universal and evolutionarily stable characteristic but its phylogenetic antiquity may be deduced from ethological studies of our closest relatives, the chimpanzees, the bonobos (pygmy chimpanzees), and the gorillas, among whom hierarchies of varying degrees of complexity are indispensable to their social organization. That the phylogenetic history of human social competitiveness has come to assume special interest for evolutionary psychiatrists is because it appears to be deeply implicated in the psychopathology of such a large number of psychiatric disorders.

Some time in the last ten million years a new form of social competition has arisen: instead of trying to intimidate rivals, a competitor seeks to attract them. This form of competition is apparent, for example, among chimpanzees, and its significance was first recognized by the primatologist, Michael Chance. In addition to threat display, male chimpanzees indulge in a form of behaviour that is not threatening at all and does not demand the submission of a subordinate. Rather it is a form of social solicitation, which, Chance noted, results in affiliative behaviour 'in which there is a continuing interaction between individuals, such as grooming, play, sexual or mothering behaviour with the displayer' (Chance and Jolly, 1970).

In the course of extensive observations on social groups of primates, Chance recognized that they had two quite distinct modes of functioning, which he termed *agonic* and *hedonic*. The agonic mode is characteristic of hierarchically organized societies where individuals are concerned with warding off threats to their status and inhibiting overt expressions of aggressive conflict; while the hedonic mode is associated with affiliative behaviour in more egalitarian social organizations where agonic tensions are absent. While acknowledging the pitfalls involved in translating animal findings to human social psychology, many researchers have come to see Chance's two modes as possessing great explanatory value.

Numerous parallels exist in the history of ideas: for example, Empedocles's distinction between love and strife, from which Freud derived his Eros and Thanatos instincts, Aristotle's distinction between the political and hedonic life, and the classical sociological distinction made by the German social theorist, Ferdinand Tonnies (1855-1936), between *Gemeinschaft* and *Gesellschaft*. In short, there is good reason to propose the existence of two major archetypal systems: that concerned with attachment, affiliation, care-giving, care-receiving, and altruism; and that concerned with rank, status, discipline, law and order, territory, and possessions. These may well be the basic archetypal patterns on which social adjustment and maladjustment, psychiatric health and sickness depend. Both can function healthily when evoked in appropriate circumstances, but either can give rise to pathology when their goals are frustrated or when they are inappropriately activated.

The evolutionary replacement of intimidation by attraction allowed the hedonic mode to emerge. In the hedonic mode, competitors seek to disarm potential rivals and attract potential mates as well as achieving status in the eyes of other members of the group. Group approbation of competitors' displays has the effect of raising their self-esteem. Should their displays be met with disapprobation, on the other hand, individuals become less attractive to potential mates, lose status in the eyes of the group, and suffer a reduction in self-esteem. Attractive people are granted prestige. They tend to assume leadership roles and have access to more resources than their successful competitors. In environments similar to the environment in which we evolved (the so-called 'ancestral environment') they tend, as with the Ache of Paraguay and the !Kung Bushmen of the Kalahari, to have more wives, sire more children, and their children are more likely to survive. Their 'fitness', in biological terms, therefore increases.

Psychopathology in a new light

Essentially, the possible outcomes of competition through dominance and attraction can be represented orthogonally, with physical competition for dominance on the vertical axis, and competition by attraction for approval and social integration on the horizontal axis.

The horizontal dimension may also be labelled approach-withdrawal, closeness-distance, friendliness-hostility, in-group/out-group

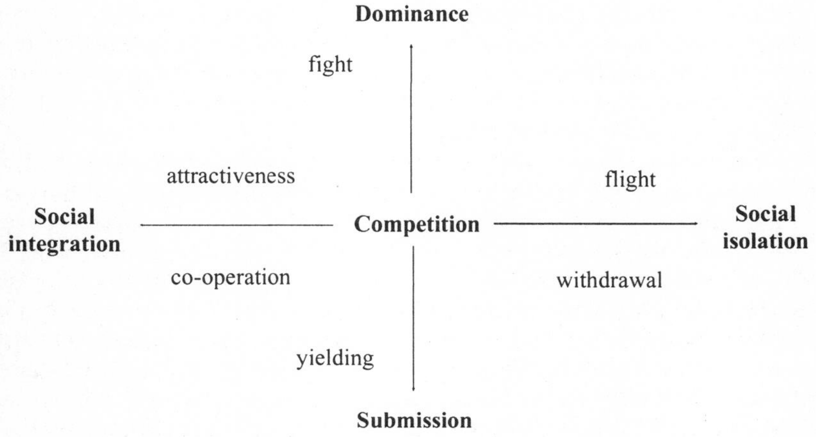

Figure 1. A schema for possible outcomes of competition through dominance and attraction

orientation, love-hate, and so on. In other words, the horizontal dimension is concerned with affiliation, while the vertical dimension is concerned with power. The horizontal needs, of course, resemble Jung's 'extraversion-introversion' dimension in his theory of psychological types.

The broad application of these basic dimensions to human psychopathology results in the following indications:

- *successful* affiliation is associated with social adjustment and mental health
- *failure* in affiliation is associated with an introverted, inner-directed mode of personality adjustment which may give rise to personality disorders of the schizoid, schizotypal, or paranoid type, or result in a schizophrenic breakdown
- *submission* is associated with low self-esteem, feelings of shame and humiliation, anxiety, depression, masochism, dependent personality disorder, and a liability to be victimized or abused
- *dominance* is associated with high self-esteem, hypomania, sadism, and a liability to abuse others.

The crucial factor determining the kind of disorder which individuals will present is whether or not they continue to feel themselves to be 'insiders' (*i.e.*, members of the in-group, committed to membership of the community, whether loved or unloved, of high status or low) or 'outsiders' (*i.e.*, not members of the in-group, not committed to membership of the community, not involved in attachment relationships or in conflicts for status). If an 'insider' develops a psychiatric disorder, it will tend to be a *disorder of attachment and rank* (e.g., anxiety disorder, affective disorder, obsessive-compulsive disorder etc.), whereas an 'outsider' will tend to develop a *spacing disorder* (e.g., schizoid personality disorder or schizophrenia). Individuals who are uncertain as to their allegiance and who hover uneasily on the cusp between 'insider' and 'outsider' status will, if they develop a psychiatric disorder, tend to present with a *borderline* state (e.g., borderline or schizotypal personality disorder).

The importance of this new classificatory schema is that it helps to move us beyond the old 'medical model', with its emphasis on the diagnosis and treatment of dubious 'mental diseases' towards an entirely new conceptual framework which defines the basic components of human nature in terms of their evolutionary origins and their essential developmental needs. The new paradigm does not contradict earlier psychiatric or psychoanalytic findings and formulations which are empirically valid, but enables them to be incorporated within a more embracing and ultimately more satisfactory explanatory system.

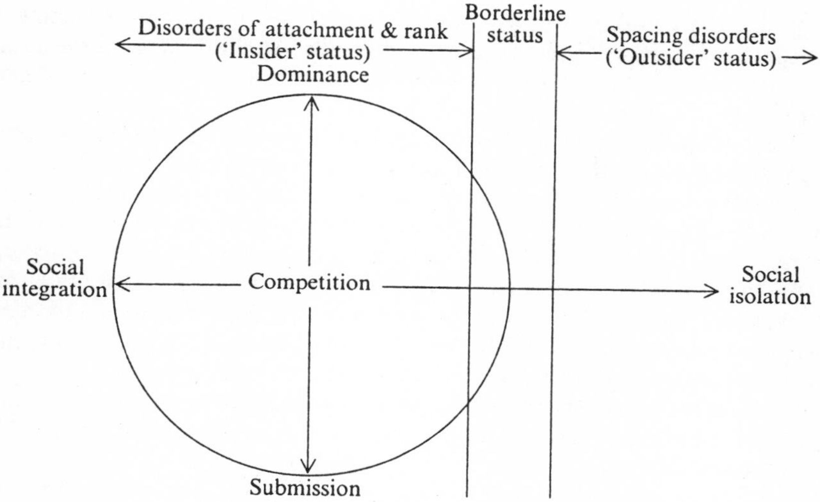

Figure 2. A schema for the classification of the major disorders

It permits the statement of a basic principle of psychopathology which may be summed up as follows: *Psychopathology results when the environment fails, either partially or totally, to meet one (or more) archetypal need(s) in the developing individual.*

This is John Bowlby's postulate, with his added corollary that the *further the rearing environment deviates from the environment of evolutionary adaptedness* (*i.e.*, the ancestral environment) the *greater is the likelihood of pathological development.* If we are to understand the psychiatric disorders from which our contemporaries suffer, then we have to take into account the ways in which Western society frustrates the needs of the paleolithic man or woman still persisting as living potential within us in our present environmental circumstances.

Many possibilities come to mind: the disruption of community-based kinship bonds as a result of migration, job mobility, experiments in town planning, and so on; the disruption of families through divorce and separation together with the rapidly increasing incidence of single-parent families; the loss of female support groups of the kind provided by traditional communities; the lack of adequate provision for the secure and intimate care of children whose mothers go out to work; the occurrence of negative life events such as losing one's job, being passed over for promotion, mortgage rate increases, house repossessions, exam or interview failures, difficulty in acquiring the necessary skills demanded by employers, and sedentary work in artificial light and controlled atmospheres; the loss of myth, ritual, and religion; the lack of contact with nature, the seasons, and the primordial environment. All these factors are potentially productive of stress, insecurity, and 'anomie' as well as distorted development.

It is not unlikely that the various neuroses, psychopathies, drug dependencies, the occurrence of child and spouse abuse, to say nothing of the ever rising crime statistics, are connected with Western society's inability to satisfy the archetypal needs of our kind. Many of these points have been impressively emphasized by Glantz and Pearce in their book *Exiles from Eden: Psychotherapy from An Evolutionary Perspective* (1989). A key factor concerned in the causation of most psychiatric illness is *stress*. The probability is that the greater the gap between archetypal needs and environmental fulfilment of those needs, the greater the stress and the more incapacitating the subsequent disorder.

The importance of kith and kin

Although many people suffering from stress come to the attention of psychiatrists, many of them, perhaps the majority, do not; nor do they necessarily manifest the signs of psychiatric illness. As early as the 1930s Jung was reporting that a good two-thirds of the patients who consulted him were not suffering from a diagnosable psychiatric disorder but from the meaninglessness and purposelessness of their lives. The same is true of the majority of people who consult psychotherapists at the present time.

What, then, has the evolutionary paradigm to offer the practising psychotherapist? The answer is that it can revolutionize the old psychoanalytic model for psychotherapy in the same way as it may replace the old medical model for psychiatry and, as a result, inaugurate a more effective as well as a more optimistic therapeutic philosophy. Freud needed to believe in resistance and in an unconscious that was atavistic, disorganized, and chaotic so that he could continue to believe in his theories and impose them on his patients. By contrast, evolutionary psychotherapy views the programmes operative in the unconscious as essentially adaptive, organized, and directed towards specific goals. It sees the patient as the primary agent of change, and seeks to activate the innate psychological mechanisms (or 'algorithms') responsible for hedonic social interaction, so as to provide support, insight, and understanding along 'kinship' lines.

Neo-Darwinian theory has thus given a new meaning to Jung's concept of 'kinship libido' and has added a whole new dimension to both the transference and the therapeutic alliance. Darwin believed that success in the struggle for survival, linked with success in competing for the attraction of sexual partners, enhanced an individual's *reproductive fitness* – that is, it increased the number of copies of his or her genetic material that the individual passed on to *direct* descendants. However the classical Darwinian view of sexual reproductive fitness focused on the *individual* and this has proved inadequate to explain certain elements of behaviour, such as self-sacrifice and altruism.

As a result, it has been found necessary to replace the Darwinian notion of reproductive fitness with the neo-Darwinian concept of *inclusive* fitness. In the contemporary evolutionary view, what matters more than the survival of the individual *per se* is the survival of that individual's genes. Inclusive fitness refers to the number of copies of their genetic material that individuals cause to be passed on, not only to their direct descendants, but to *other* than direct descendants as well – for example, to nephews, nieces, and cousins, all of whom share a proportion of their genes.

This has given rise to a variety of what are termed 'response rules', 'strategies', and 'tactics' for the performance of social behaviours which promote the probability of gene survival – for example, the care and protection of children, peer bonding and peer play, status-seeking, competing for valued resources, courtship, sexual bonding and marriage, sharing and storing food, seeking shelter, co-operating, reciprocal altruism, discriminating against strangers, the splitting of groups when they achieve a critical size, the expression of out-group hostility and in-group loyalty, cleaning, washing, grooming, teaching, ritualized tournaments, subscribing to the beliefs and practices of myth, religion, and ritual, and so on.

Since in the ancestral environment human beings lived in small groups in which some genetic relationship existed between all members, these strategies were usually directed towards kin or shared with kin, while wariness and hostility were reserved for strangers. It is within this kin-oriented matrix that the therapeutic relationship needs to operate if it is to stand any chance of success.

The positive orientation towards kin, to help, support, and succour them, so apparent in human communities throughout the world, has both 'ultimate' and 'proximate' functions. The ultimate function is to get one's genes into the next generation. Genetic 'fitness' is a relative concept: your fitness is greater than your neighbour's if more of your genes appear in the next generation. The genetic arithmetic of individual fitness is straightforward: parents share 50 per cent of their genes with each offspring and 25 per cent with each grandchild. If you have a nephew, he will share, on average, 25 per cent of your genes. One of his offspring will have 12.5 per cent of your genes. Therefore, if he has five offspring, a greater number of your genes will be replaced in the next generation than if you had only one son (12.5 per cent x 5 = 62.5 percent, as opposed to 50 percent) In practice, this gives rise to trade-offs which influence behaviour in predictable ways. Thus, parents tend to invest more in their offspring than in less genetically close relatives, and children who live with one natural and with one step-parent are more likely to be abused than children living with two natural parents.

The *proximate* consequences of this strategy of kin preference not only influence our behaviour to parents, siblings, offspring, nephews and nieces, but to people experienced and related to 'as if' they were kin. Psychological kinship thus extends further than biological kinship, and this is probably explained by the fact that we evolved to live in small communities where the majority of the members were kin. Indeed, the propensity to distinguish kin from non-kin could underlie all in-group/out-group dichotomies.

Accordingly, kinship theory offers a deeper understanding of Bowlby's attachment concept. As the evolutionary psychologist, Mark Erickson, has shown, early secure attachment to immediate kin mobilizes adaptive kin-directed behaviours in later life, such as preferential altruism and incest avoidance. Impaired attachment early in life predicts aberrant kin-directed behaviour, including diminished altruism, neglect, and an increased incidence of incest. Thus, attachment may be conceived as the primary developmental function of both the psychological experience of kinship and of the adaptive kinship behaviour that goes with it. As Erickson says, this points to an innate psychology of kinship which has evolutionary roots far more ancient than our own species. And it would seem highly probable that constellation of 'psychological kinship' within the analytic relationship is one of the most crucial factors contributing to successful outcome.

Further implications for treatment

In addition to indicating the importance of being unconsciously classified as 'kin', the evolutionary paradigm provides further guidance for the psychotherapist. Since patients are almost invariably suffering from feelings of insecurity, connected with low self-esteem and doubts about their loveworthiness, it follows that the therapist should carry out John Bowlby's prescription to provide an accepting and welcoming environment, so that the consulting room is experienced as a safe haven or 'secure base'. The therapist's attitude should essentially be one of 'care-giving' and should offer social attention and approval in such a way as to enhance the patient's sense of personal status and self-esteem. Only when these basic parameters have been established should the therapist begin to provide insight into internal models which are evidently proving dysfunctional in the life of the patient.

One defect of much psychotherapy research is that it does not take adequate account of the possibility that people with different problems may respond better to different kinds of treatment. As a result, patients with phobias, obsessions, depression, feelings of inadequacy, marital problems, and different kinds of personality disorder have, in many studies, all been lumped together and given the same kind of therapy. From the scientific standpoint, this is about as sophisticated as studying the results of administering aspirin to a group of patients with a large number of different medical disorders. As Paul Gilbert has observed, psychotherapists should not be expected to be one-club golfers: they should be equipped with a number of different clubs appropriate to the task in hand. The advantage of the evolutionary approach is that it studies each patient to discover what is the specific archetypal issue at the heart of the problem. Once that has been determined, it becomes possible to suggest what therapeutic measure is most likely to be helpful.

For people suffering from clearly established psychiatric disorders, therefore, the evolutionary perspective provides useful therapeutic indicators, as, for example, in the treatment of phobic anxiety or depression. Phobic patients invariably feel ashamed of their symptoms, believing that they are the only people in the world to be so afflicted, and that their irrational fears represent some dreadful pathological weakness in their character. The treatment offered by conventional psychiatry usually does little to alleviate this profoundly negative self-perception. When, however, such patients learn that what they are suffering is not some sick, personal aberration but a response shared as an innate defence mechanism by all humanity, it comes as a great relief to them.

Agoraphobia, for example, can be understood as an innate fear of straying from the home base. Most animals are territorial. Once they have established a territory, they defend it vigorously against all comers, and are usually victorious. Some species have a home range which they patrol and share with other members of their species. But few seem happy to leave their home range, and it is the ability to leave home *without* anxiety that is exceptional and which requires explanation.

When treating such patients it is helpful to bear in mind the association that exists in the majority of animal species between territorial ownership and the display of self-confidence and self-esteem. A rise in self-esteem can increase the range of agoraphobic patients: it is as if they feel they have a right to patrol a larger area, and, as a result, their sense of being an intruder when they stray off their home ground is reduced. Research has established that a rise in self-esteem lowers both subjective anxiety and physiological arousal. Thus, to boost the self-esteem of agoraphobic patients may be a more effective remedy than attempting to 'decondition' their anxiety by taking them into those places which they most fear – an heroic therapy which can result in a reinforcement of their conditioned aversion.

Another therapeutic measure is to encourage good relations with neighbours, so as to transform alien territory (which patients unconsciously anticipate to be agonistically defended) into a home range (which can be hedonically shared). One large group of agoraphobic patients consists of women who do not go out to work. It is helpful for these patients to be reassured that there is nothing absurd about preferring to remain safely at home instead of going out shopping on their own. After all, there were no supermarkets in the ancestral environment, and 'gathering' was almost certainly done in the reassuring intimacy of familiar groups of women.

Similarly, when confronted with a depressed patient, a therapist who appreciates the evolutionary meaning of the depressive reaction will take care to form a clear understanding of what precisely it is that the patient has lost and has, per force, to give up. As long as the patient refuses to accept the loss, and remains committed to a hopeless desire to recover what has been lost, he or she will remain depressed. Only when the loss has been truly acknowledged and accepted, is it likely that the depression will lift.

Towards a new synthesis

By far the most important function that the evolutionary approach can perform is a grand, all-embracing work of synthesis and integration. By providing a new scientific paradigm within which fundamental questions about human nature can be formed and answered, it can bring together the disparate findings of ethology, sociology, psychology, and cross-cultural anthropology within one theoretical perspective – the Darwinian perspective, which promises to become the central conceptual standpoint uniting all behavioural sciences. This trend has now moved so far that it is unlikely that any psychological explanation will stand much chance of surviving in the future if it is incompatible with the Darwinian evolutionary consensus. By allowing us to see beyond the old medical and psychoanalytic models, this wider vision must have an impact on all psychiatric and psychotherapeutic research and practice. It could succeed in reconciling the differences between 'biological', 'clinical', and 'social' psychiatry and could render obsolete the doctrinal squabbles and internecine battles between the classical schools of analysis. Already this work has begun, as with the publication of a special issue of the *British Journal of Medical Psychology* on evolutionary psychotherapy published in September 1998 and *Genes on the*

Couch: Explorations in Evolutionary Psychotherapy, edited by Paul Gilbert and Kent Bailey, due to be published in 1999.

By transcending the old differences, however, it does not follow that the knowledge and insights gained during the past century of psychiatric and analytic practice must be lost or negated; rather, they will be absorbed within a more inclusive corpus of scientific understanding. Already, evolutionary psychotherapy has greatly extended the heuristic and empirical implications of archetypal theory, conceiving archetypes as 'innate algorithms' responsible for processing emotional, non-verbal information at a largely unconscious level of experience in accordance with certain specific 'biosocial goals'.

In common with object relations and attachment theorists, evolutionary psychologists share the view that human beings are, by nature, extraordinarily sensitive to social relationships, whether these be positive (e.g., love, attachment, friendship, sex, relationship in the hedonic mode) or negative (e.g., jealousy, guilt, shame, anxiety, depression, anger, relationships in the agonic mode). But since evolutionary psychology places equal emphasis on psychological and physical events, it permits research findings from psychology, biochemistry, and neuroscience to be integrated with those of analysis and psychiatry. The elated sense of being loved and appreciated, for example, is associated with high blood levels of 5-hydroxytryptamine and with low levels of stress hormones, whereas the depressed feeling of being unloved and rejected is associated with low levels of 5-HT and high levels of stress hormones. Hence the success of Prozac and other 5-HT re-uptake inhibitors which cause 5-HT concentrations to rise and thus relieve the symptoms of depression. That the inherent strategies underlying these social experiences with their associated physiological mechanisms are evolutionarily ancient is evident from the fact that they are present in many species of animal that evolved long before *Homo sapiens sapiens*.

What comes to be fixed in the genetic structure of a species is the *predisposition* to certain 'species-specific' forms of behaviour and experience. How has evolution brought this about? Darwin's answer was through natural selection. As a result of genetic mutations, which occur spontaneously and at random, an individual may acquire a characteristic or propensity which makes it better adapted than its fellows to respond appropriately to a certain typical situation – such as, for example, attack from a predator. Being thus advantaged, this individual will tend to survive and pass its new genetic configuration to members of subsequent generations, who, possessing the desirable characteristic, will compete more effectively in the struggle for existence. As a result, the new attribute eventually becomes established as a standard component in the genetic structure of the species. It is in this manner that our archetypal propensities have become adapted to the typical situations encountered in human life. The repeated selection of fortuitous mutations, occurring through hundreds of thousands of generations and over millions of years, has resulted in the present *genome* of the human species. And the genome expresses itself as surely in the structure of the human psyche and in human patterns of behaviour as it does in the anatomy of the human physique.

Just as the ultimate 'purpose' of our existence is the perpetuation of our genes, so the transmission of our genes to the next generation is the *ultimate cause* of our behaviour. The archetypal propensities with which we are born are adapted to enable us to survive long enough in the environment in which we evolved to give our genes a fair chance of transmission to our offspring.

A central issue on which the attention of evolutionary psychologists is focused is 'What social problems have humans evolved ways of recognizing and solving?' So far there is general agreement that, as a species, we characteristically recognize and invest our resources in our own offspring, we endeavour to select 'good quality' mates, we recognize and relate to people who are likely to co-operate with rather than exploit us, and, when it comes to conflict, we tend to challenge only those whom we stand a fair chance of defeating. These characteristics have been listed as 'biosocial goals': these include *care-eliciting*, and *care-giving* (attachment behaviour), *mate selection* (sexual attraction, courtship, conception and mate retention), *alliance formation* (caring, co-operation, affiliation, aggression inhibition, friendship, and reciprocal behaviour) and, *ranking behaviour* (competition for resources, dominance and submissive behaviour, and gaining and maintaining status or rank).

From the standpoint of the historical overview which has formed the substance of this book, what is of particular interest is the fact that each of the biosocial goals detected by the evolutionary psychologists has provided the primary area of concern for the major schools of analysis – viz., care-eliciting, care-giving, and alliance formation (Klein, Winnicott, Bowlby), mate selection and sex (Freud), and rank behaviour (Adler), while the whole concept of goal-directed behaviour subserved by the archetypal components of the Self is the very stuff of analytical psychology (Jung). With the unifying perspective that evolutionary psychology offers, the empirical study of the basic programmes running in the unconscious at last becomes a scientific possibility.

Dangers ahead

Although the evolutionary paradigm evidently has a great deal to be said for it, many people entertain serious reservations about applying Darwinian insights to human nature. They fear that psychology could degenerate into a form of biological fundamentalism, conceiving everything in terms of genetic determinants, encouraging a cold, ruthless scientific objectivity that would result in the denial of feeling, ethics, values, and morality. Not only would this lead to immensely destructive kinds of psychotherapy, but it would constitute a cultural disaster of incalculable proportions, compounded by the use of scientific procedures such as those designed to assess positive therapeutic outcome purely in terms of economic cost effectiveness. Many would argue that we have already moved too far in this direction, and that the attempt to systematise and regulate psychotherapeutic techniques in the form of 'manuals' is a frightening indication of what could be in store for us. I find myself much in sympathy with these arguments, and, while I am excited by the heuristic possibilities offered by the new paradigm, I would agree that we must be vigilant to protect ourselves from the dangers involved in embracing it.

The gravest threat could come from those fanatics, thrown up by every theoretical system, who believe they know what is best for humanity and who, placing themselves on the highest intellectual and moral ground, seek to impose these beliefs on everyone else, entirely 'for their own good'. Darwin would have been horrified by the thought that anyone could turn his discovery to such ends. To him it would have been inconceivable that scientists should use the facts of our biological nature to make rules about how we 'ought' to live our lives. Unlike Marxism, Darwinism is not a manifesto; and, unlike Freudianism, it is not a doctrine. Darwinism gives us profound insights into the facts of how our bodies, minds, and typical behaviours evolved, but it can never dictate how we should live or how we should organize society. It can provide us with useful information about the nature of our innate psychic propensities and the sort of environmental circumstances they evolved to adapt us to, and this knowledge may help psychiatrists and psychotherapists to make more enlightened decisions than hitherto about how best to treat their patients: but evolutionary theory should never be applied further than that. The most crucial of our evolved capacities is consciousness, with its associated capacities to perceive meaning, to make ethical judgements, and to override the basic programmes that evolution has equipped us with. It is consciousness that provides us with our most precious asset – the freedom to choose.

Secondly, it is essential that psychology should not fall into the trap of promoting itself as a branch of sociobiology, embracing a simplistic view of human beings as mere fitness-maximizing genetic vehicles, for this obliterates the psychological level of analysis altogether. So much human experience and behaviour results from working out complex variations on sets of archetypal themes, and these just cannot be explained as expressions of 'the strategy of the genes'. Men, for example, do not look at erotic photographs in order to maximize their fitness, but because they are equipped with evolved psychological mechanisms which cause them to find images of nubile females sexually stimulating. By exciting themselves with erotic images, they are manipulating components of the psychosexual system (which *can* result in reproduction) purely for their own enjoyment. As the evolutionary psychologist, Paul Gilbert, has observed, 'what humans excel at is not only the type of competencies they possess, but the range of stimuli they can direct their mentalities to. For example, caring behaviour can be directed to other people, animals, plants (gardening), inanimate objects (one's car or house) and also oneself. And we gain pleasure from engaging in all of these ... It is this opening up of mentalities (like caring) to a wide field of things ... that may well have been important to human evolution' (Gilbert, 1998). Moreover, archetypal systems exist in us as ever-present potential which may or may not be activated in our life-time: a man may remain celibate, never get involved in a fight, never go hunting, or never go to war. A woman may never have a child. Though our genes are powerful influences, they do not turn us into unconscious automata. The social matrix in which we grow up, its rules, values, language, customs, and ideals are mediating factors between our basic human nature and the kind of individual human being we become.

A compass and a new orientation

Our capacity for consciousness may have evolved to enable us to monitor environmental events in the interests of survival and reproductive success, but it also makes us aware of the meaning and quality of those events as they occur. In the words of St Augustine, we both exist and know that we exist, and rejoice in this existence and this knowledge. Evolutionary theory not only provides insights into the natural history of this extraordinary achievement but at the same time grants a wide therapeutic perspective in which it is possible to relate peoples' sufferings to the totality of human experience, as it is now and always has been.

To those psychotherapists working within the Jungian tradition, the evolutionary approach is particularly appealing since it provides the phylogenetic basis of the collective unconscious. It amplifies the archetypal concept, extending it downwards into its biological roots and outwards into the realm of social behaviour. This is a necessary compensation for Jung's own contribution, constrained as it inevitably was by his psychological type and personal experience. Jung extended archetypal theory upwards into the spiritual realm and inwards into the realm of the introverted, symbolic life arising from the unconscious. The evolutionary perspective enables us to fill out the picture, furthering the enterprise which Jung began. It also reaffirms Jung's transpersonal view of the human situation. Instead of seeing personal problems as merely the product of familial and social circumstances, it examines them in the context of the evolved goals, needs, and strategies that have determined human behaviour since our species came into existence on the African Savannah.

From the evolutionary standpoint, a psychiatric disorder is not a medical disaster like cancer or a stroke, but an ancient adaptive response which for some contemporary reason has become maladaptive to the detriment of the patient's emotional and social life. For like the Jungian, the evolutionary psychiatrist looks beyond the personal predicament and relates it to the story of humankind. Both appreciate that what has traditionally been classified as 'illness' is often a consequence of a potentially healthy organism struggling to meet the demands of life: symptom formation is itself an adaptive process. Both the Jungian and the evolutionary approaches are thus conducive to therapeutic optimism. Instead of forms of futile suffering, symptoms are seen as the growing pains of people struggling to adjust to the demands that life has put on them.

The evolutionary view also affirms Jung's insight that every human being is richly endowed with the archetypal potential of the species. This means that however disordered, one-sided, or constricted an individual's psychological development may be, the *potential* for further growth and better adaptation is nevertheless there, implicit in the psychophysical structure of the organism. As a result, patients may be helped to grow beyond the defective or inadequate form of adjustment that their personal history has permitted.

This perhaps is the most important conceptual contribution that evolutionary psychotherapy has to make: it grants an expanded view of the self. The self is not just the sum total of one's personal life experiences as the object relations theorists and self psychologists maintain, but the product of many millions of years of development. Within each one of us the vast potential of humanity is contained. This provides an added dimension to the *individuation* process of becoming as complete a human being as one's circumstances allow: it is about integrating ontogeny with phylogeny, uniting one's personal experience with the potential experience of humanity. It means making the most of the mentalities with which natural selection has equipped us and bringing them to fulfilment in our lives. Success in this endeavour will depend on the therapist's skill in releasing the unused creative potential in the patient's personality.

A model for this is provided by classical Jungian analysis, which seeks to mobilize archetypal components of the phylogenetic psyche by encouraging patients to dream, to fantasize, to paint, to open themselves to relationships with new friends, and to find new ways of relating to old ones, as well as becoming conscious of the strategies and conflicts that have been controlling their lives in the past. To make headway in such demanding work, therapists have to develop their own personality and creative abilities if they hope to do much more than patch up their patients and enable them to go on existing. As Jung observed, 'an analyst can help his patient just as far as he himself has gone and not a step further.' It is a heavy responsibility, but it makes the work of a committed therapist one of the most challenging and rewarding professions it is possible to embrace.

Whatever upheavals may be in store for us as a result of theoretical revisions, outcome studies, clinical audits, and research on the biochemistry of the brain, the primary duty of the psychotherapist will remain the same: to put empathy, knowledge, and professional skill at the service of the patient. To adopt an evolutionary approach is not to espouse a political cause, to submit to biological determinism, or to abandon a proper concern for ethical values. What such an approach does provide is a compass and a new orientation to steer us through the immense complexities of human psychology, its disorders, and their treatment. New psychotherapies continue to appear: new forms, new methods, new theories, new organizations, all offering new trainings, most of them under-researched and under-evaluated. It is likely, as we have seen, that all successful psychotherapies are based on a small number of principles which have been known to be effective in bringing psychological relief and personal change for many generations. What is needed now is a corpus of informed knowledge about the relationships between individual experience, social influences, and the phylogenetic propensities which guide and inform all human development. This is the programme which Freud and Jung embarked upon at the beginning of the twentieth century. Now, as a new century dawns, we are, perhaps, in a better position to bring it to fruition.

Glossary

Abreaction: the discharge of emotion associated with disturbing experiences suffered in the past; advocated by Joseph Breuer and Sigmund Freud as the most effective treatment for hysteria. Their claims for the success of the method have subsequently proved to be exaggerated. Abreaction is still used, however, albeit in modified form, in the treatment of post-traumatic stress disorder.

Aetiology: that part of medical science which investigates the causes of disease.

Agonic mode: a mode of social interaction characteristic of hierarchically organized societies where individuals are concerned with warding off threats to their status and inhibiting overt expressions of aggressive conflict.

Algorithm: a genetically acquired learning mechanism which organizes experience into adaptive patterns specific to certain typical activities, such as mate selection, predator avoidance, site selection, and so on.

Amplification: a technique advocated by Jung for working with symbolical material (arising from dreams, fantasies, paintings, etc.). Whereas free association may reveal much about the personal context of a dream, amplification educes parallels from myth, literature, art, religion, and anthropology to 'make ample' the symbolism involved and extend its range of meaning to the human condition as a whole.

Analytical psychologist: an analyst who subscribes to the theories and who practices the therapeutic techniques devised by C.G. Jung. To be distinguished from psychiatrist, psychoanalyst, psychologist, and psychotherapist.

Ancestral environment: the environment of evolutionary adaptedness; the environment in which our species evolved and in which it is adapted to live.

Anxious attachment: a term introduced by John Bowlby to describe the state of those who suffer from the fear that their attachment figures may either be lost of prove inaccessible to them.

Archetypes: a term introduced by C.G. Jung to denote innate neuropsychic centres possessing the capacity to initiate, control, and mediate the common behavioural characteristics and typical experiences of all human beings irrespective of race, culture, creed, or historical epoch. In the Jungian scheme of things, archetypes are the components of the collective unconscious.

Attachment: a tie of affection formed by one person or animal for another; in the sense used by Bowlby, the tie formed between an infant and its mother or mother-substitute.

Attachment behaviour: the characteristic forms of behaviour by which attachment bonds between individuals are expressed.

Basic trust: a term introduced by Erik Erikson for the conviction that a good maternal figure can engender in a child, through the development of a strong attachment bond, that it can trust her, the world, and itself.

Behavioural systems: a term introduced by John Bowlby for goal-directed mechanisms operating cybernetically (like electronic systems, through positive and negative feedback) in both mother and child, which are responsible for attachment behaviour and for mediating the development and maintenance of attachment bonds.

Behaviourism: a theoretical approach to animal and human psychology which focused on the objective study of actual behavioural responses while largely ignoring the existence of feelings or states of mind, since these are not public and not objectively verifiable.

Biosocial goals: the social goals for which we are biologically equipped to strive, such as care, protection, love, and status.

Borderline personality: a concept applied to individuals whose abnormal personalities combine features of neurotic and psychotic symptomatology.

Catharsis: a term which literally means 'purging'; used in classical psychoanalysis to describe the therapeutic effect of abreaction.

Charisma: a term derived from New Testament Greek meaning the gift of grace; introduced into sociology by Max Weber to describe an 'extraordinary quality' possessed by persons or objects, which is thought to give them unique and magical power.

Collective unconscious: a term introduced by C.G. Jung to designate those aspects of the psyche which are common to all humanity; synonymous with phylogenetic psyche.

Complex: a group or cluster of interconnected ideas and feelings which exert a dynamic effect on conscious experience and on behaviour. Complexes are to the ontogenetic psyche (or personal unconscious) what archetypes are to the phylogenetic psyche (or collective unconscious), the one being dependent on the other in the sense that complexes are 'personations' of archetypes.

Countertransference: the analyst's transference onto the patient.

Delusion: a false belief; characteristic of psychosis.

Denial: a mechanism of ego-defence whereby a painful experience or an aspect of the self is denied and disowned.

Ego: the part of the personality which one consciously recognizes as 'I' or 'me'.

Ego-defence mechanism: a mechanism by means of which the ego defends itself from threats emanating from the id, the superego, or the environment. Examples are denial, projection, rationalization, reaction-formation, and repression.

Environment of evolutionary adaptedness: see ancestral environment.

Epigenesis: a term derived from Greek epi = upon + genesis = generation; a biological theory of development proposed by C.H. Waddington (1957). It holds that the development of all biological characteristics, whether they be relatively sensitive or insensitive to environmental variation, is governed by the genome.

Epistemology: study of the basis of knowledge.

Ethology: the study of the behaviour of organisms living in their natural habitats.

Fixation: the process by which libido remains attached to an object appropriate to an earlier state of development. As a result of such fixation, a person will continue to indulge in immature patterns of behaviour, or regress to such behaviour when subjected to stress.

Free association: the patient's response to the basic rule of psychoanalysis to allow every thought to arise and be expressed freely, without censorship or conscious inhibition. When the free flow of associations comes to an end, this is considered to be the result of resistance.

Free-rider: an individual who seeks to acquire an undue proportion of the group's resources without first satisfying the usual requirement of achieving high social rank.

Gene: the basic unit of heredity.

Genome: the complete genetic constitution of an organism; the entire genetic programme characterizing the species.

Hallucination: a false sensory perception in the absence of external stimuli: characteristic of psychosis.

Hedonic mode: a mode of social interaction in which underlying dominance relations are not being challenged and agonic tensions are consequently absent, permitting individuals to be affiliative and to give their attention to recreational or task-oriented activities.

Hermeneutics: the art or discipline of interpretation.

Homeostasis: maintenance of balance between opposing mechanisms or systems.

Hysteria: a disorder characterized by the presence of physical symptoms in the absence of any evidence of a physical cause. The symptoms, nevertheless, perform some psychological function which provides the patient with a 'secondary gain'. So-called conversion hysteria presents in a variety of apparent neurological disturbances, such as paralyses, losses of sensation, convulsions, and blindness. The condition is encountered much less frequently today than it was in the time of Charcot, Breuer, and Freud.

Id: Latin for 'it'; used by Freud's translators for 'das Es'. 'We approach the id with analogies: we call it a chaos, a cauldron full of seething excitations ... it is filled with energy reaching it from the instincts, but it has no organization, produces no collective will, but only a striving to bring about the satisfaction of instinctual needs subject to the observance of the pleasure-principle'. (Freud, 1933).

Inclusive fitness: refers to the number of copies of an individual's genetic material that survive him, not only in his direct descendants, but in other than direct descendants as well – e.g., nephews, nieces, cousins, brothers and sisters, all of whom share a proportion of his genes.

Individuation: a term used by C.G. Jung to designate the process of personality development which leads to the fullest possible actualization of the archetypal endowment of an individual: 'Individuation means becoming a single, homogeneous being, and, insofar as "individuality" embraces our innermost, last, and incomparable uniqueness, it also implies becoming one's own self. We could therefore translate individuation as "coming to selfhood" or "self-realization"' (*CW* 7, para. 266).

Internal working model: a hypothetical construct introduced by John Bowlby; an inner, psychic representation of the self as capable (or incapable) of giving and receiving care and affection and of forming lasting bonds of attachment.

Kin-selection: refers to the selection of genes which cause individuals to favour close kin on account of the high probability that they will share those genes. Strictly speaking 'kin' should include direct offspring (sons and daughters), but many biologists have come to apply the term 'kin-selection' solely to kin other than offspring (e.g., nephews and nieces).

Lamarckism: the discredited theory originally advanced by the French biologist, Jean-Baptiste Lamarck (1744-1829), which held that experiences or characteristics acquired by one generation could be transmitted genetically to the next.

Libido: a term used by analysts of all schools to designate a hypothetical form of mental energy. It was originally conceived by Freud as energy derived from the sexual instinct; Jung rejected this as unduly narrow, preferring to conceive libido as general psychic energy which could be expressed in a great variety of forms, of which sexuality was one.

Mandala: Sanskrit word for 'magic circle', a geometric figure incorporating both a circle and a square, divided up into four (or multiples of four) segments radiating from the centre. The mandala stands as a symbol for the wholeness of the Self, the deity, and the cosmos.

Natural selection: the principle mechanism of evolutionary change, originally proposed by Darwin (1859). The theory holds that of the range of different individuals making up the population of a given species, those individuals possessing certain advantageous characteristics contribute more offspring to the succeeding generation (*i.e.*, they have greater reproductive success) than those lacking these characteristics. Provided these advantageous attributes have an inherited basis, they will eventually become established as standard components of the genetic structure of the species (*i.e.*, they will be selected by a natural process).

Neurosis: a term dating from the second half of the eighteenth century which originally meant a disease of the nerves; as a result of the work of Charcot and Freud on hysteria towards the end of the nineteenth century, however, neurosis came to be applied precisely to mental disorders which were not diseases of the nervous system. Although used less frequently than hitherto, neurosis remains a convenient term for a group of psychiatric disorders which do not involve hallucinations, delusions, or loss of insight.

Numinosity: a term introduced into psychology by Jung, who borrowed it from the German theologian, Rudolf Otto. Otto used it to describe what he regarded as the fundamental experience common to all religions – namely, the sense of awe and exaltation generated by the feeling of being in the presence of the Creator.

Object: in psychoanalytic parlance, the term is used to refer to a person, or to part of a person, or to a symbol of one or the other.

Object relations: refers to the social need of a subject to establish and maintain a relationship with an object (usually a mother-figure) and later with other significant people in the subject's life. An object relationship may be with an actual person in outer reality or with the mental representation of that person in the subject's psyche.

Objective psyche: Jung sometimes referred to the collective unconscious as the objective psyche in order to stress its conaturality with all existence: it is as real and as existent as anything in nature. For this reason Jung held that the fundamental natural laws, like the principles of adaptation, homeostasis, and growth, apply to the psyche just as surely as to any other biological phenomenon.

Obsessive-compulsive disorder: a fear that things will get out of control and that some catastrophe will ensue; obsessional symptoms and compulsive behaviours arise as quasi-superstitious means to prevent this from happening.

Thus, patients feel that they 'have got to' think certain thoughts or perform certain acts. Such compulsions can become severely distressing when, as is often the case, they cannot be controlled by voluntary effort.

Oedipus complex: a cluster of largely unconscious ideas and feelings of wishing to possess the parent of the opposite sex and eliminate the parent of the same sex. Freud derived the term from the classical Greek story of Oedipus, who slay his father, Laius, and married his mother, Jocasta, without realizing that they were his parents. Freud believed the complex to be universal and phylogenetically determined.

Ontogenetic psyche: those psychic attributes which are dependent for their functional development on the personal history of the individual.

Ontogeny: the development of an organism through the course of its life cycle.

Operant conditioning: learning to perform certain acts which initially occur as random or spontaneous movements through rewards (e.g., food) or punishments (e.g., electric shock).

Paradigm: a term given a technical meaning by T.S. Kuhn in his *The Structure of Scientific Revolutions* (1962). Denying that scientific theories are mere products of induction from sensory experience, Kuhn argued that theories give meaning to facts rather than simply arising out of them. A paradigm is the theoretical framework within which all thinking in a given scientific discipline proceeds. A paradigm shift occurs when one theoretical framework is replaced by another.

Persona: the mask worn by an actor in classical times; Jung used the term to describe the 'packaging' with which we present ourselves to the world. The persona is 'a functional complex that comes into existence for reasons of adaptation or personal convenience, but is by no means identical with the individuality' (*CW* 6, para.801).

Phylogenetic psyche: those psychic structures and functions which are characteristic of all members of the human species; synonymous with Jung's term collective unconscious.

Phylogeny: the evolutionary origin and development of a species.

Pleasure principle: Freud conceived the psyche in infancy as being motivated entirely by the desire to experience pleasure and avoid pain; only later, when the ego had developed, was the pleasure principle modified by the reality principle. In Freud's view the pleasure principle operated throughout life as a built-in propensity to keep instinctual tensions at a minimal level.

Projection: the unconscious process by which aspects of the self, or feelings or ideas associated with those aspects, are experienced as if they were located in someone or something external to oneself. Projection commonly functions in association with another ego-defence mechanism, denial, in that one denies the existence in oneself of the beliefs, motives, or intentions that one attributes to the person, animal, or thing on to whom or which one projects them.

Proximate cause: a term used in evolutionary psychiatry to denote an aetiological factor which operates on and through the constitution and the life experience of the individual.

Psyche: the totality of all mental processes, unconscious as well as conscious, as opposed to mind, which is conventionally applied to conscious processes only. 'The psyche is not of today,' wrote Jung; 'it's ancestry goes back many millions of years. Individual consciousness is only the flower and the fruit of the season, sprung from the perennial rhizome beneath the earth ...' (*CW* 5, p.xxiv).

Psychiatrist: a medically qualified practitioner who specializes in the treatment of mental illness. Only a small minority of psychiatrists are also analysts.

Psychoanalyst: an analyst who subscribes to the theories and who practices the therapeutic techniques devised by Sigmund Freud and developed by his followers. Only a minority of psychoanalysts are medically or psychiatrically qualified.

Psychologist: a pure scientist who studies all behaviour, normal and abnormal, human and animal.

Psychopathology: the study of psychiatric disorders and the provision of theories to account for their existence and development in individual patients.

Psychosis: a broad term used to discover those relatively severe psychiatric disorders in which hallucinations and delusions occur in people with relatively poor insight into their condition.

Psychotherapist: a generic term for therapists who use their own minds to treat the minds of others, with or without reference to unconscious processes or using the techniques of any particular school of analysis.

Rationalization: the finding of bad reasons to justify what one does on impulse.

Reaction-formation: the ego-defence mechanism whereby an unacceptable impulse is mastered and discharged by an exaggerated expression of its opposite. Thus, hostility may be discharged through excessive kindness.

Reality principle: a term used by Freud to designate the environmental constraints imposed on fulfilment of the pleasure principle. Freud believed that the reality principle developed in the course of ontogeny, whereas the pleasure principle was innate and present at birth.

REM sleep: rapid eye movement sleep, which at regular intervals during the night is reliably associated with the experience of dreams and with characteristic physiological changes in the body of the dreamer.

Repression: the ego-defence mechanism by which an unacceptable impulse or idea is rendered unconscious.

Reproductive success: the number of surviving offspring produced by an individual.

Resistance: a term introduced by Freud to account for the unwillingness of his patients to accept his interpretations – an unwillingness which he invariably attributed to their reluctance to face the unpleasant nature of their unconscious wishes rather than to the possibility that his interpretations could be wrong.

Schizoid personality: a type of personality structure characterized by a reluctance to enter into close personal relationships, a preference for solitary activities, and displaying a marked degree of emotional detachment.

Self: a term introduced by Jung for the dynamic nucleus of the core of the personality responsible for the process of individuation: the Self incorporates the entire archetypal potential of the unconscious psyche.

Separation anxiety: anxiety experienced at the prospect of becoming separated from a person to whom a bond of attachment has been formed.

Shadow: Jung's term for the aspect of the Self which remains unconscious because it is repressed by the superego or unactivated because of deficiencies in the life experience of the individual.

Sociobiology: a term introduced by E.O. Wilson for his approach to the study of behaviour; it is based on the assumption that the survival of the gene ultimately determines the form of the behaviour studied.

Superego: a term originally introduced by Freud which has come to designate that inner moral authority or ethical complex which monitors individual behaviour in such a way as to make it acceptable first to the parents and later to society.

Transcendent function: Jung's term for the mutual influence which is exerted between the ego and the Self in the course of personality development and individuation.

Transference: the process whereby a patient transfers onto the person of the analyst feelings, anticipations, and notions, which derive from important figures related to in the past. Freud came to view transference as an essential part of the therapeutic process. By remaining detached, and declining to fulfil the patient's anticipations, the analyst seeks to create a novel situation through which it may be possible to interpret to the patient that he or she is behaving as if the analyst were his or her father, mother, grandparent, sibling, etc. This transference relationship is to be distinguished from the analytic relationship (which refers to the total relationship, both conscious and unconscious, between analyst and patient) and the therapeutic alliance (which refers to their collaborative effort to confront and resolve the problems which brought the patient into analysis).

Ultimate cause: a factor contributing to the structure of the human genome over millions of years of selection pressure and determining the biosocial goals to the fulfilment of which human behaviour is directed.

Yielding subroutine: a behavioural programme adopted by a contestant losing in a ritual agonistic encounter or tournament. It terminates challenge by signalling submission and it facilitates voluntary yielding by inducing a mental and behavioural state of 'giving up', 'giving in', and 'giving way'. When prolonged it may manifest as a depressive state.

Bibliography

Ainsworth, M., Blehar, M., Waters, E., and Wall, S. (1978) *Patterns of Attachment: Assessed in the Strange Situation and at Home*. Lawrence Erlbaum Associates, Hillsdale, NJ.

Arlow, J.A. (1982) 'Psychoanalaytic education: a psychoanalytic perspective', *Annual of Psychoanalysis*, 10, pp.5-20.

Aveline, M., and Shapiro, D.A. (eds), (1995) *Research Foundations for Psychotherapy Practice*. John Wiley & Sons, New York.

Balint, Michael (1959) *Thrills and Regressions*. London: The Hogarth Press.

Baynes, Godwin (1949) *Mythology of the Soul*. Methuen, London.

Bennet, E.A. (1982) *Meetings with Jung*. London: Anchor.

Bergin, Allen E., and Garfield, Sol L., (eds) (1994) *Handbook of Psychotherapy and Behavior Change* (Fourth edition). JohnWiley & Sons, New York.

Bowlby, John (1944) 'Forty-four juvenile thieves: their characters and home life', *International Journal of Psycho- Analysis*, 25: pp.1-57 and 207-228.

——— (1951) *Maternal Care and Mental Health*. World Health Organization, Monograph Series No. 2.

——— (1969) *Attachment and Loss*, Vol.1, *Attachment*. The Hogarth Press, New York: Penguin Books, 1971.

——— (1979) *The Making and Breaking of Affectional Bond*. Tavistock Publications, London.

——— (1988) *A Secure Base: Clinical Applications of Attachment Theory*. Routledge, London.

Casement, Ann (1995) 'A brief history of Jungian splits in the United Kingdom', *Journal of Analytical Psychology*, Vol.40, No.3, pp.327-42.

Chance, M.R.A., and Jolly, C. (1970) *Social Groups of Monkeys, Apes and Men*. Jonathan Cape/E.P. Dutton, New York and London.

Crews, Frederick. 'The Unknown Freud', *New York Review of Books*, 18 November 1993, pp.55-66

——— 'The Revenge of the Repressed', *New York Review of Books*, Part I, 17 November 1994, pp.54-60: Part II, 1 December 1994, pp.49-58.

Dawes, Robyn, M. (1994) *House of Cards: Psychology and Psychotherapy Built on Myth*. The Free Press, New York and London.

Denman, Chess (1995) 'Questions to be answered in the evaluation of long-term therapy' in M. Aveline, and D.A. Shapiro (eds), *Research Foundations for Psychotherapy Practice*. John Wiley & Sons, New York.

Diamond, Jared (1991) *The Rise and Fall of the Third Chimpanzee*. Vintage, London.

Ellenberger, Henri (1970) *The Discovery of the Unconscious*. Basic Books, New York

——— (1993) *Beyond the Unconscious: Essays of Henri F. Ellenberger in the History of Psychiatry*, edited by Mark S. Micale, Princeton University Press, Princeton, NJ.
Erikson, E.H. (1962) *Young Man Luther: A Study in Psychoanalysis and History*. Norton, New York.
Erickson, Mark (in press) 'Rethinking Oedipus: the evolution of incest avoidance and psychological kinship', in *Genes on the Couch: Explorations in Evolutionary Psychotherapy*, edited by Paul Gilbert and Kent Bailey, Psychology Press, Hove, East Sussex.
Esterson, Allen (1993) *Seductive Mirage: An Exploration of the Work of Sigmund Freud*. Open Court, Chicago.
Eysenck, H.J. (1952) 'The effects of psychotherapy: an evaluation', *Journal of Consulting Psychology*, 16, pp.319- 24.
Fairbairn, W.R.D. (1952) *An Object-Relations Theory of the Personality*. Basic Books, New York.
——— (1994) *From Instinct to Self: Selected Papers of W.R.D. Fairbairn* (Vols.1-2), edited by E.F. Birtles and D.E. Scharff. Aronson, Northvale, NJ.
Ferenczi, Sandor (1988) *The Clinical Diary of Sandor Ferenczi*, edited by Judith Dupont, Harvard University Press, Cambridge, Mass.
Fordham, Michael (1994) *The Making of an Analyst*. Free Association Books, London.
Freud, Anna (1927) 'Four Lectures on Child Analysis' in *Introduction to Psychoanalysis*. The Hogarth Press, London (1974).
——— (1936) *The Ego and the Mechanisms of Defence*. The Hogarth Press, London.
——— (1966-80) *The Writings of Anna Freud* (8 Volumes). International Universities Press, New York.
Freud, Sigmund (1953-74) *The Standard Edition of the Complete Psychological Works of Sigmund Freud*, edited by James Strachey, The Hogarth Press and The Institute of Psycho-Analysis.
——— (1893-95) *Studies on Hysteria* (Vol.2).
——— (1900) *The Interpretation of Dreams* (Vols.4 and 5). Penguin, 1976.
——— (1910) *Five Lectures on Psycho-Analysis* (Vol.11).
——— (1913) *Totem and Taboo* (Vol.13).
——— (1920) *Beyond the Pleasure Principle* (Vol.18).
——— (1923) *The Ego and the Id* (Vol.19).
——— (1927) *The Future of an Illusion* (Vol.21).
——— (1930) *Civilization and its Discontents* (Vol.21).
——— (1933) *New Introductory Lectures on Psycho-Analysis* (Vol.22).
——— (1937) *Analysis Terminable and Interminable* (Vol.23)
——— (1939) *Moses and Monotheism* (Vol.23).
——— (1939) *An Outline of Psycho-Analysis* (Vol.23).
——— 'The Freud/Fliess Letters', see Masson, Jeffrey (ed.).
——— 'The Freud/Jung Letters', see McGuire, William (ed.).
Frosh, Stephen (1998) *For and Against Psychoanalysis*. Routledge, London.
Gay, Peter (1988) *Freud: A Life For Our Time*. J.M. Dent & Sons, London and Melbourne.
Gilbert, Paul (in press) 'Evolutionary psychopathology: why isn't the mind designed better than it is?' Special issue of the *British Journal of Medical Psychology* on Evolutionary Psychopathology.
Gilbert, Paul, and Bailey, Kent (eds), (in press) *Genes on the Couch: Explora-*

tions in Evolutionary Psychotherapy. Psychology Press, Hove, East Sussex.
Glantz, K., and Pearce, J. (1989) *Exiles from Eden: Psychotherapy from an Evolutionary Perspective*. Norton, New York.
Gomez, Lavinia (1997) *An Introduction to Object Relations*. Free Association Books, London.
Grosskurth, Phyllis (1986) *Melanie Klein: Her World and her Work*. Hodder & Stoughton, London; Harvard University Press, Cambridge, Mass.
——— (1998) 'Psychoanalysis: a dysfunctional family?' *Journal of Analytical Psychology*, Vol.43, No.1, January, pp.87-95.
Grünbaum, Adolf (1984) *The Foundations of Psychoanalysis: A Philosophical Critique*. University of California Press.
Guntrip, H. (1971) *Psychoanalytic Theory, Therapy and the Self*. Basic Books, New York; Karnac, London (1977).
——— (1975) 'Analysis With Fairbairn and Winnicott: (How Complete a Result Does Psycho-Analytic Therapy Achieve?)', *International Review of Psycho-analysis* 2: pp.145-56.
Hartmann, Heinz (1939) *Ego Psychology and the Problem of Adaptation*. International Universities Press, New York.
Hazell, J. (1996) *H.J.S. Guntrip: A Psychoanalytic Biography*. Free Association Books, London and New York.
Henry, William P., Strupp, Hans H., Schacht, Thomas E., and Gaston, Louise (1994) 'Psychodynamic approaches', in Bergin, Allen E., and Garfield, Sol L., (eds), *Handbook of Psychotherapy and Behavior Change* (Fourth edition). John Wiley & Sons, New York.
Hobson, J. Allan (1988) *The Dreaming Brain*. Basic Books, New York.
Holmes, Jeremy (1993) *John Bowlby and Attachment Theory*. Routledge, London.
Jones, Ernest (1953-7) *Sigmund Freud: Life and Work*, (3 vols). The Hogarth Press, London.
Jung, C.G. The majority of quotations in the text are taken either from *The Collected Works of C.G. Jung* (1953-78) edited by H. Read, M. Fordham and G. Adler and published in London by Routledge, in New York by Pantheon Books (1953-60) and the Bollingen Foundation (1961-7) and in Princeton, New Jersey by Princeton University Press (1967-78), or from *Memories, Dreams, Reflections* (1963), published in London by Routledge & Kegan Paul and in New York by Random House. Sources of quotations from The *Collected Works* are indicated by the volume number followed by the number of the paragraph from which the quotation is taken, e.g., *CW* 10, para.441. Quotations from *Memories, Dreams, Reflections* are indicated by the page number thus: *MDR*, p.111.
——— (1911-12) *Transformations and Symbols of the Libido*: originally published in German, now available in English as *Symbols of Transformation* (*CW* 5) published in 1956.
——— (1921) *Psychological Types*: originally published in German, now available in English as *Psychological Types* (*CW* 6) published in 1971.
——— (1933) *Modern Man in Search of a Soul*. Kegan Paul, London.
Kantrovitz, J. (1995) 'Outcome research in psychoanalysis: review and reconsiderations', in T. Shapiro and R. Emde (eds), *Research in Psychoanalysis: Process, Development, Outcome*. International Universities Press, Madison, Conn.
Klein, M. (1932) *The Psycho-Analysis of Children*. The Hogarth Press, London.

——— (1940) 'Mourning and its relations to manic- depressive states', in *Love, Guilt and Reparation*, The Hogarth Press, London, (1975).
——— (1957) *Envy and Gratitude and Other Works: 1946-63*. The Hogarth Press, London (1975).
Kohut, H. (1971) *The Analysis of the Self*. International Universities Press, New York.
——— (1977) *The Restoration of the Self*. International Universities Press, New York.
Kuhn, T.S. (1962) *The Structure of Scientific Revolutions*. University of Chicago Press, Chicago.
Lakoff, R.T., and Coyne, J.C. (1993) *Father Knows Best: The Use and Abuse of Power in Freud's Case of "Dora"*. Teachers College Press, New York.
Macmillan, Malcolm (1997) *Freud Evaluated: The Completed Arc*. The MIT Press, Cambridge, Mass., and London, England.
Masson, Jeffrey (1984) *The Assault on Truth: Freud's Suppression of the Seduction Theory*. Farrar, Straus & Giroux Inc., New York; reissued with a new preface as The Assault on Truth: Freud and Child Sexual Abuse, HarperCollins (1992).
——— (1990) *Against Therapy: Emotional Tyranny and the Myth of Psychological Healing*. Fontana, London.
Masson, Jeffrey (ed.), (1985) *The Complete Letters of Sigmund Freud to Wilhelm Fliess 1887-1904*. Harvard University Press, Cambridge, Mass.
McGuire, William, (ed.), (1974) *The Freud/Jung Letters: The Correspondence Between Sigmund Freud and C.G. Jung*, trans. Ralph Manheim and R.F.C. Hull, Princeton University Press, NJ.
McGuire, William, and Hull, R.F.C. (1977) *C.G. Jung Speaking*. Princeton University Press, Princeton, N.J.
Medawar, P.B. Review of Irving S. Cooper's *The Victim is Always the Same*, New York Review of Books, 23 January 1975.
Meltzoff, J., and Kornreich, M. (1970) *Research in Psychotherapy*. Atherton Press, New York.
Mitchell, Stephen, A., and Black, Margaret J. (1995) *Freud and Beyond: A History of Modern Psychoanalytic Thought*. Basic Books, New York.
Neumann, Erich (1955) *The Great Mother: An Analysis of the Archetype*. Routledge & Kegan Paul, London.
——— (1973) *The Child: Structure and Dynamics of the Nascent Personality*. Hodder & Stoughton, London.
Noll, Richard (1994) *The Jung Cult: Origins of a Charismatic Movement*. Princeton University Press, Princeton, NJ.
——— (1997) *The Aryan Christ: The Secret Life of Carl Jung*. Random House, New York.
Parry, G. (1966) *NHS Psychotherapy Services in England*. NHS. Executive, 135-155 Waterloo Road, London.
Roazen, Paul (1992) *Freud and His Followers*. Da Capo Press, New York.
Roth, A., and Fonagy, Peter, (1996) *What Works For Whom? A Critical Review of Psychotherapy Research*. The Guilford Press, New York.
Rutter, Michael (1981) *Maternal Deprivation Reassessed* (second edition). Penguin, London.
Ryle, Anthony (1990) *Cognitive Analytic Therapy: Active Participation in Change*. John Wiley & Sons, Chichester.
Samuels, Andrew (1985) *Jung and the Post Jungians*. Routledge & Kegan Paul, London.

Shapiro, David A. (1996) Foreword to *What Works For Whom? A Critical Review of Psychotherapy Research* by Anthony Roth and Peter Fonagy, The Guilford Press, New York.

Shapiro, T., and Emde, R. (eds), (1995) *Research in Psychoanalysis: Process, Development, Outcome*. International Universities Press, Madison, Conn.

Sloane, R.B., Staples, F.R., Cristol, A.H., Yorkston, N.J., and Whipple, K. (1975) *Short-Term Analytically Oriented Psychotherapy vs. Behavior Therapy*. Harvard University Press, Cambridge, Mass.

Stevens, Anthony (1982) *Archetype: A Natural History of the Self*. Routledge & Kegan Paul, London and William Morrow & Co., New York.

——— (1991) *On Jung*. Penguin, London.

——— (1996) *Private Myths: Dreams and Dreaming*. Penguin, London.

Stevens, Anthony, and Price, John (1996) *Evolutionary Psychiatry: A New Beginning*. Routledge, London.

Storr, Anthony (1979) *The Art of Psychotherapy*. Secker & Warburg, London.

——— (1996) *Feet of Clay: A Study of Gurus*. HarperCollins, London.

Sulloway, Frank, J. (1979) *Freud, Biologist of the Mind: Beyond the Psychoanalytic Legend*. Burnett Books/Andr Deutsch, London.

——— (1991) 'Reassessing Freud's Case Histories: The Social Construction of Psychoanalysis', *Isis*, Vol.82. pp.245-75.

Sutherland, J.D. (1980) 'The British Object Relations Theorists: Balint, Winnicott, Fairbairn, Guntrip', *Journal of the American Psychoanalytic Association*, Vol.28, No.4, pp.829-60.

——— (1989) *Fairbairn's Journey Into the Interior*. Free Association Books, London.

Waddington, C.H. (1957) *The Strategy of the Genes: A Discussion of Some Aspects of Theoretical Biology*. George Allen & Unwin, London.

Wallerstein, R. (1986) *Forty-two Lives in Treatment*. Guilford, New York.

Webster, Richard (1997) *Why Freud Was Wrong: Sin, Science and Psychoanalysis*. HarperCollins, London.

Wenegrat, Brant, (1982) *Sociobiology and Mental Disorder*. Addison-Wesley, Menlo Park, California.

Wilcocks, Robert (1994) *Maelzel's Chess Player: Sigmund Freud and the Rhetoric of Deceit*. Rowman and Littlefield, Lanham, Maryland.

Winnicott, D.W. (1958) *Through Paediatrics to Psychoanalysis*. The Hogarth Press, London.

——— (1965) *The Maturational Process and the Facilitating Environment*. International Universities Press, New York.

——— (1991) *Playing and Reality*. Penguin, London.

Index